AF575161

TO CATCH THE WIND

A PHOTOGRAPHER'S JOURNEY

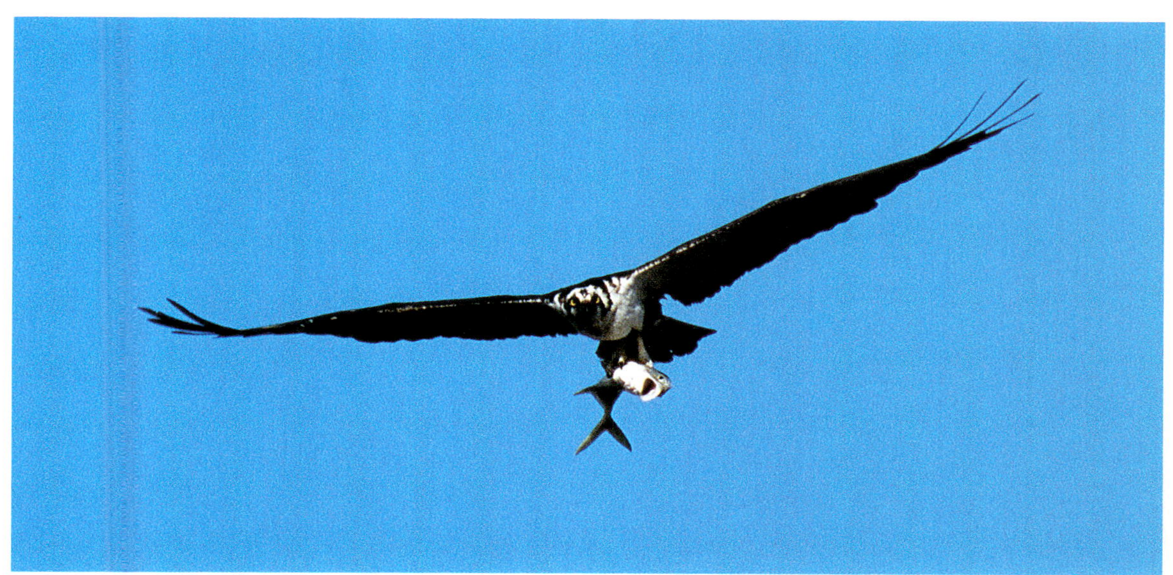

STEPHEN KIRKPATRICK

TO CATCH THE WIND

A PHOTOGRAPHER'S JOURNEY

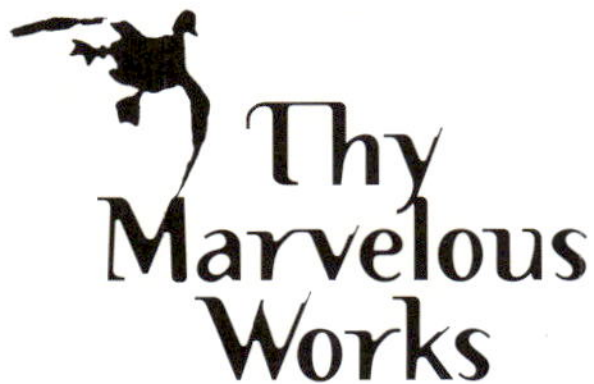

P.O. Box 31414
Jackson, MS 39286

ISBN # 0-9619353-9-1
Library of Congress Catalog Card # 97-90236
First Edition

Printer: Friesens, Canada
Prepress & color separations: K&W Prepress, Jackson, MS
Designer: Heidi Flynn Allen, Flynn Design, Jackson, MS
Editor: Marlo Carter Sibley, Madison, MS

Printed in Canada

To all those who are "in search of lost bearings."

"I would have despaired unless I had believed that I would see the goodness of the Lord in the land of the living. Wait for the Lord; be strong and let your heart take courage."

PSALM 27: 13 & 14

It is hard to thank everyone who has made the following pages come to life without forgetting someone. There is so much more to a project like this than direct contributions to getting photographs. Without family to help me in "many" ways, I would be much less the person you see. Thank you Susan, Penny, Ted, Julia, & O.L.

Sean, Ryan, & Ian: No man could have better sons.
I am blessed by the mere mention of your names!

Heidi Allen: The joy in your smile is reflected in the pages.
Marlo Carter Sibley: Your talent became the panacea to my journals.
Wayne & Fran Kirkpatrick: Your music, hospitality, & love left one set of footprints.
Bobby McCain: Friends are supposed to be like you.
Don & Denise Quick: Your prayers are being heard.

A special thanks to those of you directly responsible for the success of some of the enclosed photos: Tommy Smith, Hardin Phillips, Charlie Shorter, Herb Cilley, Paul Hartfield, Kelly Williams, Cliff Covington, Jimmy Bullock, Edmond McIlhenny, & Maureen Merchant.

Also the following organizations:

Delaware Nature Conservancy
Half Crown Island, Que.
Chevron Corporation, MS
Remington Farms, MD
Tara Wildlife, MS
Premier Camera, MS
Union Camp, S.C.
Avery Island, LA
Anchorage Audubon Society, AK
Mississippi Department of Wildlife, Fisheries & Parks

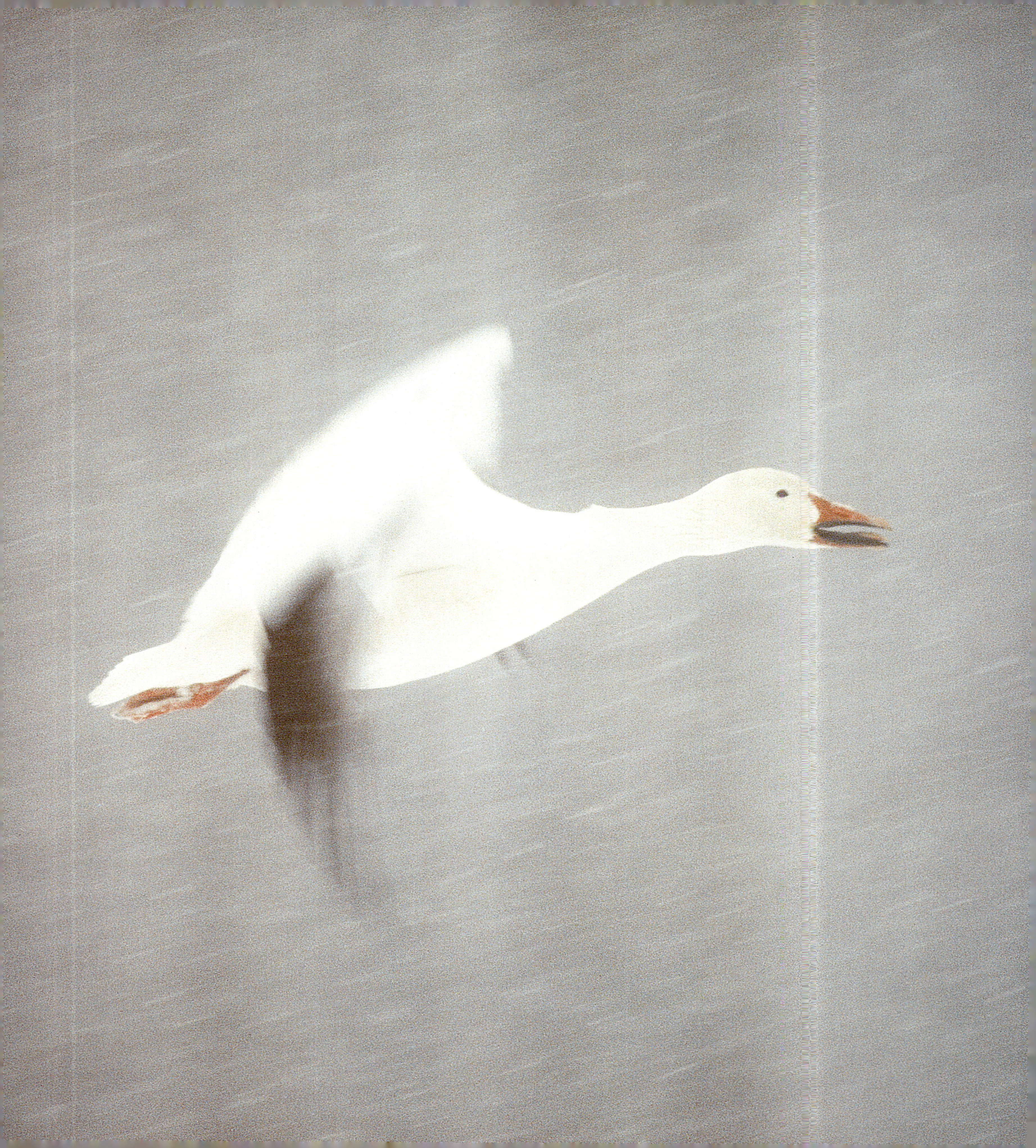

"The bitter winds of life blow their silent rage against the calming fragrance of hope, never knowing they merely scatter its aroma like the feathers of a dandelion."

STEPHEN KIRKPATRICK, 1997

SNOW GOOSE IN SNOW STORM, DELAWARE, JANUARY 1996

"Times in the past have been tough, real tough from the outside, but now they seem to call from deep within. A chamber inside that constantly echoes the cry, 'Help me, Lord, I need your help.'"

Over a period of three years, I experienced several life changes.

The strain and heartbreak of a divorce, separation from my three sons, frustration with my work, and the particular pressures that come from making my living sitting in trees and wading through swamps all caused me to ask fundamental questions about the direction my life was taking.

During these months of personal and professional upheaval, I kept a journal. As I waited for that perfect shot, searching for the light that would make it all worthwhile, I jotted down my random thoughts and pointed questions, my conversations with God, and some quirky observations about life in general. That journal became the basis for this book.

To Catch the Wind features many of my favorite photos, shot in locations throughout North America over the course of my career as a wildlife photographer. As you peruse the pages of *To Catch the Wind,* you'll share my journey – not only a photographic journey across the continent, but an emotional and spiritual journey that reaches into previously unexplored locales in my own heart and soul.

Did I discover the answers to my questions, reach a state of perfect nirvana in my personal and professional life, and find a cure for cancer? Of course not. But while questions still remain – and no doubt always will – I can look back over those three years with a sense of resolution and peace that wasn't there when I first put pen to paper in the spring of 1994.

Now, don't say I didn't warn you. Some of the reflections contained here are a bit intense, and the journey was a long one. But to steal a line from my own journal, "*One tiring step at a time is not the way we want to move, yet it is in each of these steps that we 'experience' our accomplishments.*"

So if you're ready, let's head on out. Grab your gear and focus your lens. And don't forget to pack both an adventurous spirit and a more contemplative side – trust me, you'll need both.

Oh, just one more thing. Thanks for embarking on the journey with me. Hopefully, it'll be a trip to remember.

PHOTO BY TOMMY SMITH

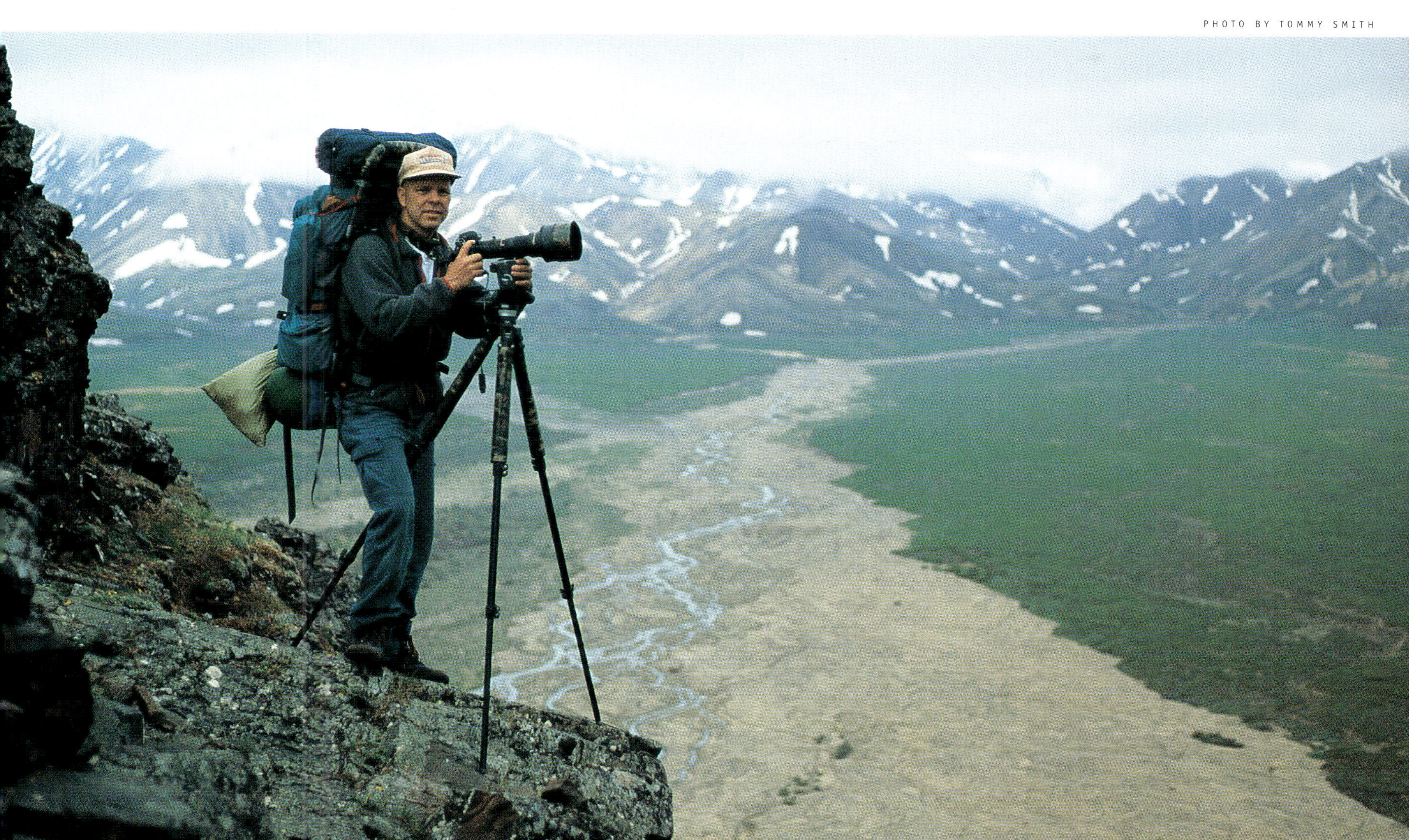

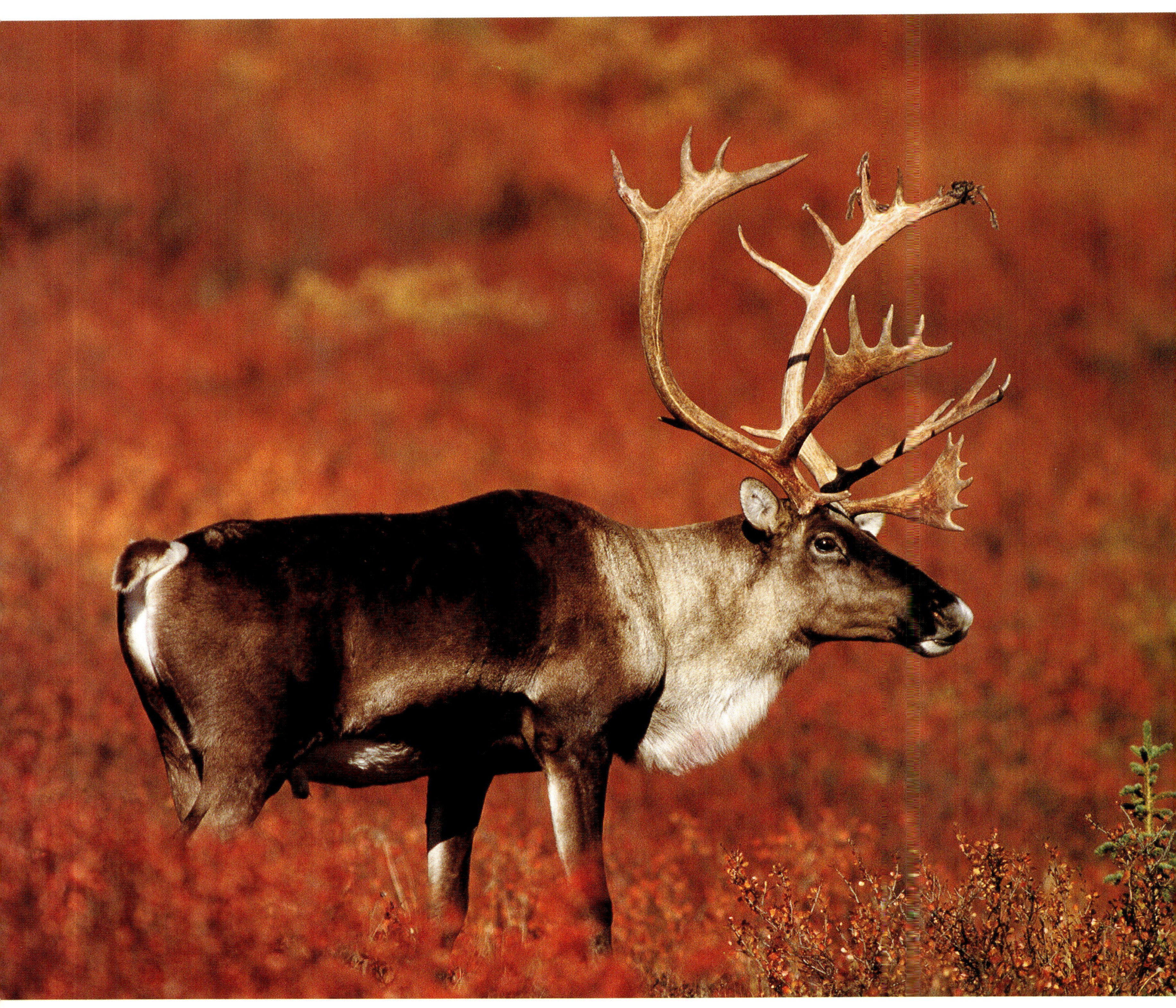

CARIBOU IN FALL COLOR, ALASKA, SEPTEMBER 1996

SPRING 1994

journal entry

"As much as anything, I am a seeker. Always digging, probing for truth, love, compassion. Always fighting against my own insecurities, my own pain, my own ego. These are poisons. A big enough dose will kill you, or at least make you worthless."

I suppose the catalyst behind this intense period of soul-searching was the divorce.

The break-up of my family wreaked havoc upon the familiar choreography of my day-to-day existence. A lifetime of dreams evaporated before my eyes. My personal universe, once so orderly and predictable, suddenly seemed random and haphazard.

"Tonight is a low one. Quiet, pacing, pensive, reflective. Adagio for Strings *is playing, but tonight it brings no comfort. The children's distance is killing me."*

My very sense of *who I was* was shaken to the core.

With so much in my life so suddenly changed, it was difficult to believe *any* part of me was still the same.

I was separated from my family, but I was still a photographer, still expected to do the same job, still expected to find the same beauty in the world as though nothing had changed. How could that be? Was that really what I *wanted* to be?

What did God say? What did I hear?

"I am uninspired and feel more pressure and stress than I wish to think about. Over the past eight years, I've logged more than one thousand speaking engagements, and I am quite simply exhausted. The work continues to inspire my audiences, but for me, the thrill is gone."

GREAT EGRET IN SUNSET, MISSISSIPPI, JANUARY 1988

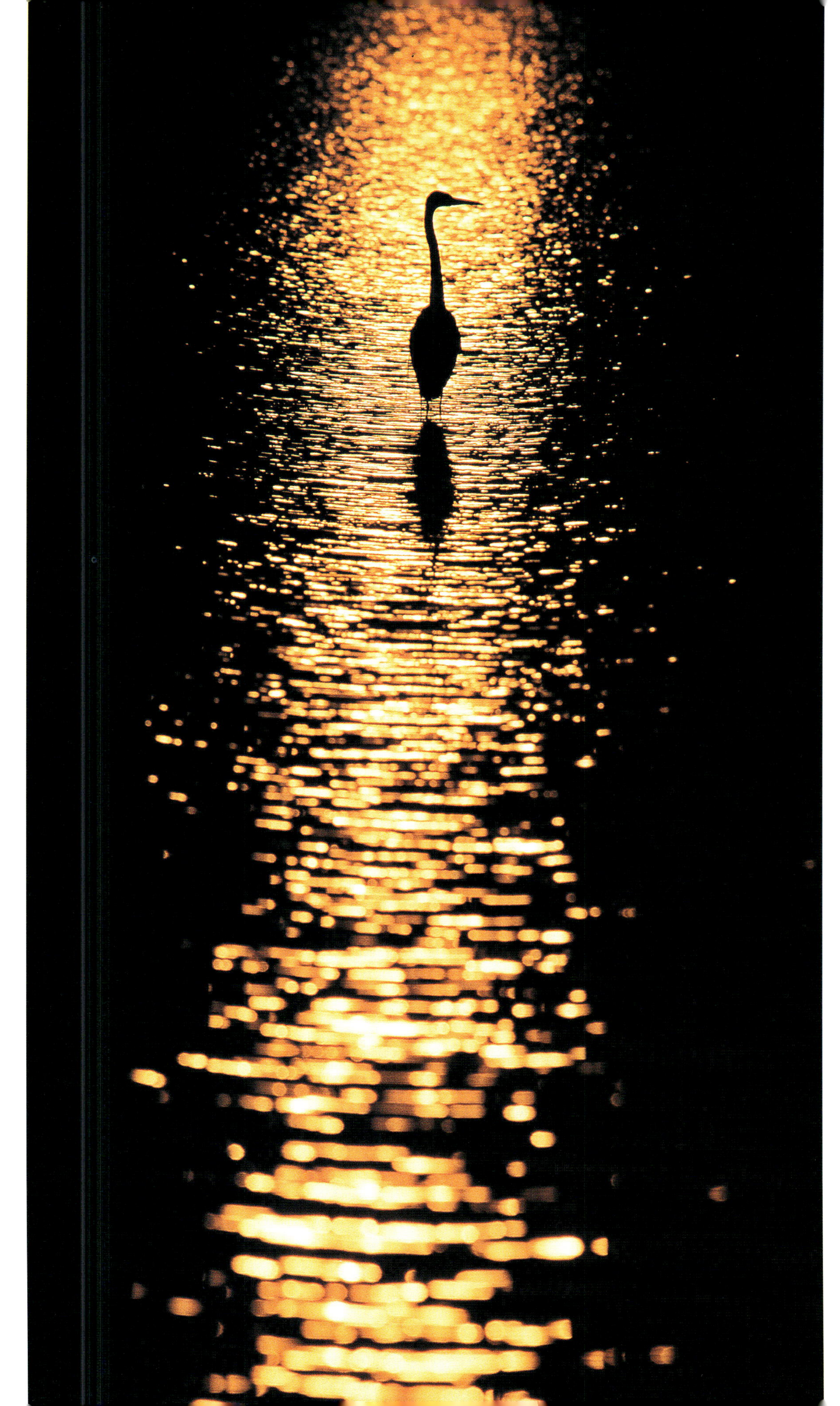

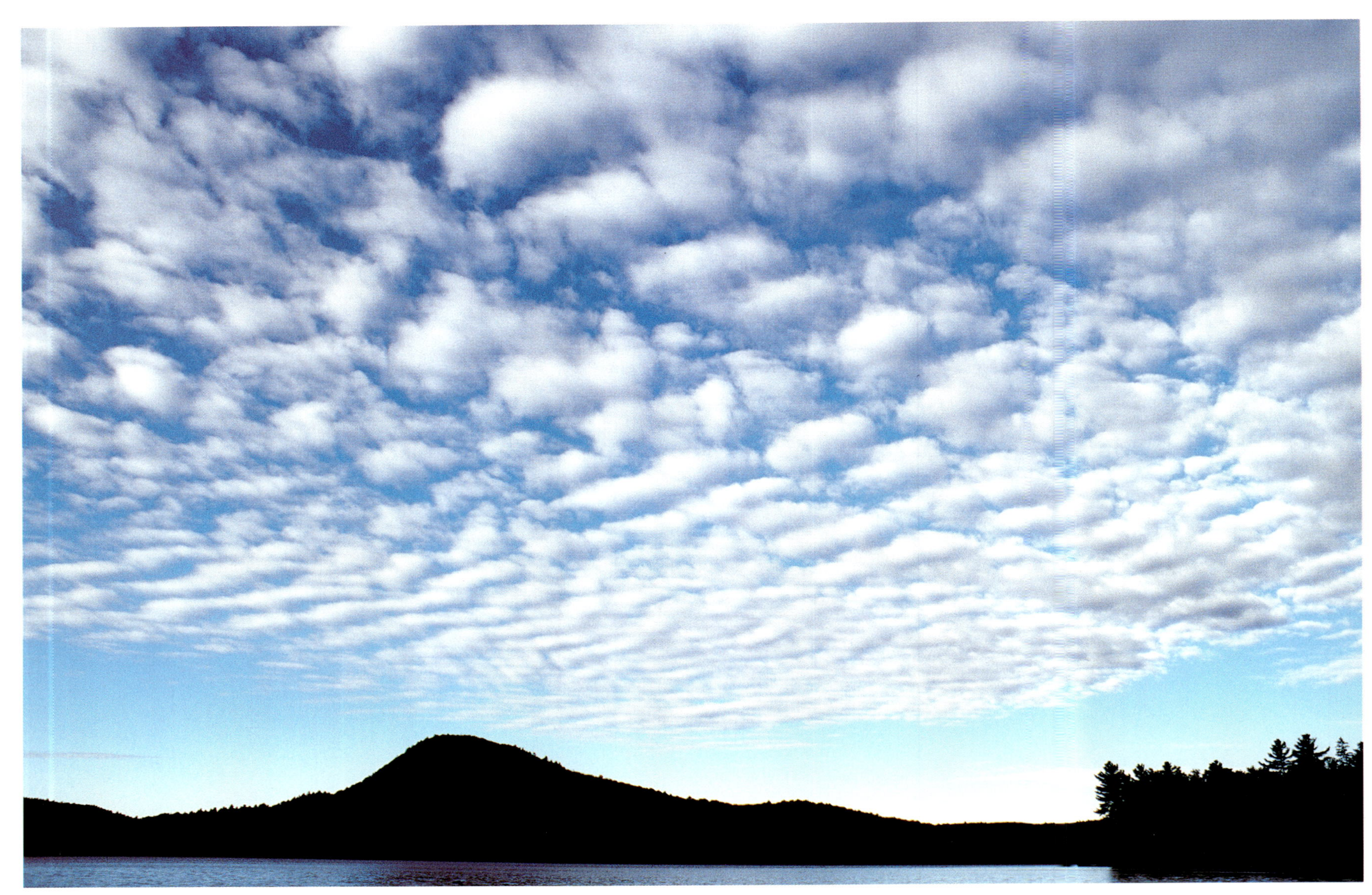

THIRTY-ONE-MILE LAKE AND CLOUDS, QUEBEC, OCTOBER 1994

"I sometimes dream of moving to another state, selling all my camera gear, giving up my business, and going to work as a laborer. I know I could never really do it. I just like to run away sometimes – I guess we all do."

And so it was in this frame of mind that I set out for a quiet lake in Quebec to finish work on my loon book, *In Wilderness Song*. I'd spent twelve magical summers photographing the majestic loons who inhabited that serene lake, but I knew this expedition would be different.

There would be no loving notes or cheerful chiclets tucked into my bags, no silly cards from the boys hidden there to brighten up the nights spent alone in the wilderness. And even when the shoot came to an end, my longing for home would remain unfulfilled.

This assignment would be no different from the many that had preceded it. Seek out the loons, shoot the scenics, take advantage of opportunities waiting in the wilderness.

But while the *trip* would be much the same, a much different *man* would be making the journey.

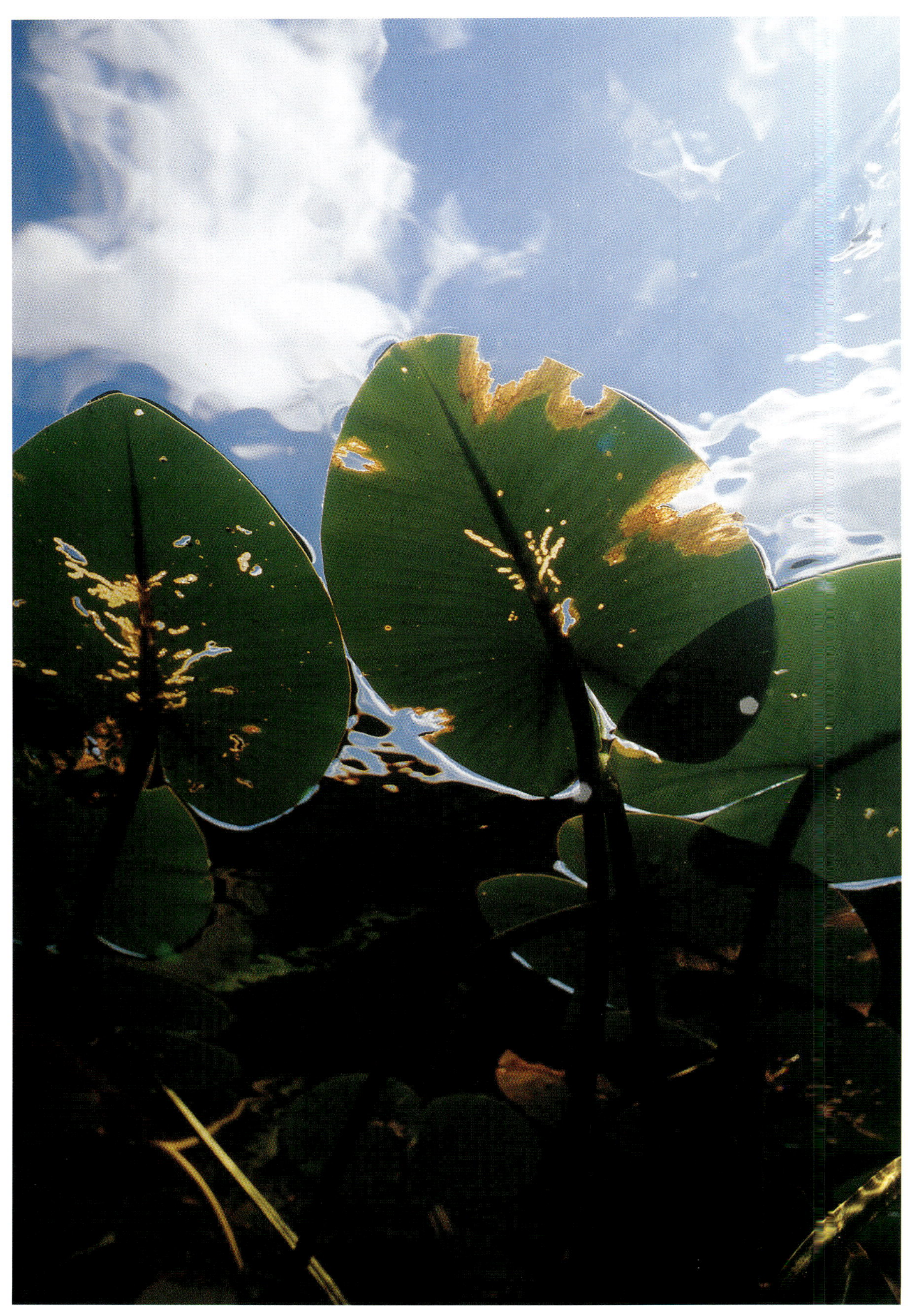

LILY PADS FROM BELOW, QUEBEC, JULY 1996

SNAPPING TURTLE UNDERWATER, QUEBEC, JULY 1994

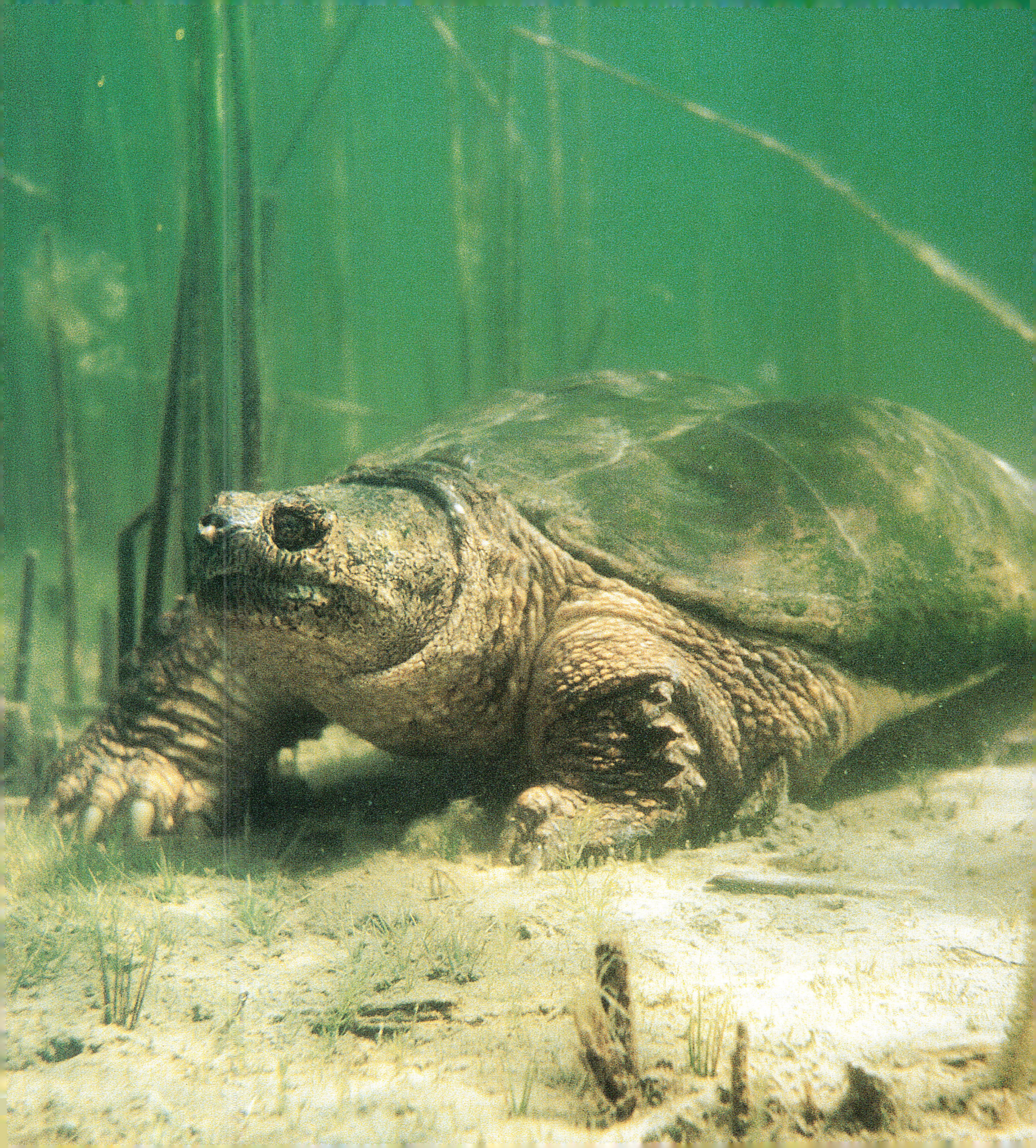

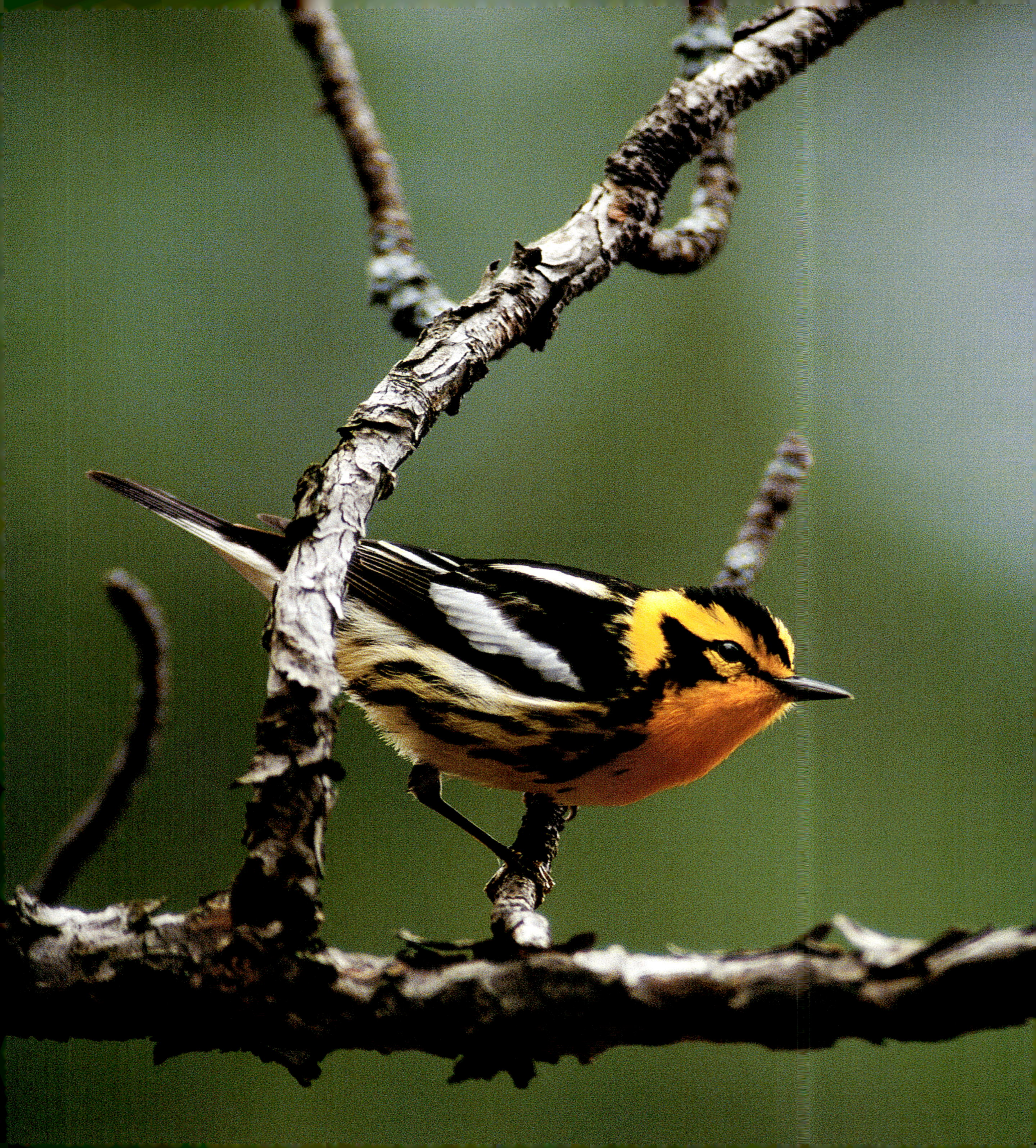

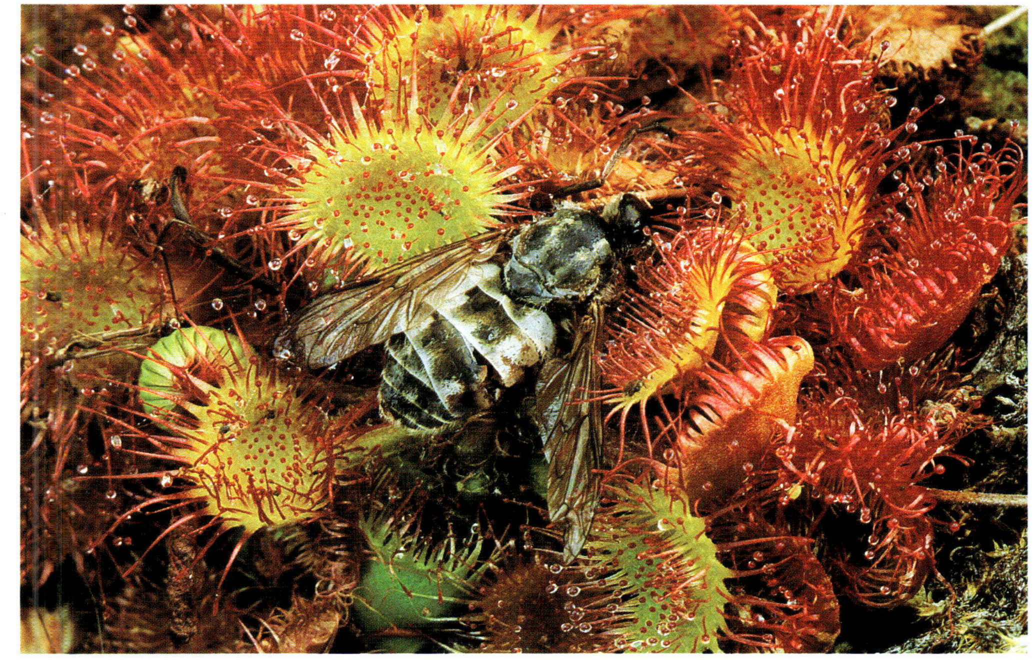

FLESH FLY IN SUNDEW, QUEBEC, AUGUST 1991

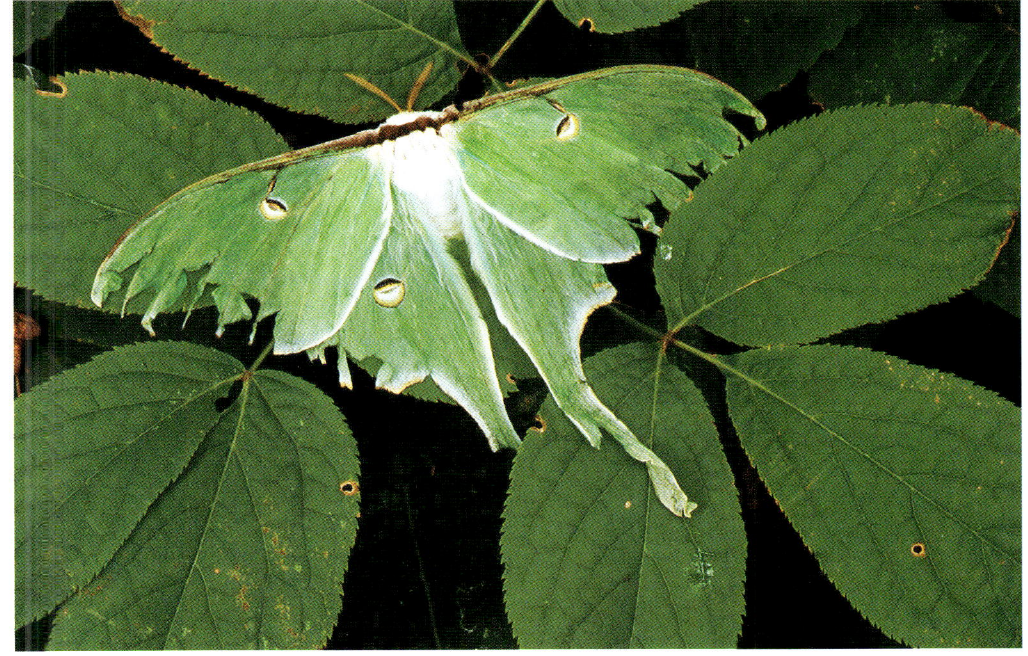

DYING LUNA MOTH, QUEBEC, JULY 1994

BLACKBURNIAN WARBLER, QUEBEC, JUNE 1996

"Being asked to put a wonderful image of nature on film is a bit like being asked to catch the wind. We can see its effect, but we can never put it in a box. We do not capture it, we only borrow it for a while."

Over the course of my sixteen-year career as a wildlife photographer, I've taken nearly half a million photographs. Like any artist, I have my favorites.

There's the rare shot of normally cautious does and a fawn wading in an open stream – I waited a decade to find that shot. Or the snow goose flying in a blinding snow storm, a technical feat I could never have pulled off ten years ago.

There's the colorful portrait of the only blue frog I've ever seen, and the frozen moment just before the grizzly bear catches the leaping salmon.

But while I have my personal favorites and a number of crowd-pleasers, there's one shot missing from my portfolio.

A shot that will once and forever define my career.

A shot that will reveal the majesty and truth of God's creation in a way that everyone in the world can understand.

One shot that's still out there, waiting.

I will capture that photograph the same day I catch the wind.

"Since the beginning, I have sought a feeling in my photography that seems to elude me. Every once in a while I see it show up, but not nearly often enough. It's turned into a project I have no control over. Capturing this feeling, whatever it is, is driving me on."

"There are no great moments in still photography, only great fractions of seconds. This is obvious in high action shots – deer charging across a swamp, mallards taking flight, orcas rising to the surface.

"But even those moments which seem *timeless are, in reality, fleeting.*

"The snow-laden spider web seems literally frozen in time, yet disintegrates in an instant, crushed by the same snow that accentuates its delicate lines. A flower bursts into vivid bloom amidst perfect light, then just as quickly fades into a memory. The perfect leaf falls upon the perfect log, but is soon carried away by the wind. Even a sunrise, reliably repeated every day, achieves its most achingly brilliant color only for a heartbeat."

WHITE-TAILED DEER, MISSISSIPPI, NOVEMBER 1985

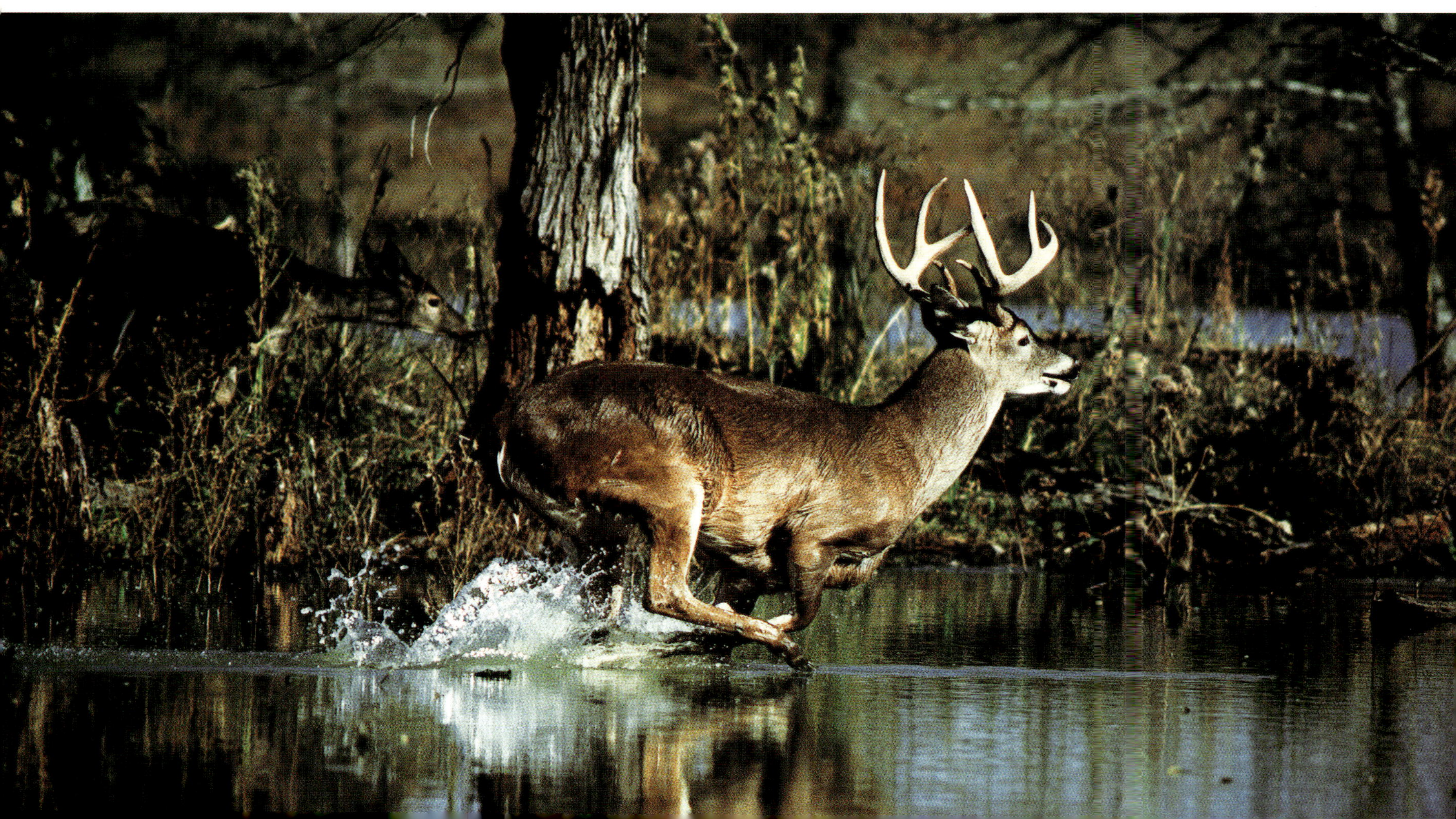

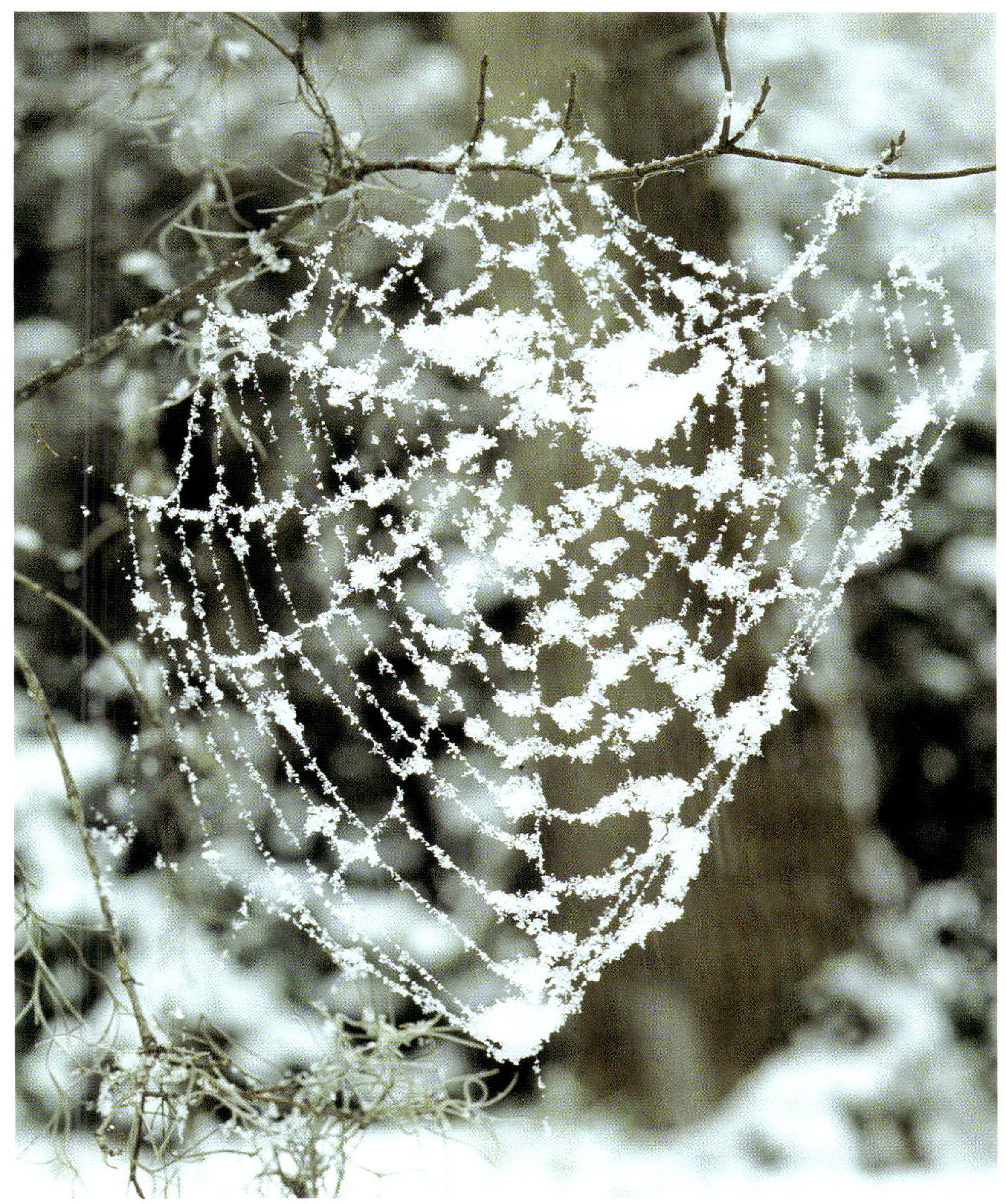

SPIDER WEB IN SNOW, MISSISSIPPI, DECEMBER 1996

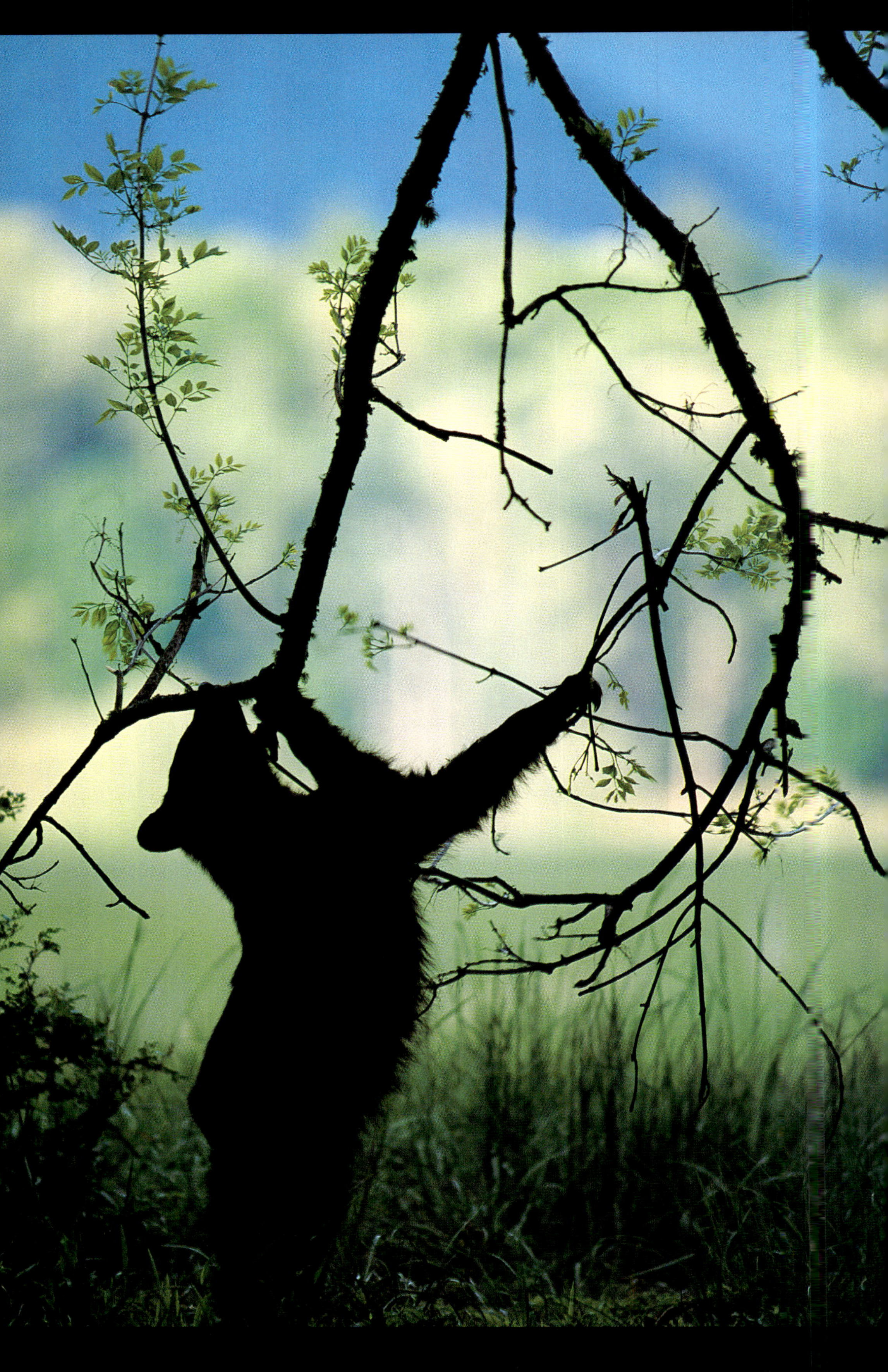

Take away the long days I spent watching and waiting, the unbroken hours stretched end to end. Take away all of the preparation and the patience. Take away the shots I missed, lost forever in the blink of an eye.

Now count only the split second of exposure, the instant when the shutter explodes and the image is captured.

One hundred of the images in this book combined represent a mere ten seconds of actual recorded time.

Searching for answers to questions that haunt our hearts and fill our souls is much the same as seeking that single, elusive photograph. Every now and then we gain some insight, glimpse a perfect truth, or experience a sudden realization that makes us say, "That's it. I've got it now."

But as soon as it's answered, another question arises to tease us, to lead us a little further down the path of internal discovery. And sooner or later, we realize the quest to catch the wind is a never-ending one, and that along the journey, not one, but a multitude of truths will be revealed.

"For one who seeks such answers is a seeker by nature. Finding is but a result to the exercise, and the preparation for the exercise is often more exhilarating than the actual event itself. My spontaneous nature has often robbed me of these rapturous time lapses, yet it is still the enticement of never knowing that draws me, excites me."

BLACK BEAR CUB FEEDING, TENNESSEE, MAY 1995

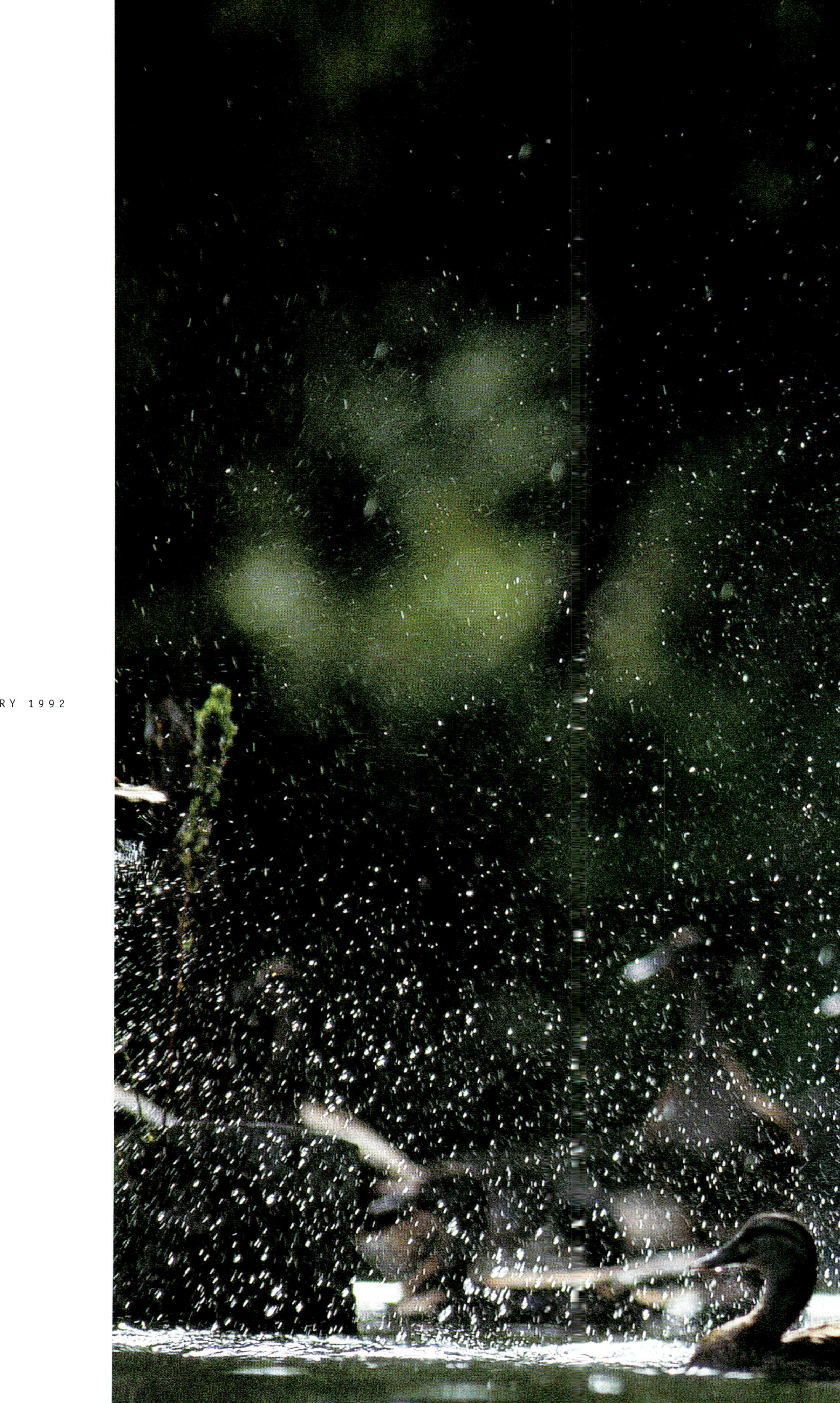

MALLARDS IN SPRAY, MISSISSIPPI, FEBRUARY 1992

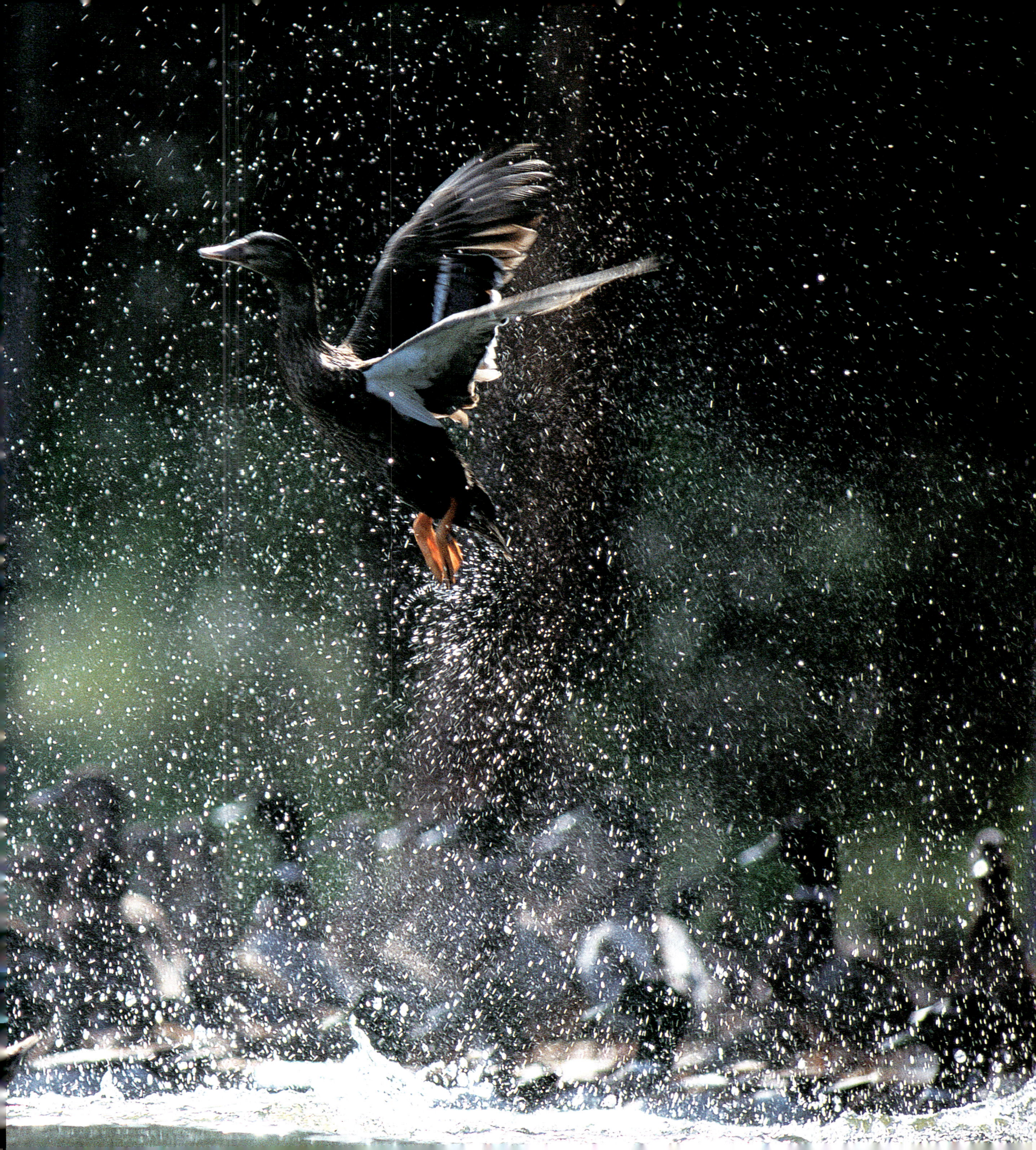

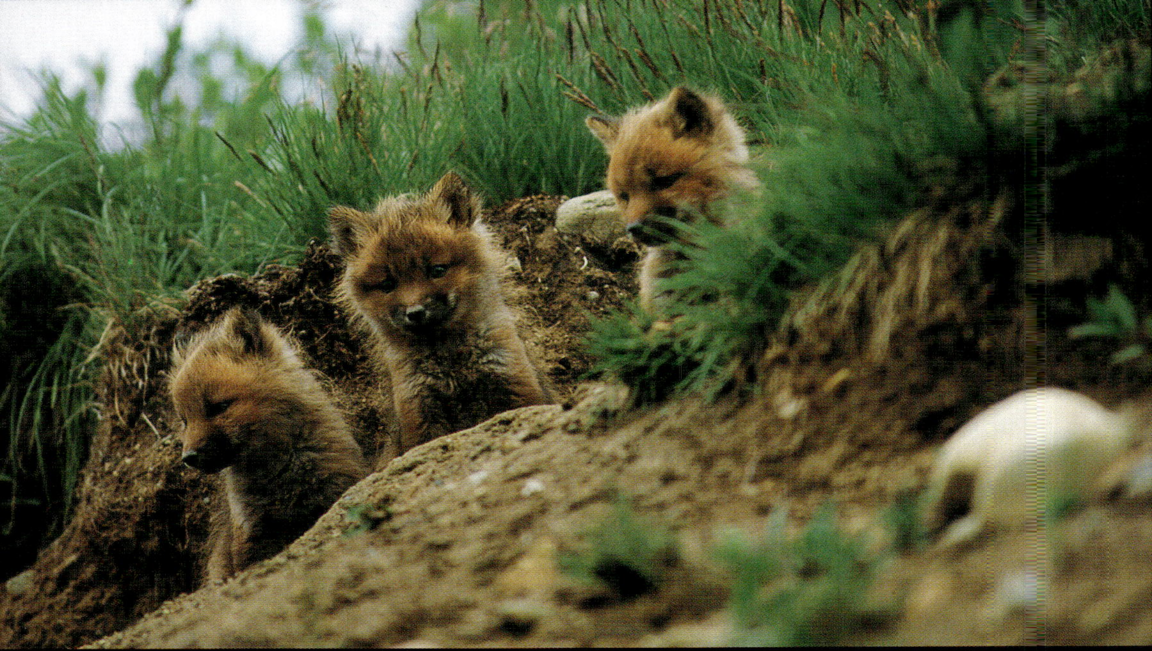

RED FOX KITS AT DEN, ALASKA, JUNE 1992

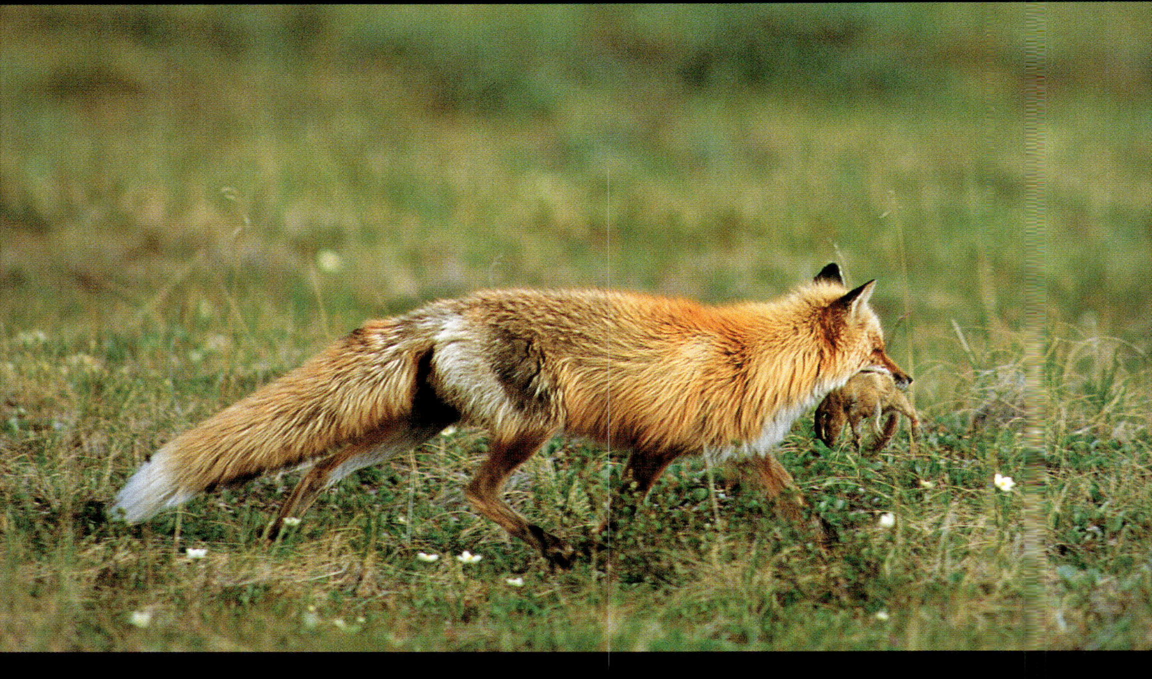

RED FOX WITH ARCTIC GROUND SQUIRREL, ALASKA, JUNE 1992

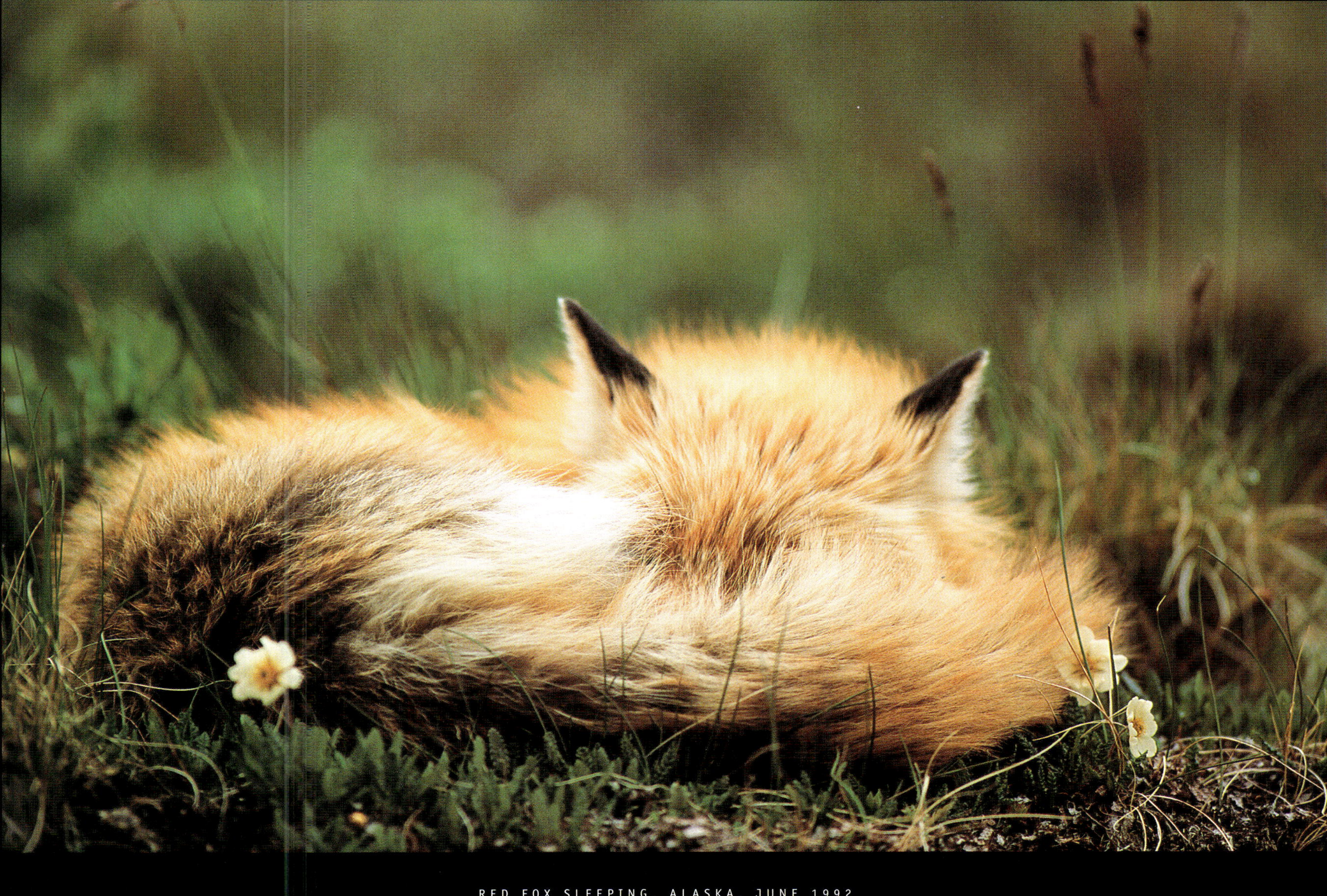

RED FOX SLEEPING, ALASKA, JUNE 1992

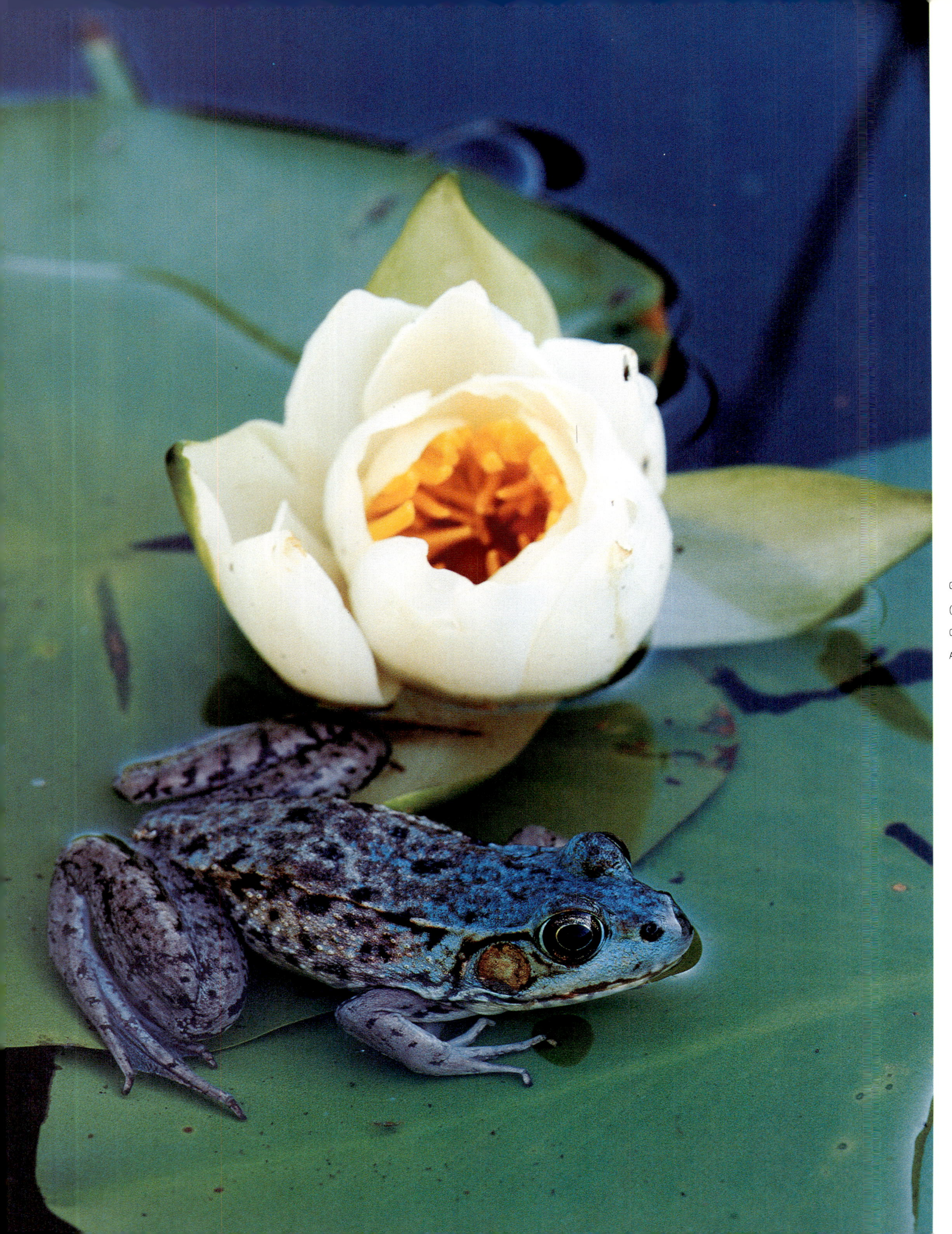

GREEN FROG
(BLUE PHASE),
QUEBEC,
AUGUST 1996

"Moving inside this man is a mystery. A drive of sorts that sends me on journeys, a searching out of wonder. Why it is there, I do not know. The dichotomy is that even though I'm looking for it, it's as if I don't really want to find it."

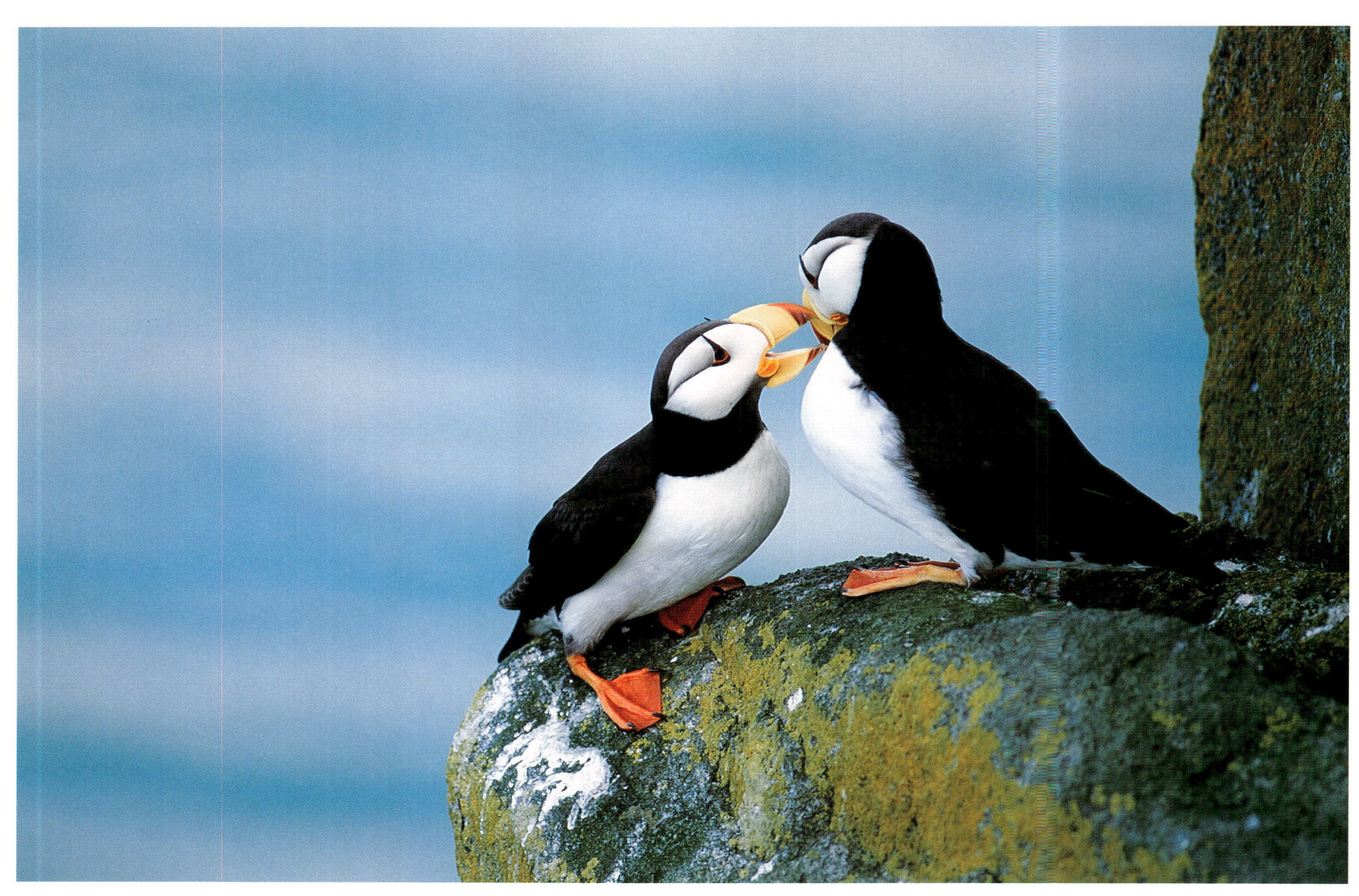

HORNED PUFFINS GREETING, ALASKA, JULY 1992

If this were a work of fiction, I'd tell you how I went into the woods on a rainy day, communed with nature, survived a near-fatal snake bite, and came out a changed man just as the sun was breaking through the clouds.

If only it were that easy. Real life, however, is not a cliché, a Walt Disney film, or a tightly-written novel with a neatly-wrapped ending.

Real change comes only as a result of a great deal of soul-searching, a great deal of prayer, and a great deal of time.

Real life is not a destination, but a journey.

"The ability to set your sights on a target and move toward it exists very seldom these days. To do this correctly, you must have a vision, a sensitive nature, and a burning passion that can blaze through the toughest times."

While there's no doubt that many people have experienced dramatic conversions and sudden, inspirational bolts from the blue, I think the more common experience is one of God whispering directly to your heart, moving you toward the answers you seek not with a single, forceful push, but with gentle, persistent nudges.

What begins as an indistinct impression gradually takes shape and solidifies, growing quietly in the heart until one day you see it very clearly, and realize it's been there all along.

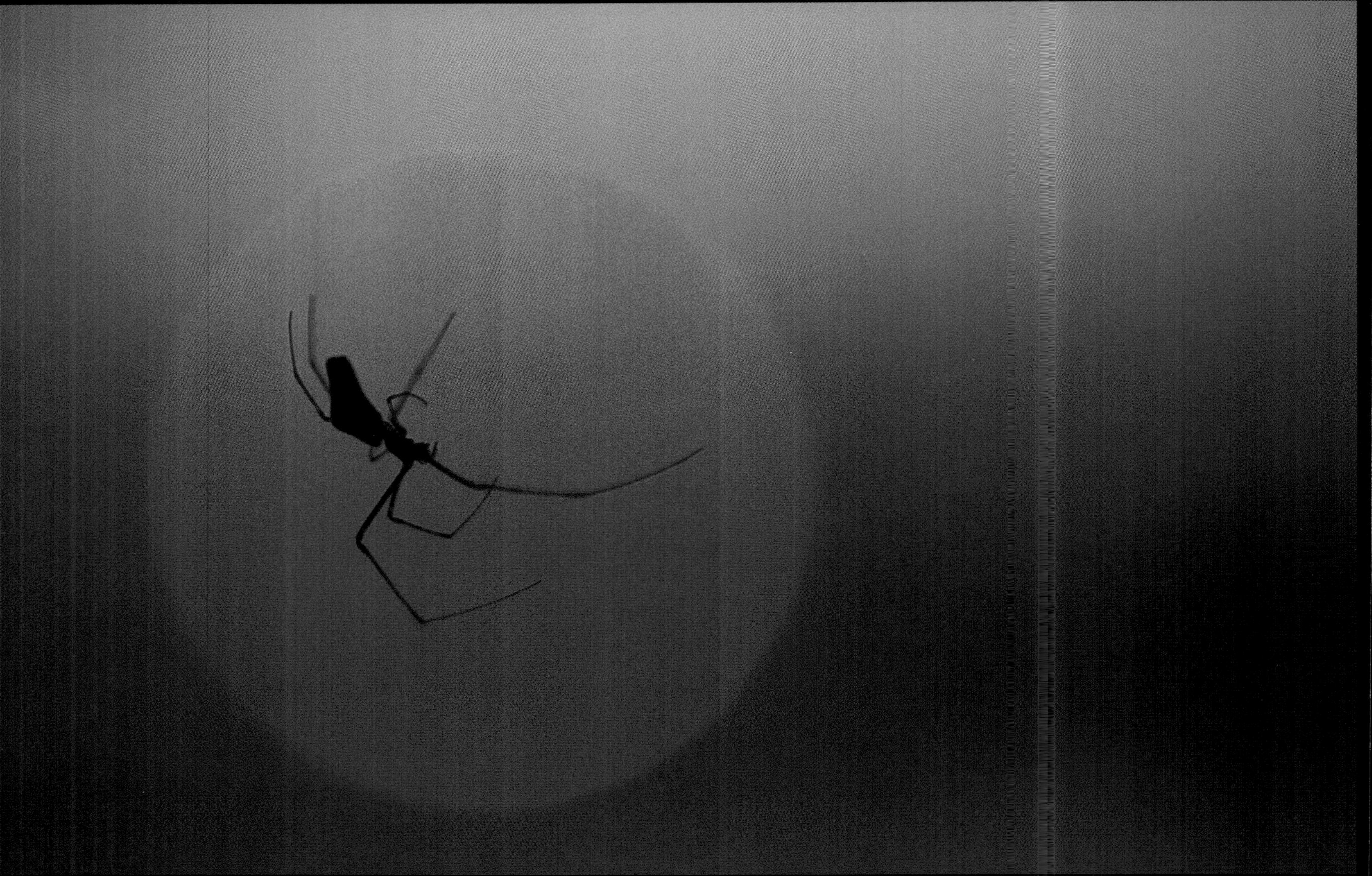

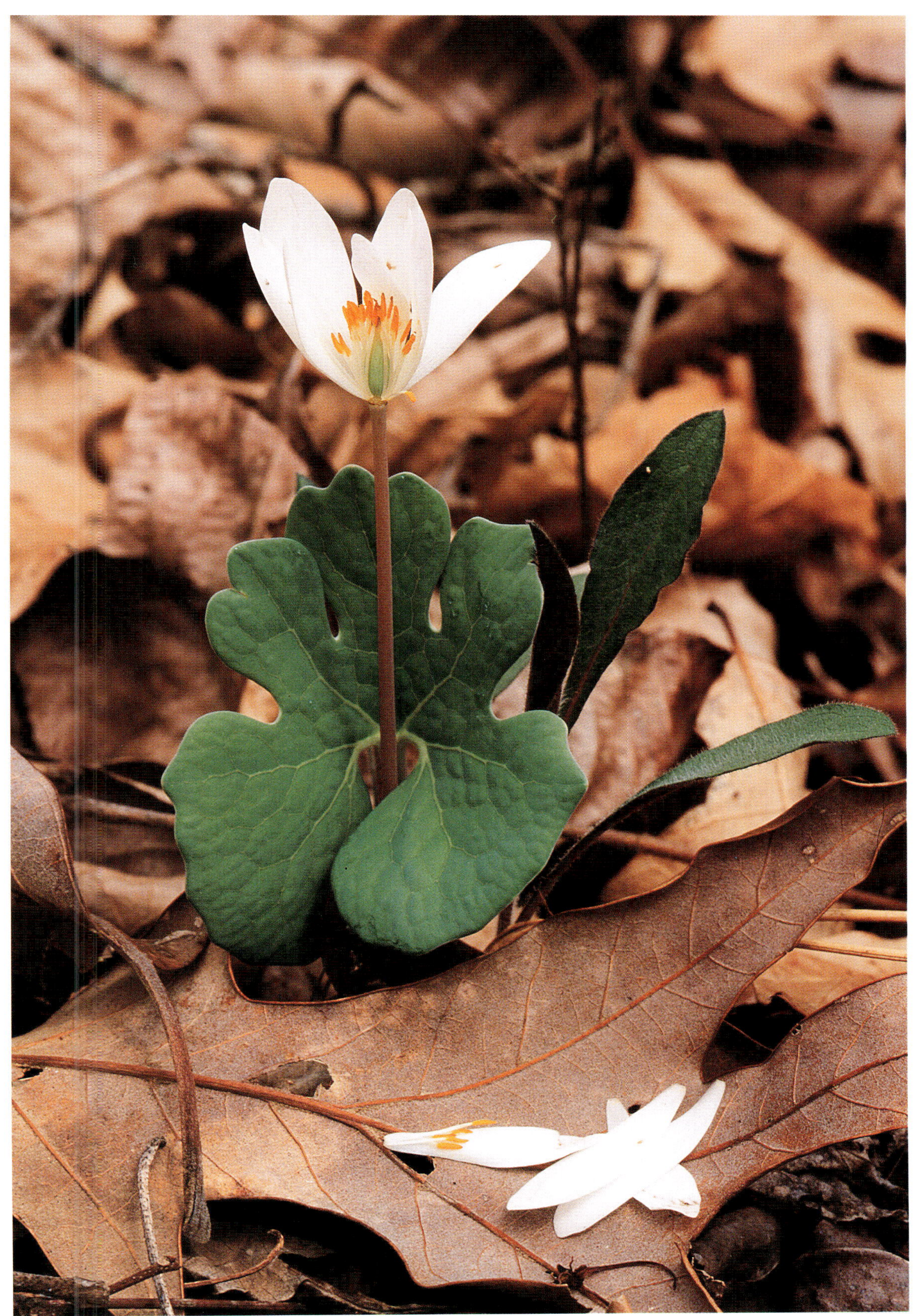

BLOODROOT, MISSISSIPPI, APRIL 1993

"The heart – the core of human existence. It is the place faith inhabits, the depths of the soul. A volcano comes to mind, the core burning hot and making its way to the surface where it becomes visible and changes the landscape, even though the coolness of the atmosphere hardens it."

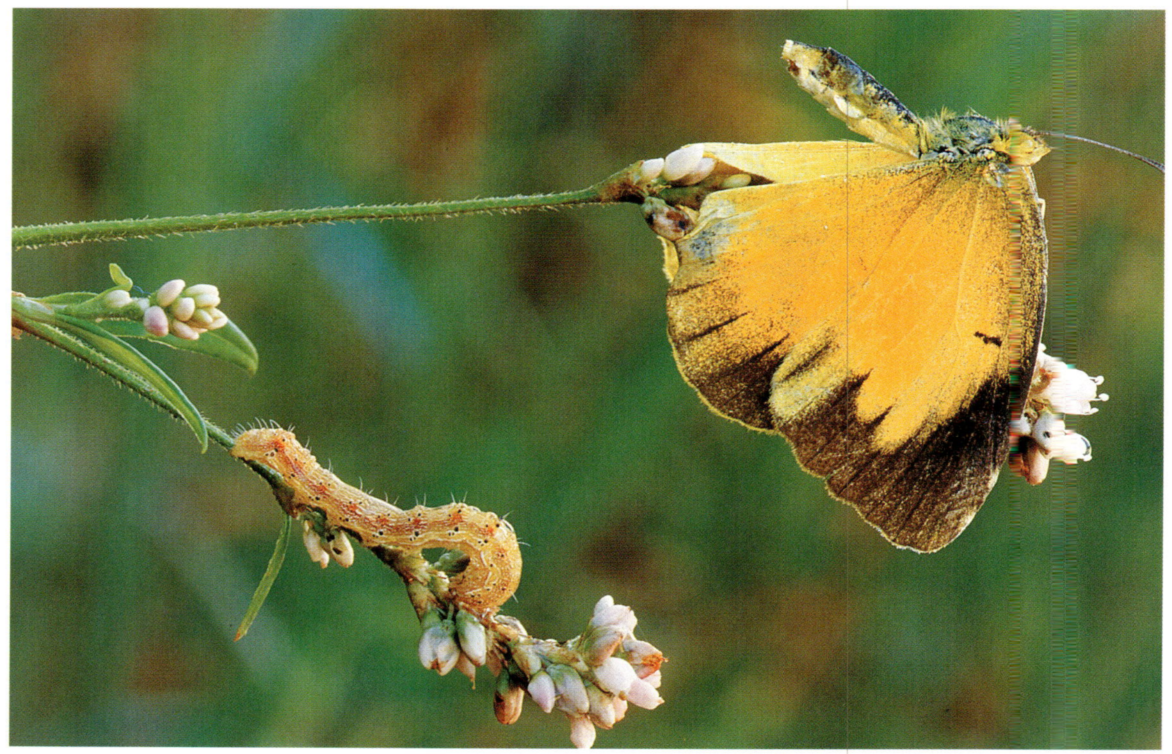

SULPHUR BUTTERFLY AND CATERPILLAR, MISSISSIPPI, SEPTEMBER 199

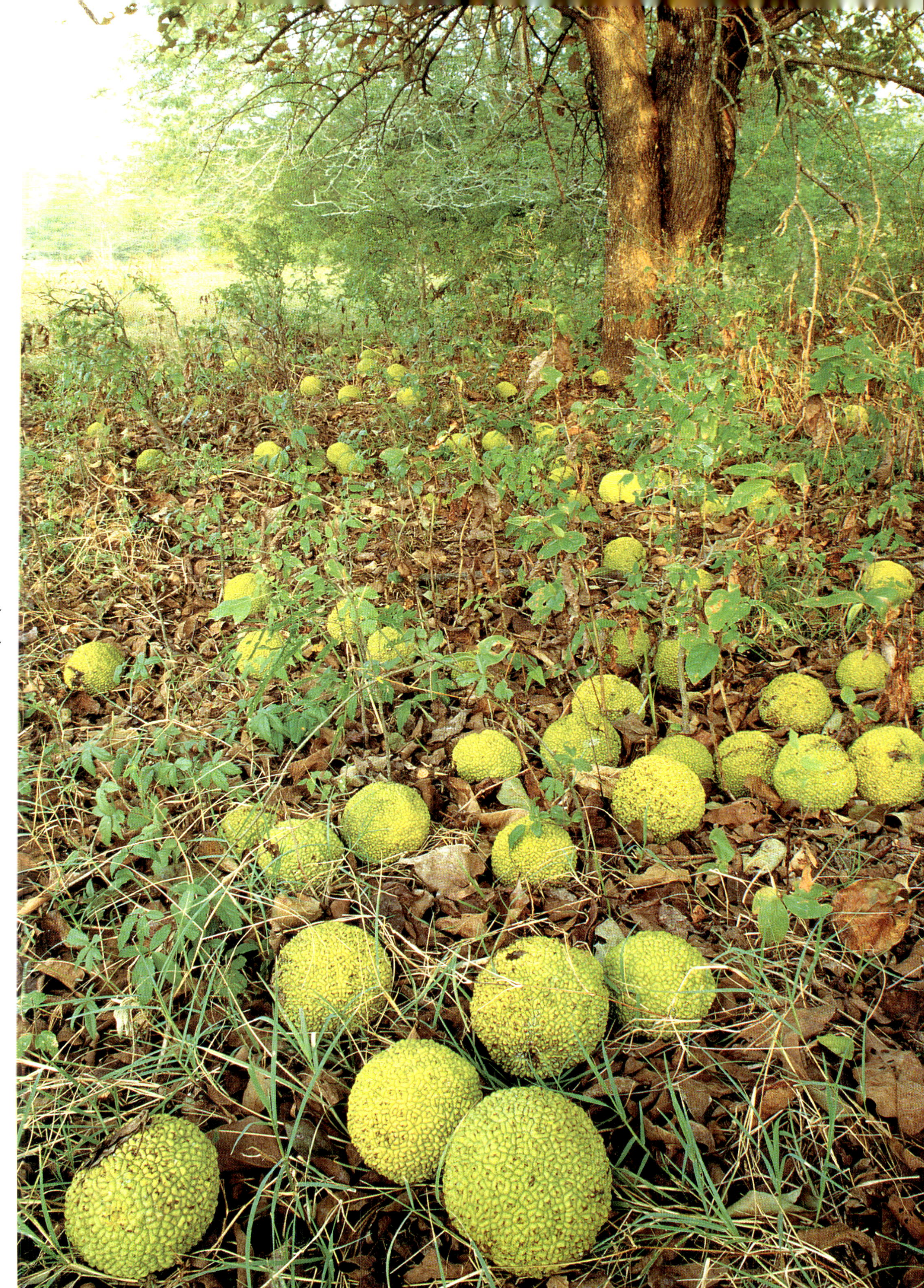

OSAGE ORANGE,
MISSISSIPPI,
OCTOBER 1995

"I see my mind as a busy street that cannot be rerouted. My friends describe it as a traffic jam. There is, however, no doubt that it is always 'on' and in gear. I constantly search for a way to disengage it. Once in a while I manage to get it into neutral. These times seem to involve wilderness and fatigue. What does that tell you?"

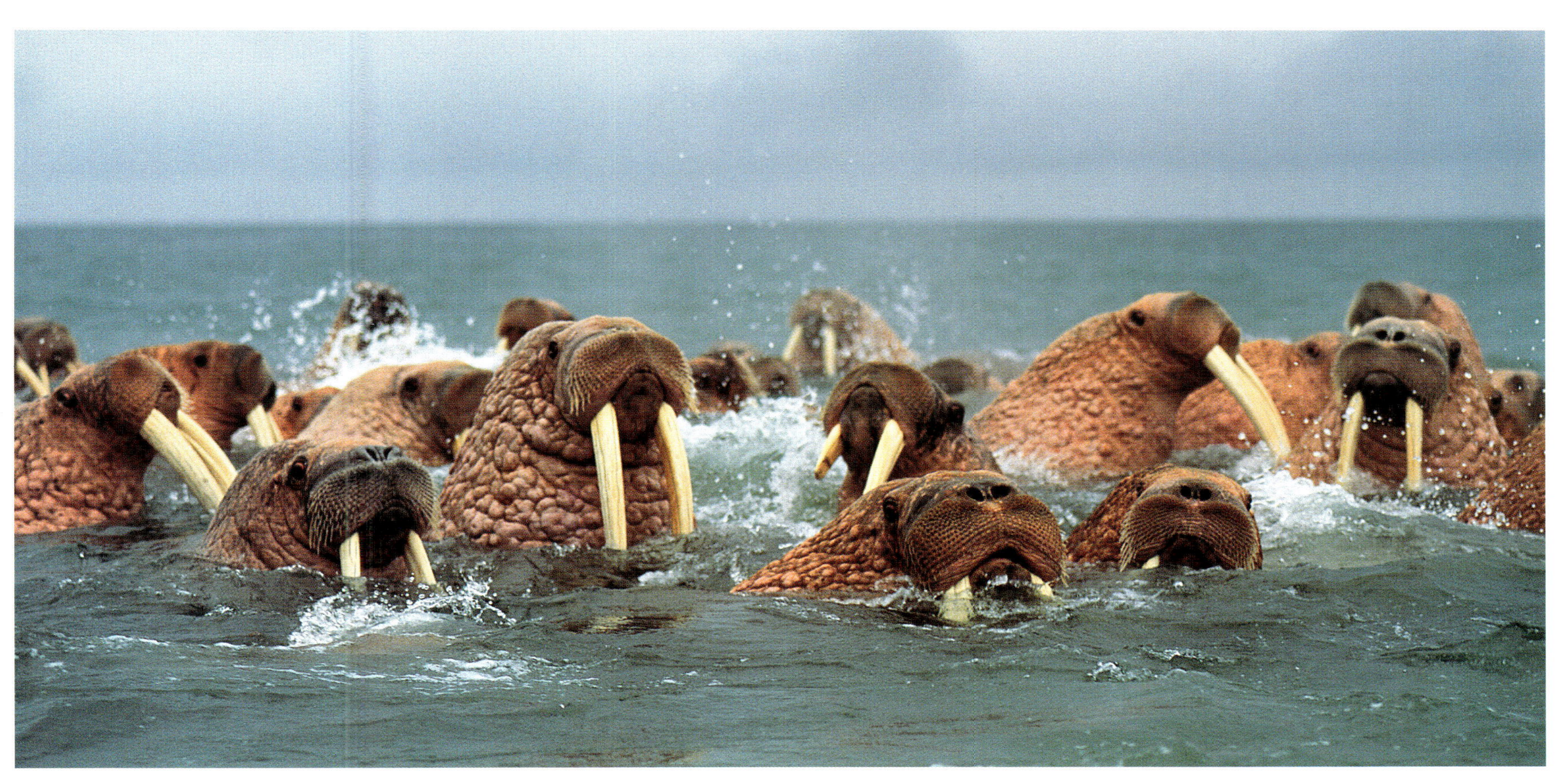

MALE WALRUS SWIMMING, ALASKA, JULY 1992

While I can't pretend that a walk in the woods is a balm for all of life's problems, it sure does help. After all, what force other than nature can be dependable yet ever-changing, calming and inspiring, all in the same instant?

"Nature is my quiet place, my home, if you will.... It's so steady. You can depend on it. There are beautiful, tranquil days and there are scary, stormy days, but at least there will continue to be days."

"Nature is not always kind, but nature is always honest. It doesn't change for you just because you are unhappy, in a bad mood, or feeling great. No, you take what it gives you, plain and simple. It's true, honest, and will never deceive you. You never have to second-guess its motives or emotions. It has none, and that's fine with me."

The thing you love most is a clue to your calling and talent – a mental bill-board shouting "*This is* what you were put here to do!"

Most people assume I was a photographer first, an outdoorsman second. The opposite is true.

The Lord instills in each of us gifts to use in our own lives and to glorify Him. I may have learned to use a camera, but the first gift God gave to me was a love of the outdoors.

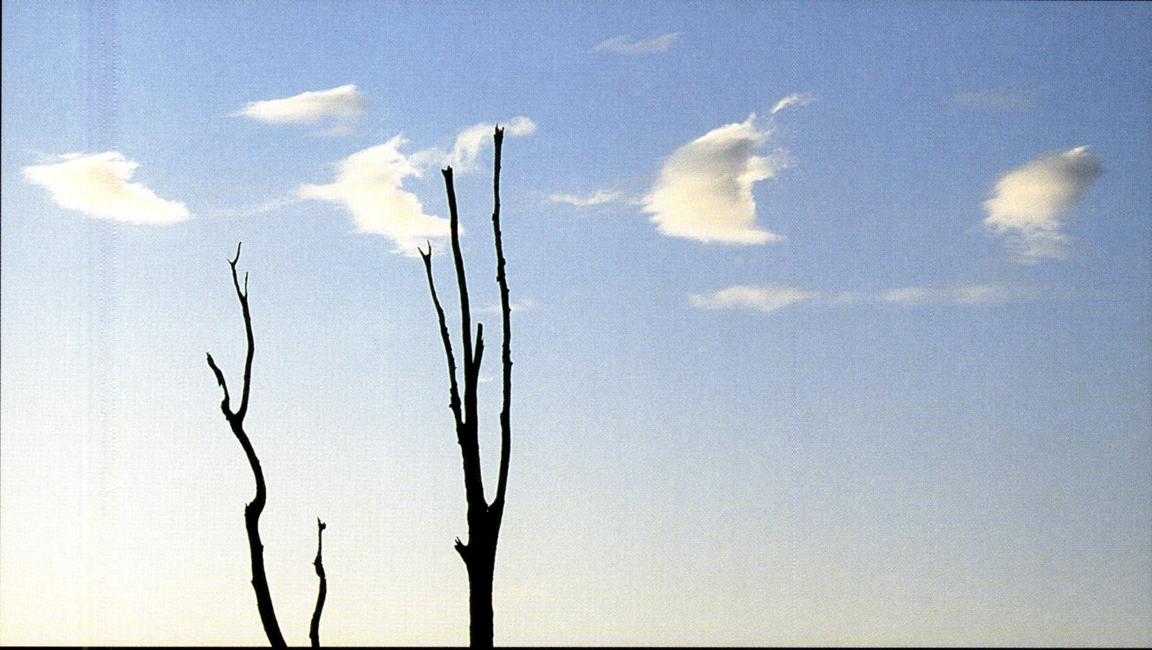

TREE AND CLOUDS, MISSISSIPPI, SEPTEMBER 1992

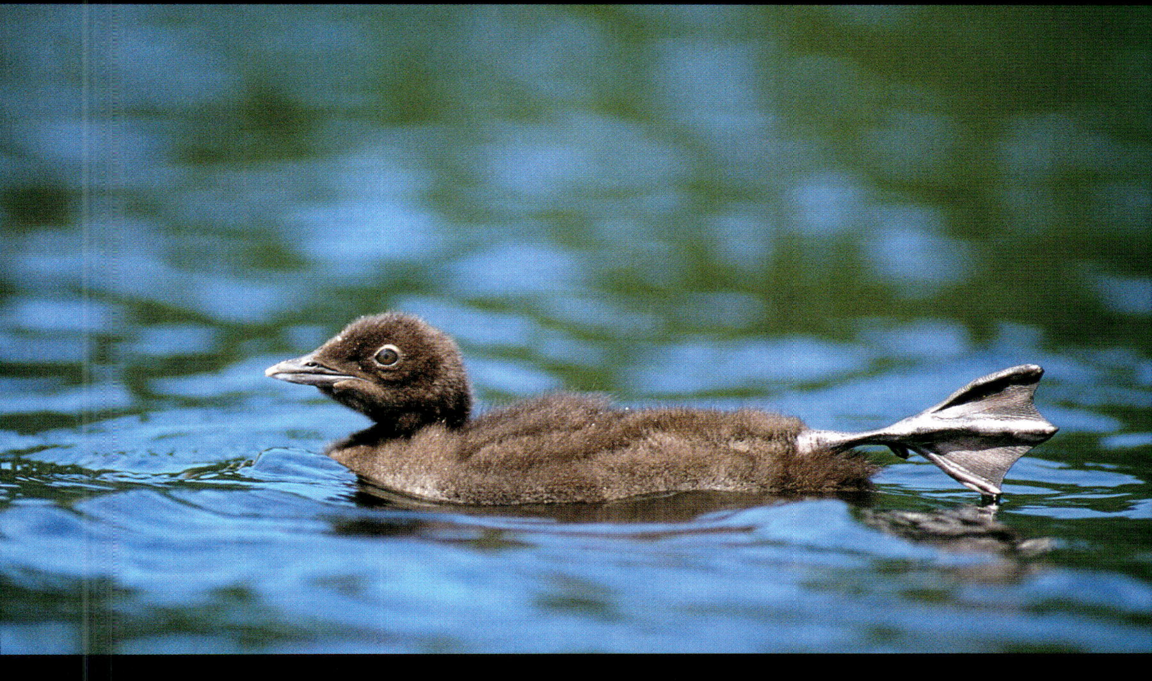

COMMON LOON CHICK STRETCHING, NEW HAMPSHIRE, JUNE 1995

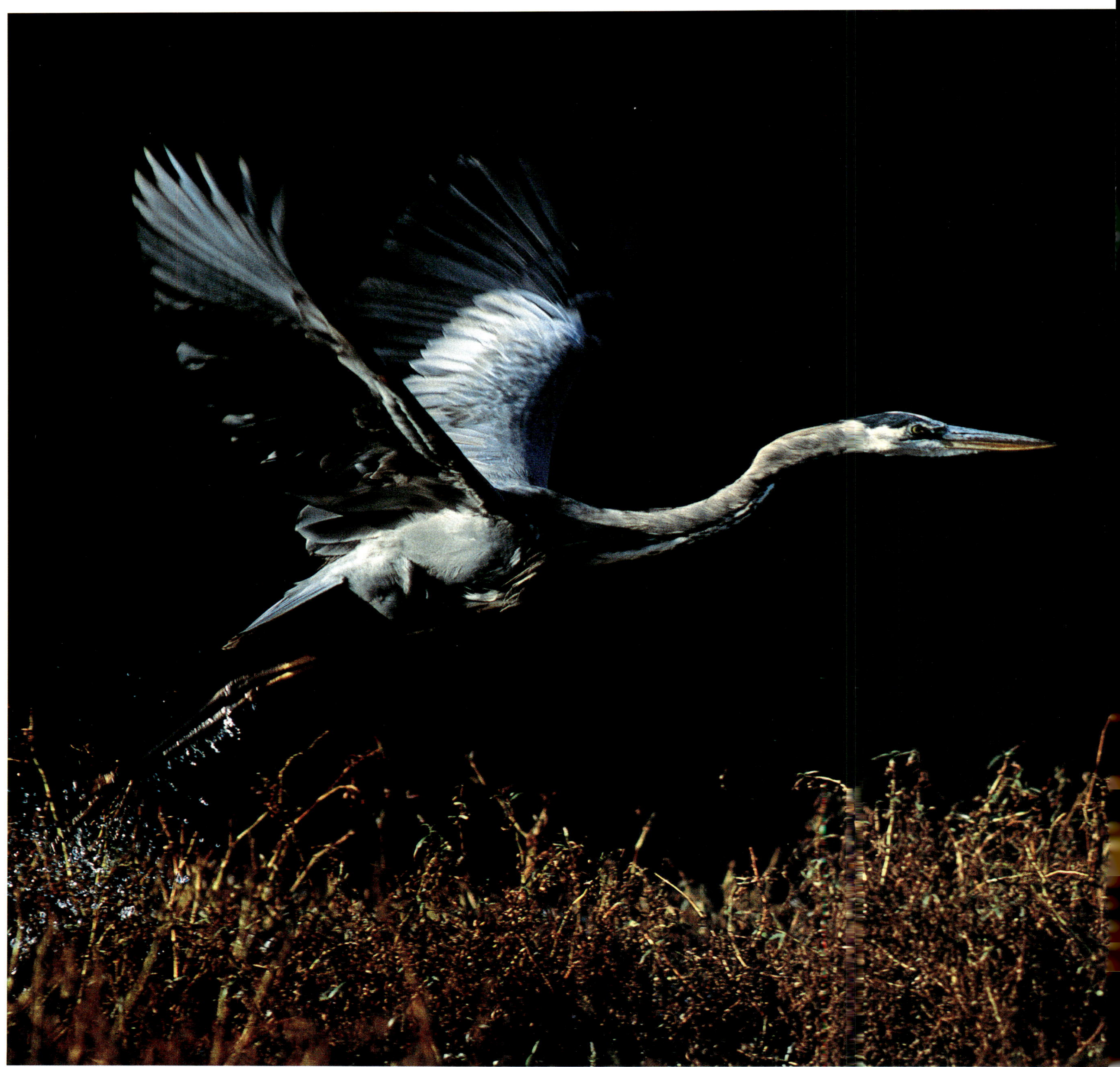

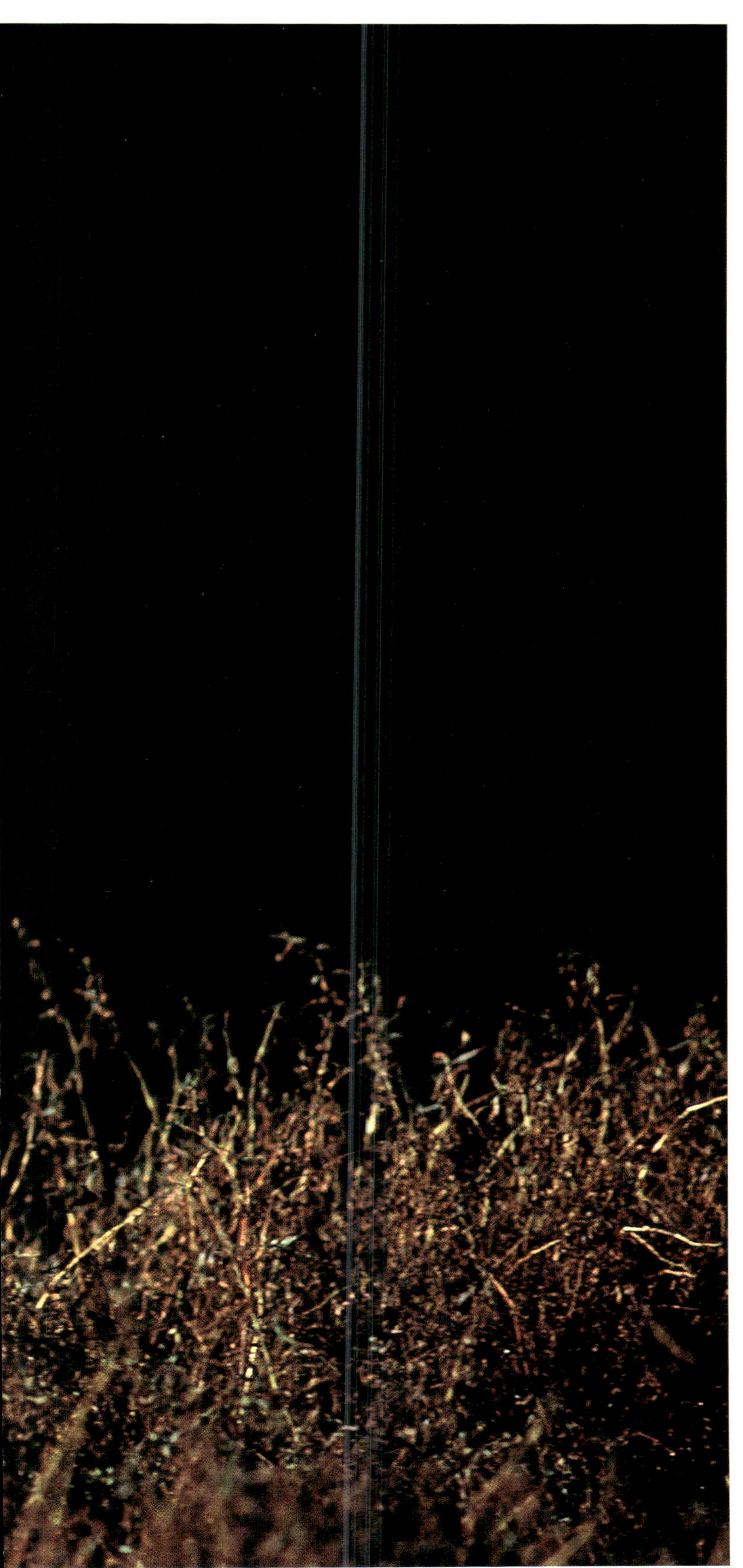

GREA¯ BLUE HERON, MARYLAND, OCTOBER 1992

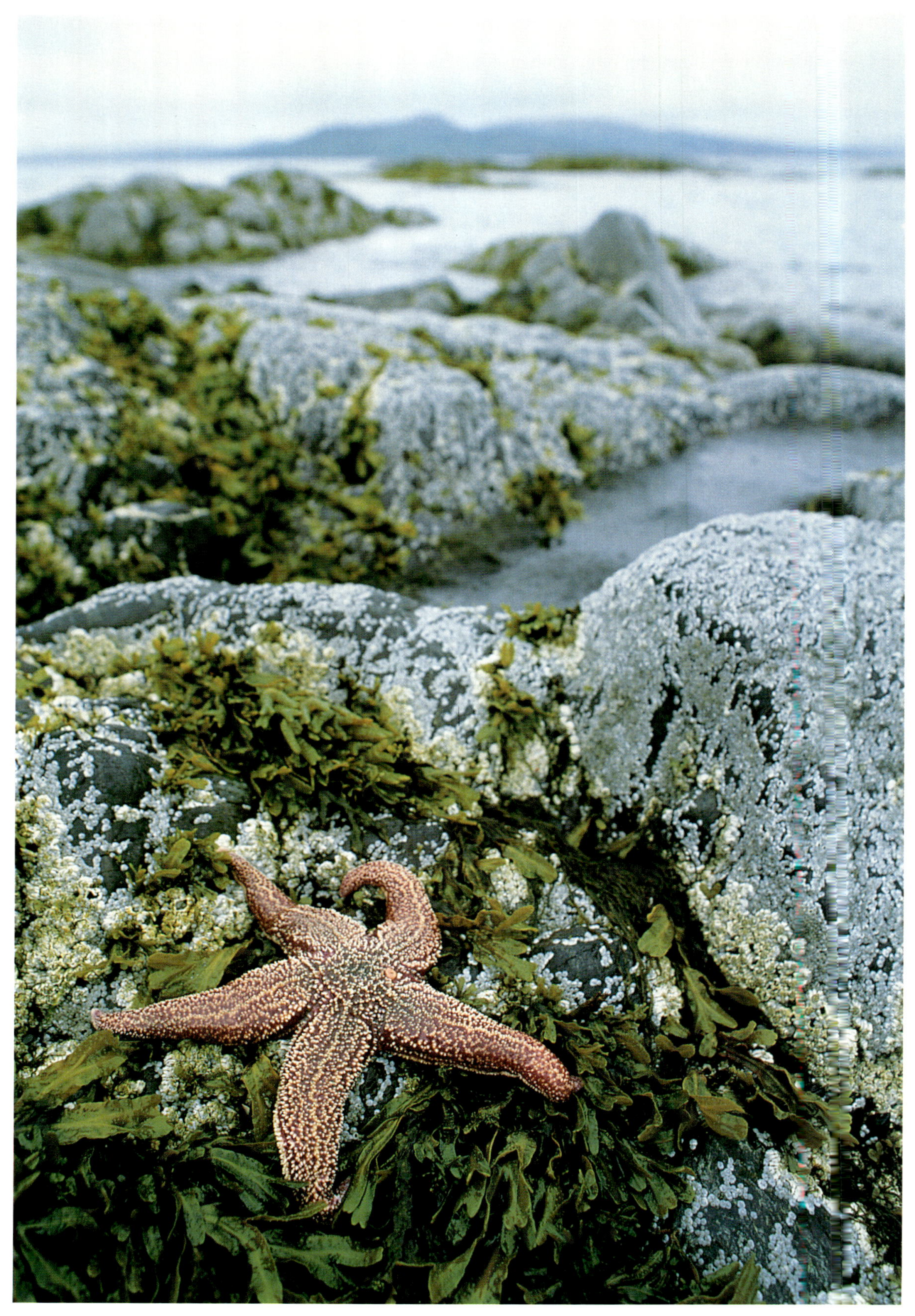

STARFISH ON SUMMIT ISLAND, ALASKA, JULY 1992

"I am an outdoorsman – that not *being defined as 'one who lives with bears.'*

"The term 'outdoorsman' is not necessarily a person who has a cottage on a northern lake among fragrant balsams with a boat or two for fishing. It cannot be defined simply as one who sleeps in a tent on a sandy shore, waking to a smoldering fire.

"The title isn't reserved for the lone explorer paddling through the ethereal surroundings of a foggy southern swamp. Pursuits of mountain tops or lost rainforests cannot make you one.

"An outdoorsman cannot be defined by mere outward appearances. For the heart of an outdoorsman lies not in the outdoors, but in the awareness *of the outdoors. It simply is part of his or her being, and no amount of luxury, or poverty, or education can change it."*

SCARLET KINGSNAKE,
MISSISSIPPI,
OCTOBER 1995

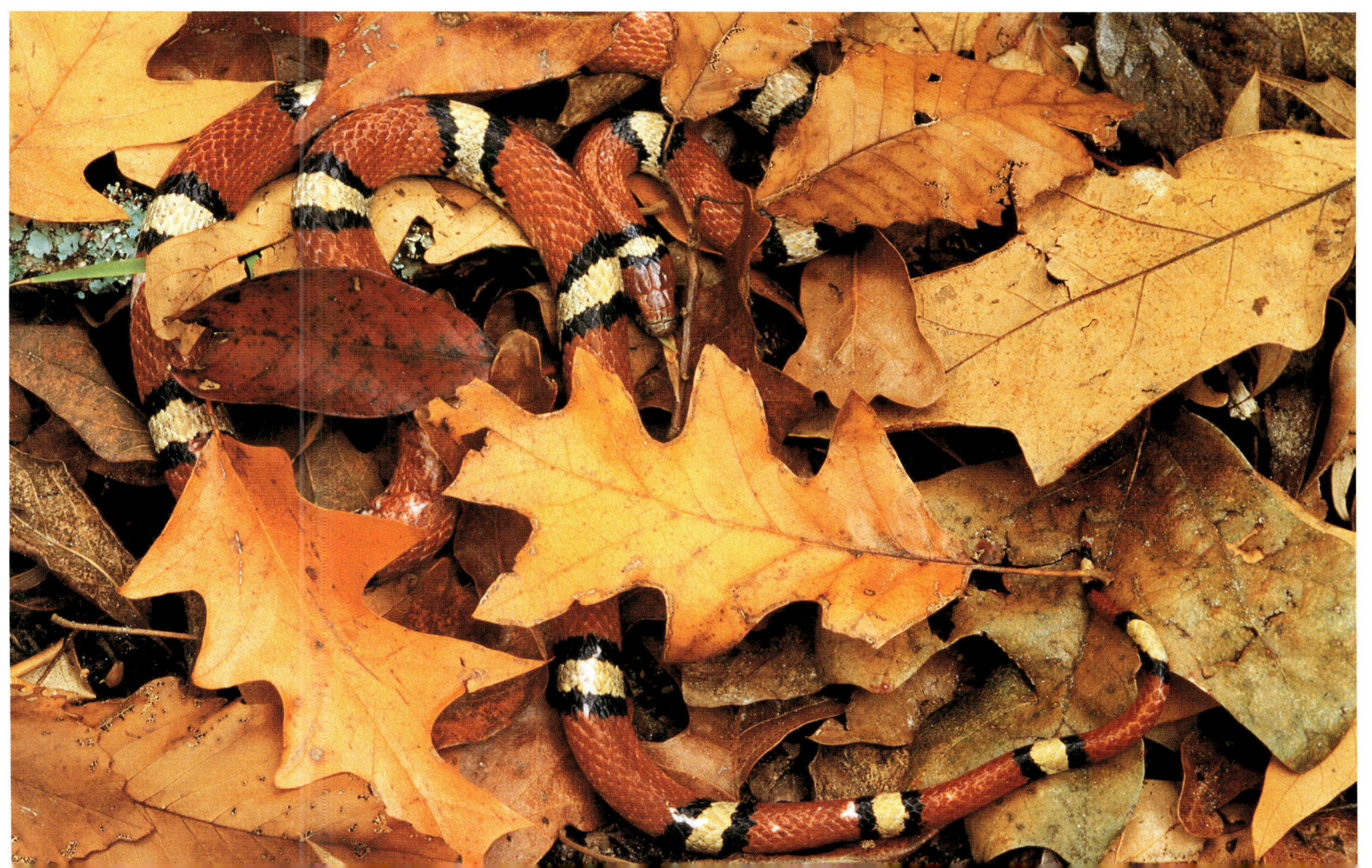

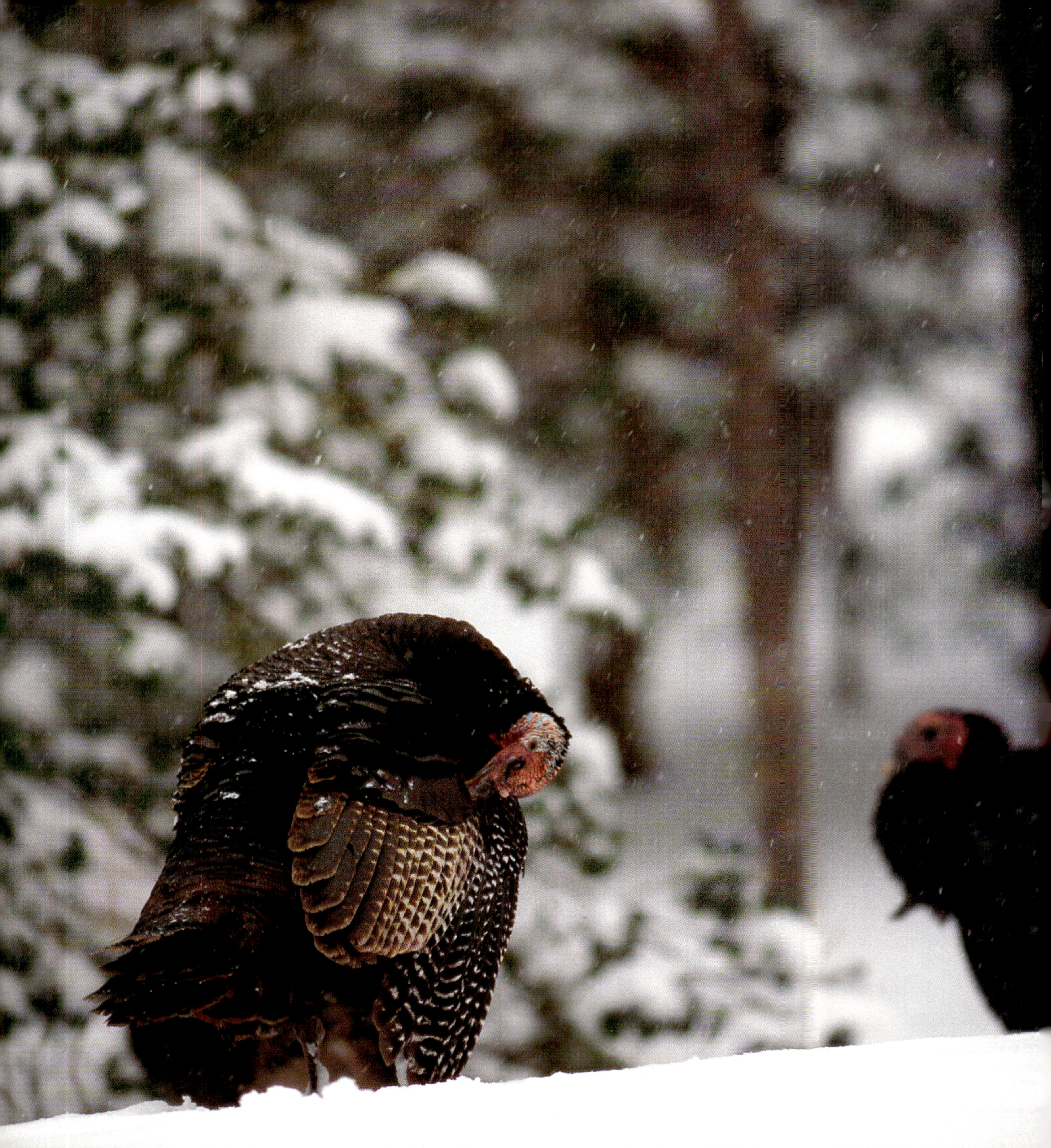

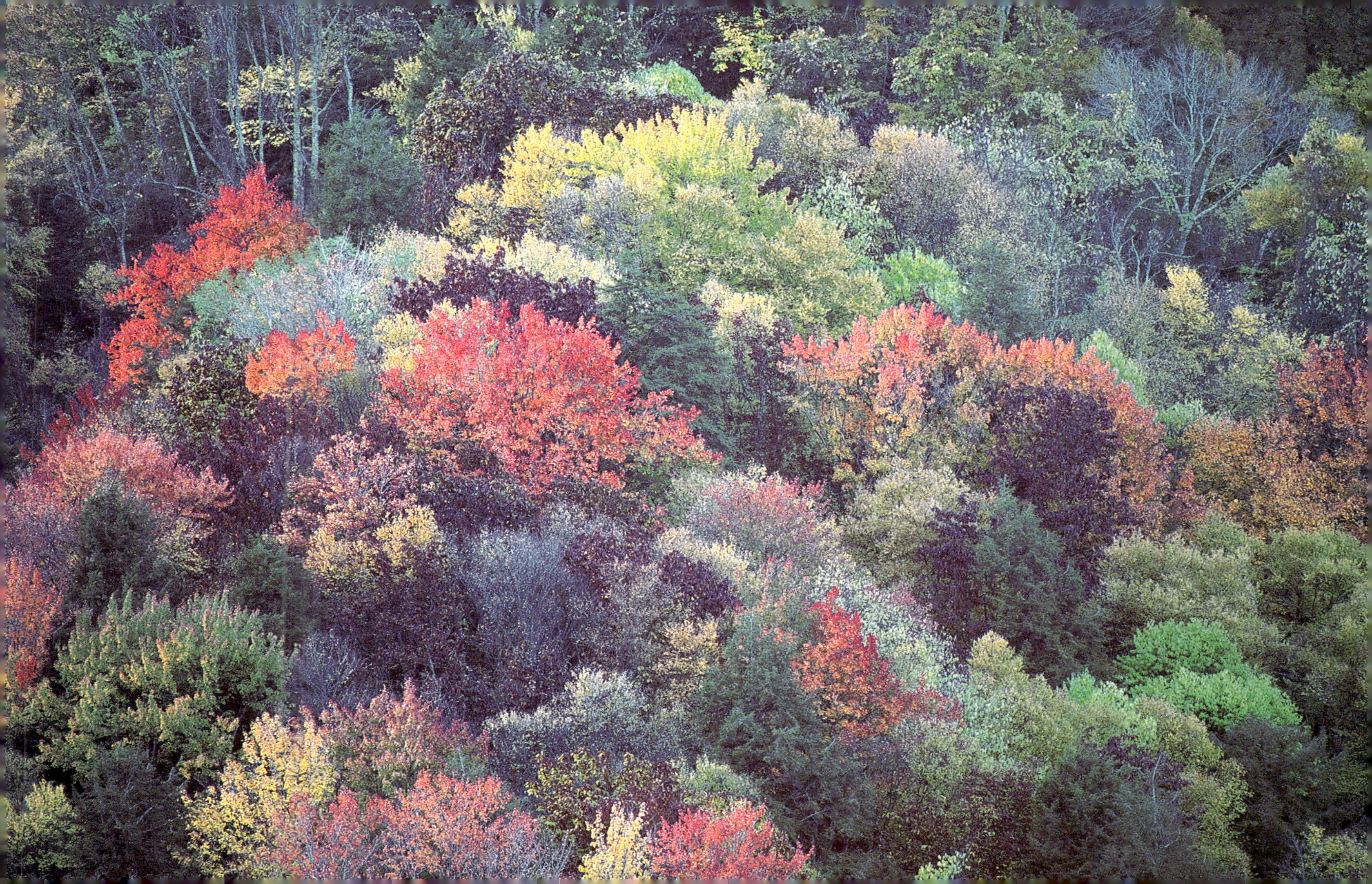

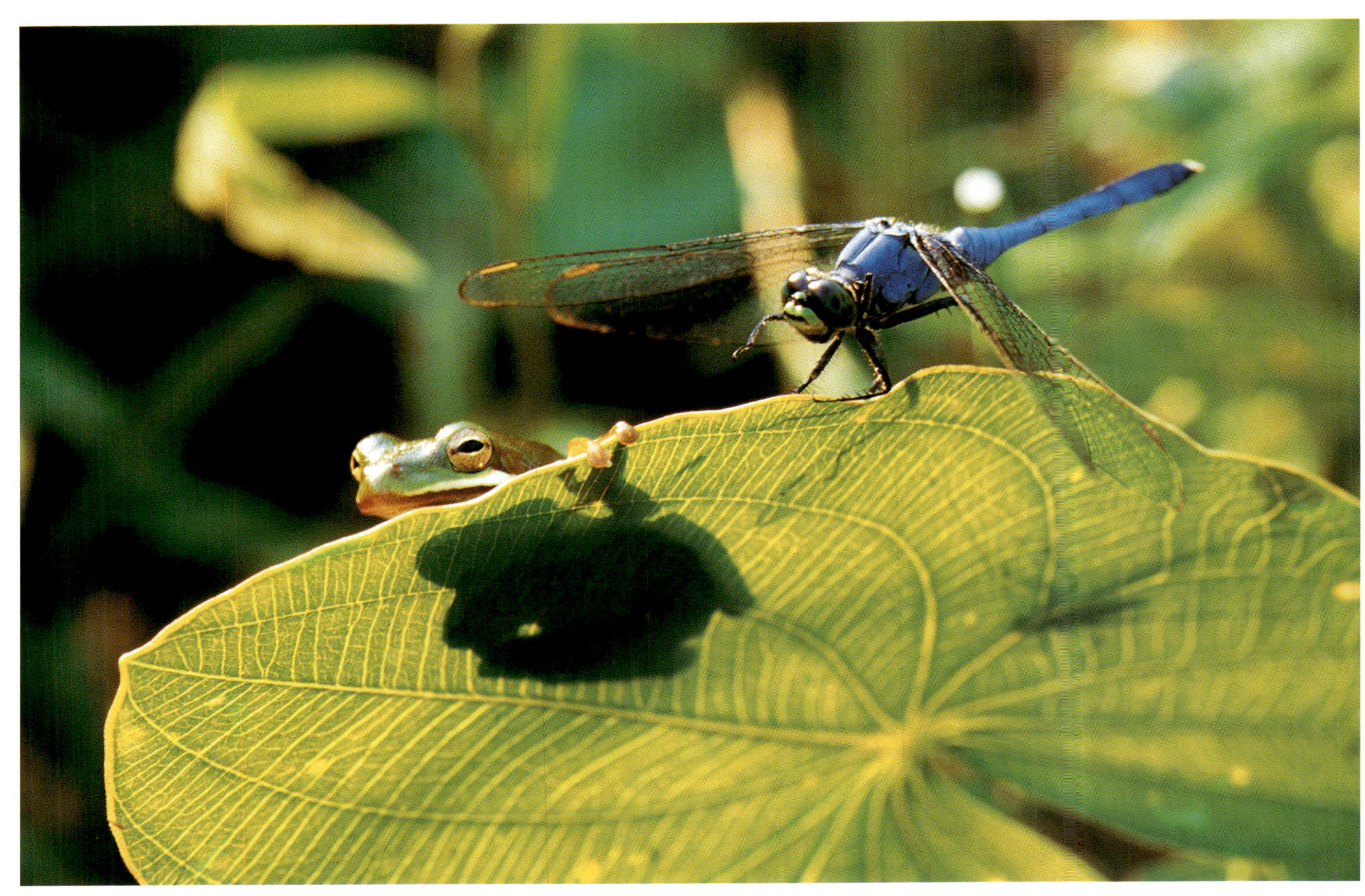

GREEN TREEFROG AND DRAGONFLY, MISSISSIPPI, NOVEMBER 1995

"Sincerity is not an indicator of truth or accuracy. Truth is not a point of view. Even in a 360-degree examination, the truth remains the same."

Heading into the wilderness with a fishing pole, a canoe, and a handful of environmental guides does *not* make one an outdoorsman, much less a naturalist. Too many people who call themselves "nature lovers" merely use the outdoors with no real understanding of it.

"The wilds seem to provide privileges but no obligations? Is this right? In my mind it isn't. It's simply a one-for-one trade – one without the other does not exist.

"The real irony lies in the fact that even when we realize we have an obligation, we're not sure what it is."

We tend to discriminate in our efforts to "save" the wilds, separating nature into parts. We're sincere in our efforts, with the best of intentions, but we're simply too small and finite to have an accurate view of the entire "web of life."

"Strand by strand it's disappearing – the insects, the mussels, the seemingly 'insignificant' little threads. Because their absence doesn't lessen the web's visual beauty, we don't notice it's sending a message of trouble within the structure. Even when we do, we focus our attention on a single strand while the web collapses around us.

"We do not possess the silk to repair the tears. The web's integral parts were spun by a divine hand. We will never understand its full complexity until we're in touch with its Creator."

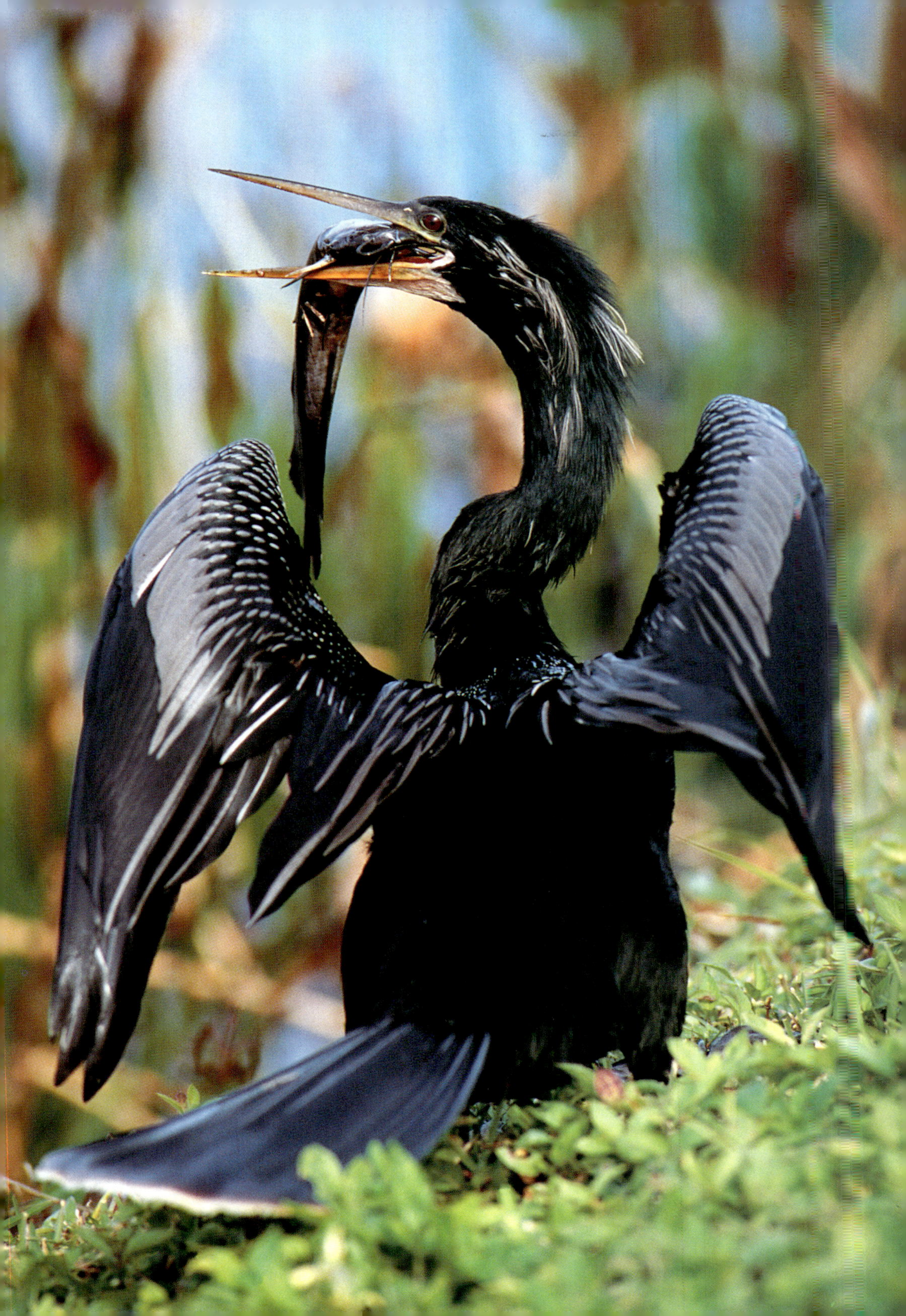

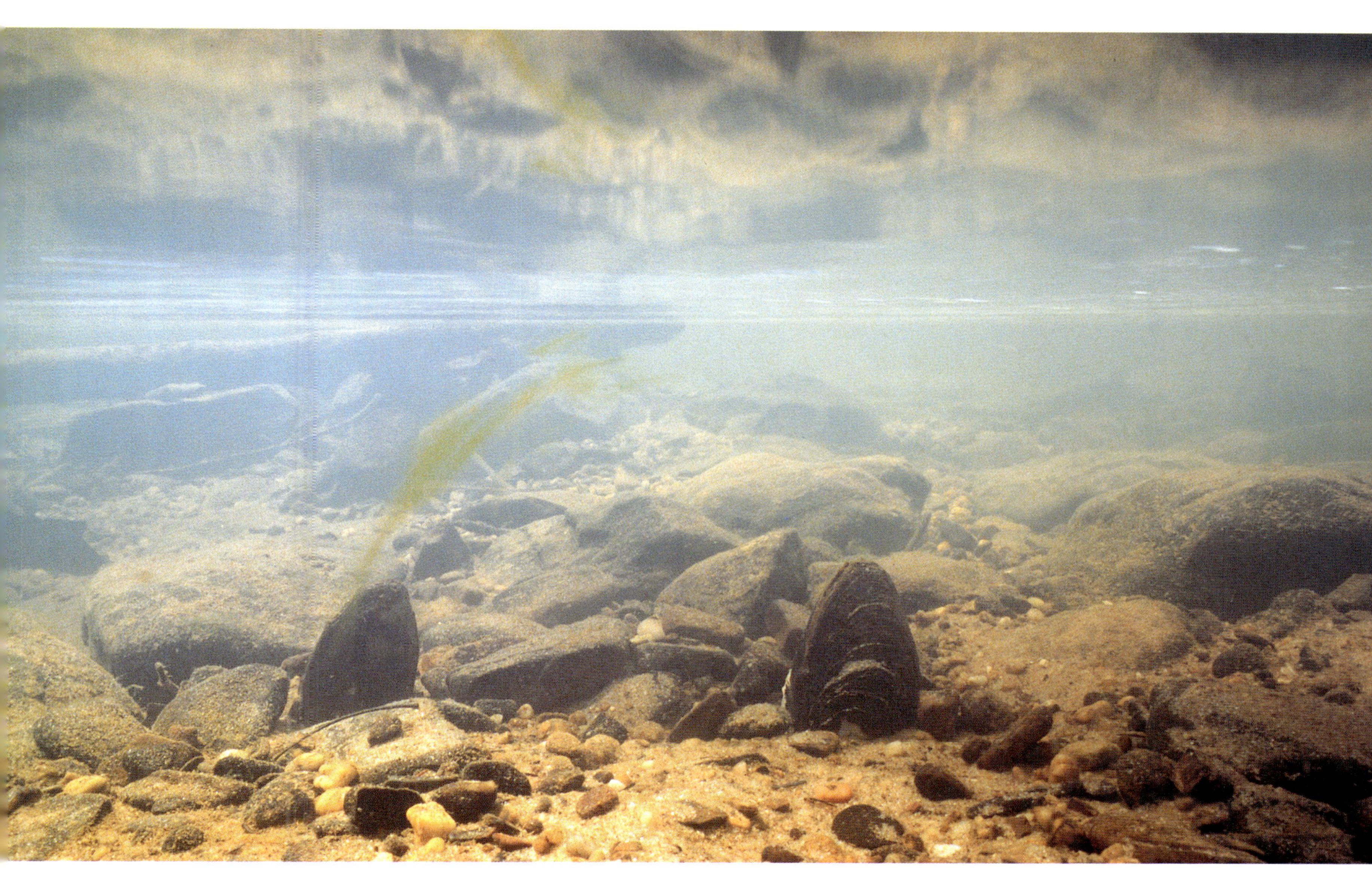

ALABAMA CREEK MUSSEL SPERM RELEASE, ALABAMA, MARCH 1994

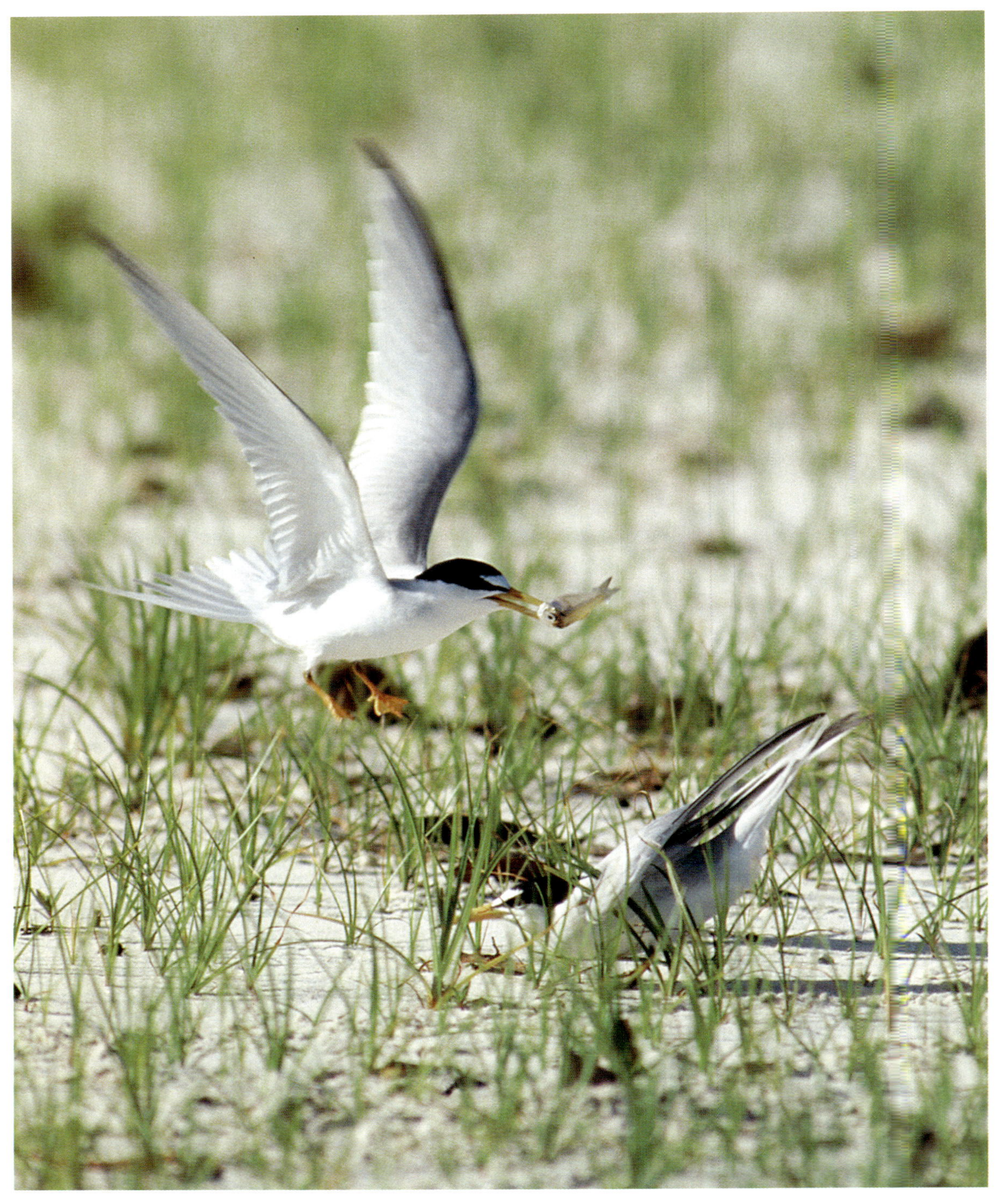

LEAST TERNS COURTING, MISSISSIPPI, JUNE 1996

WHITE-TAILED DEER, TENNESSEE, AUGUST 1996

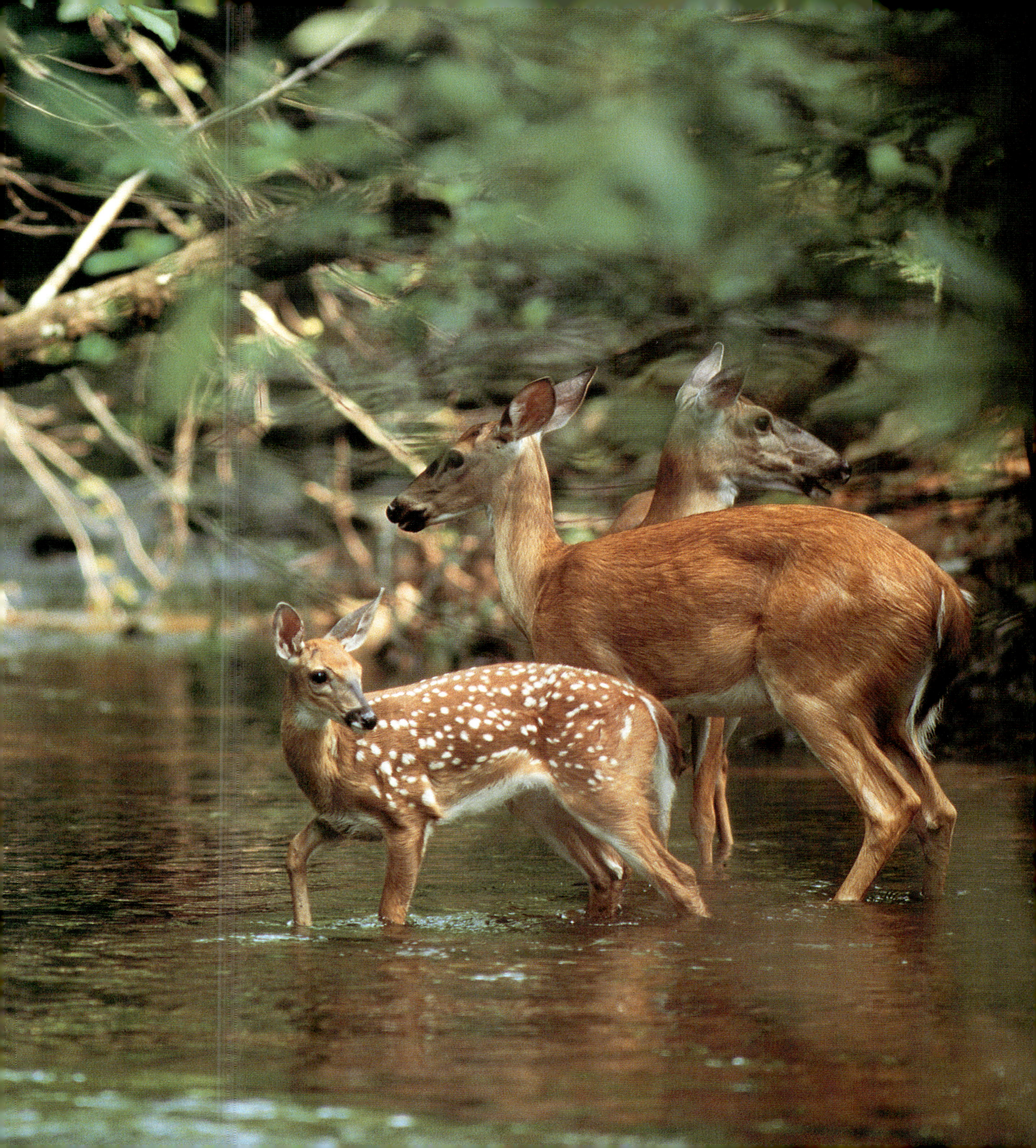

SPRING 1995

journal entry

"We need more natural aspects to our lives. There are no powers that can hurry up a sunrise, the growth of a forest, or the twenty-four hours the day takes to expend itself. The Creator has planted a desire in my heart to slow down, to move at a pace established not by mortals, but by my Maker."

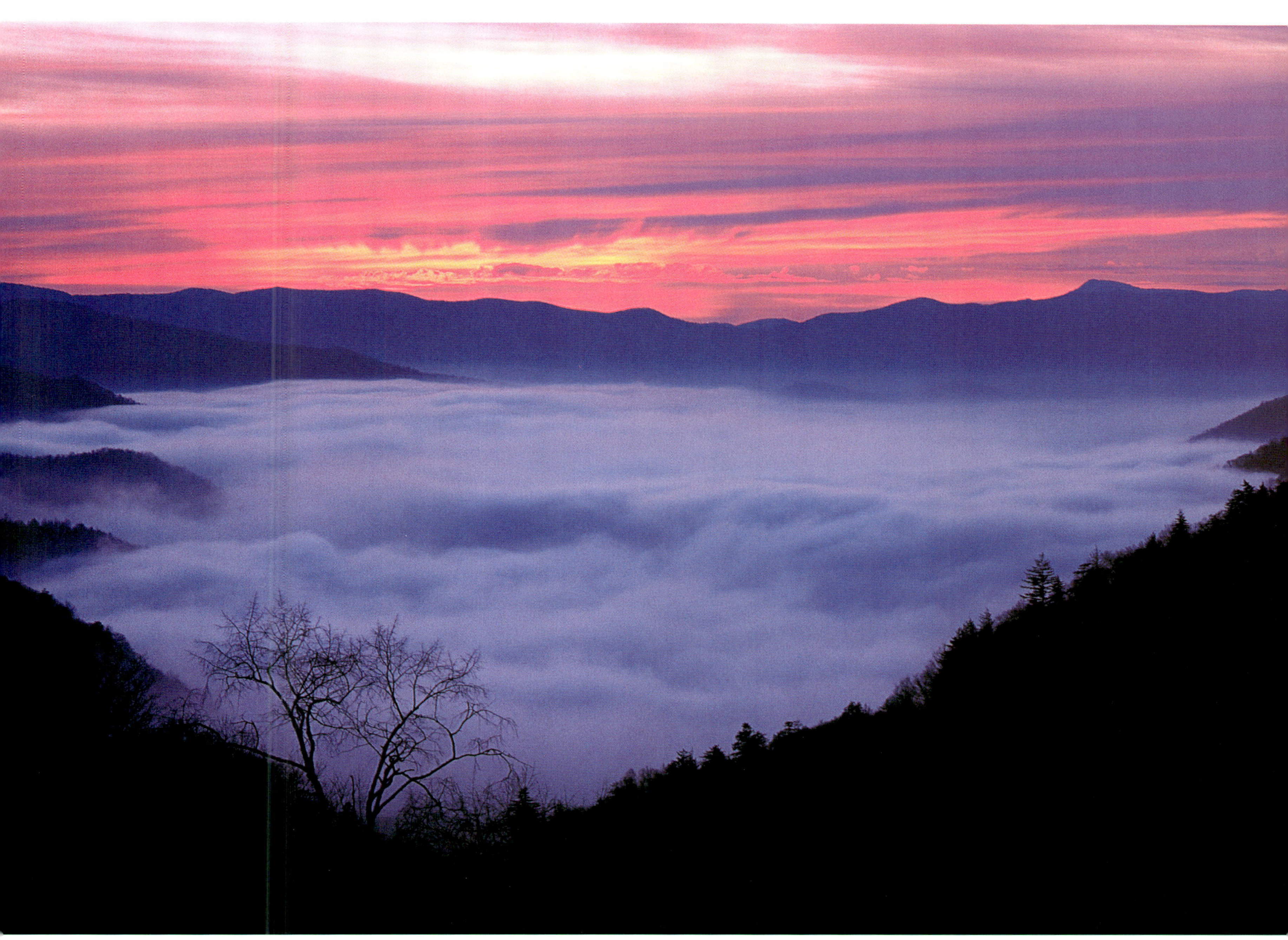

SMOKY MOUNTAIN SUNRISE, NORTH CAROLINA, NOVEMBER 1991

Paperwork, ringing telephones, and the mundane details of daily life that crowded my mind provided a diversion that was sometimes welcome, but more often a trap. A series of never-ending distractions that occupied the conscious level of my thinking, leaving more important ideas to simmer in my subconscious.

"We all want everything now. *Whatever happened to the slow, steady climb? Sometimes I wonder whether the fight I put up to keep contact with a slower pace is actually extracting more energy than it would require to simply keep up with the rest of the world. Overachieving to underachieve! Maybe I should give in.*

"But that simply will not work. My heart rebels when it comes to thoughts like these. How preposterous to even consider such a dishonorable surrender – fight 'til the death! Commitment!"

Alone in the wilderness, I worked on *nature's* timetable. There were no distractions, nothing pulling at my attention, nothing to break my focus. The jumble of thoughts and impressions generated by my overworked subconscious seized the opportunity to rise to the surface.

I had no choice other than to adapt, slow down, and wait for it all to come to me.

MALLARDS DEPARTING, MISSISSIPPI, JANUARY 1995

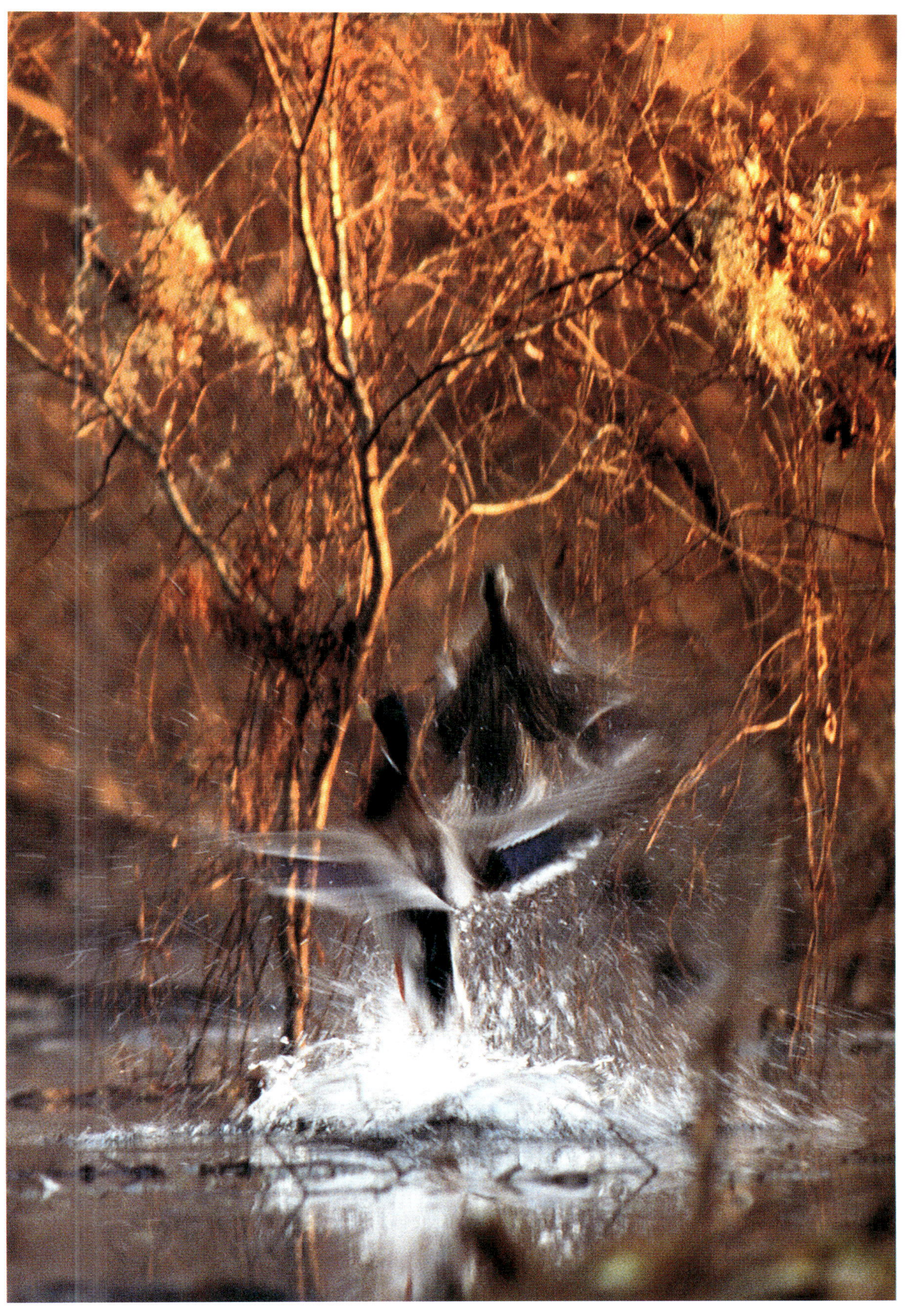

ASKA, SEPTEMBER 1996

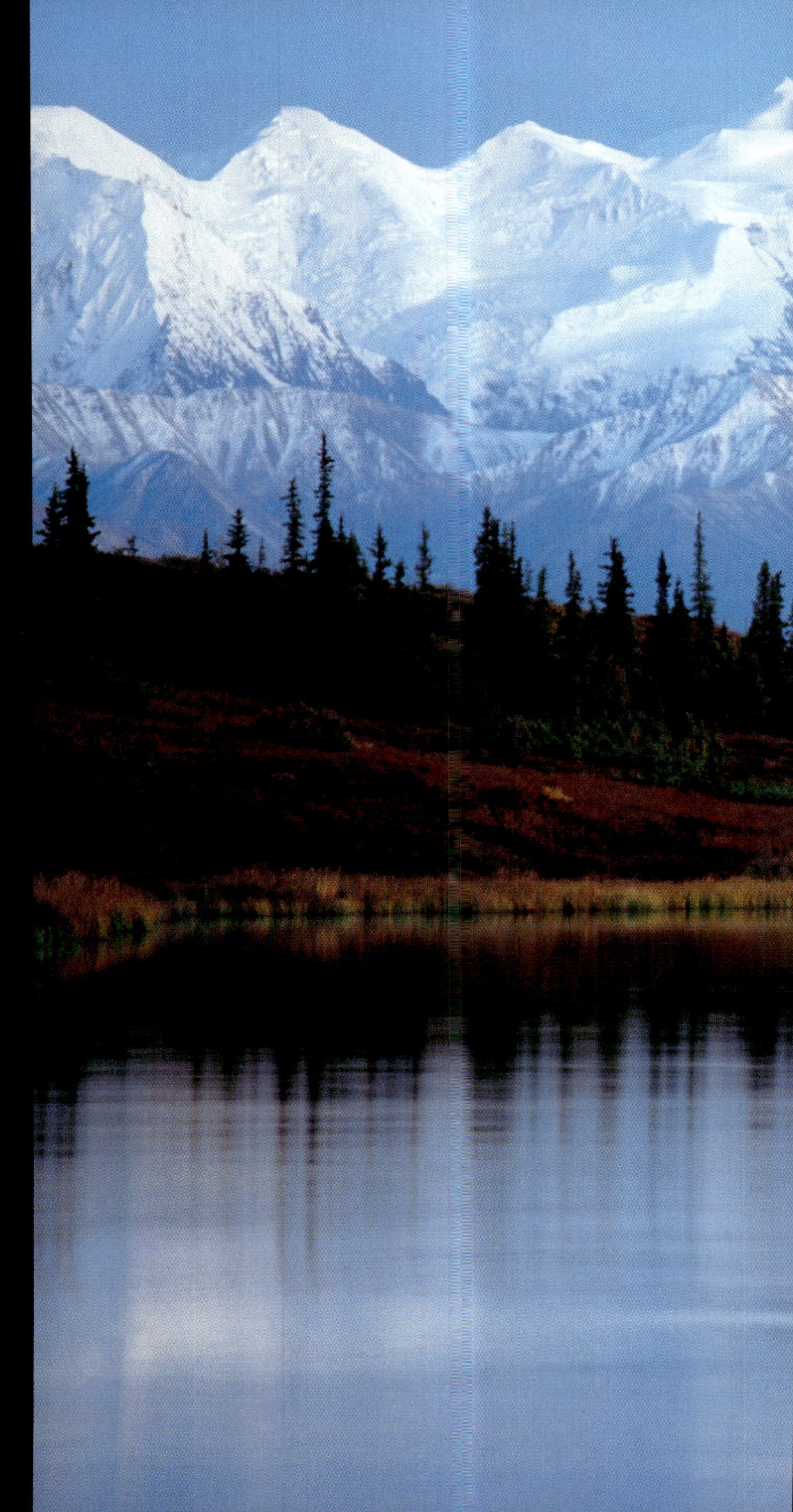

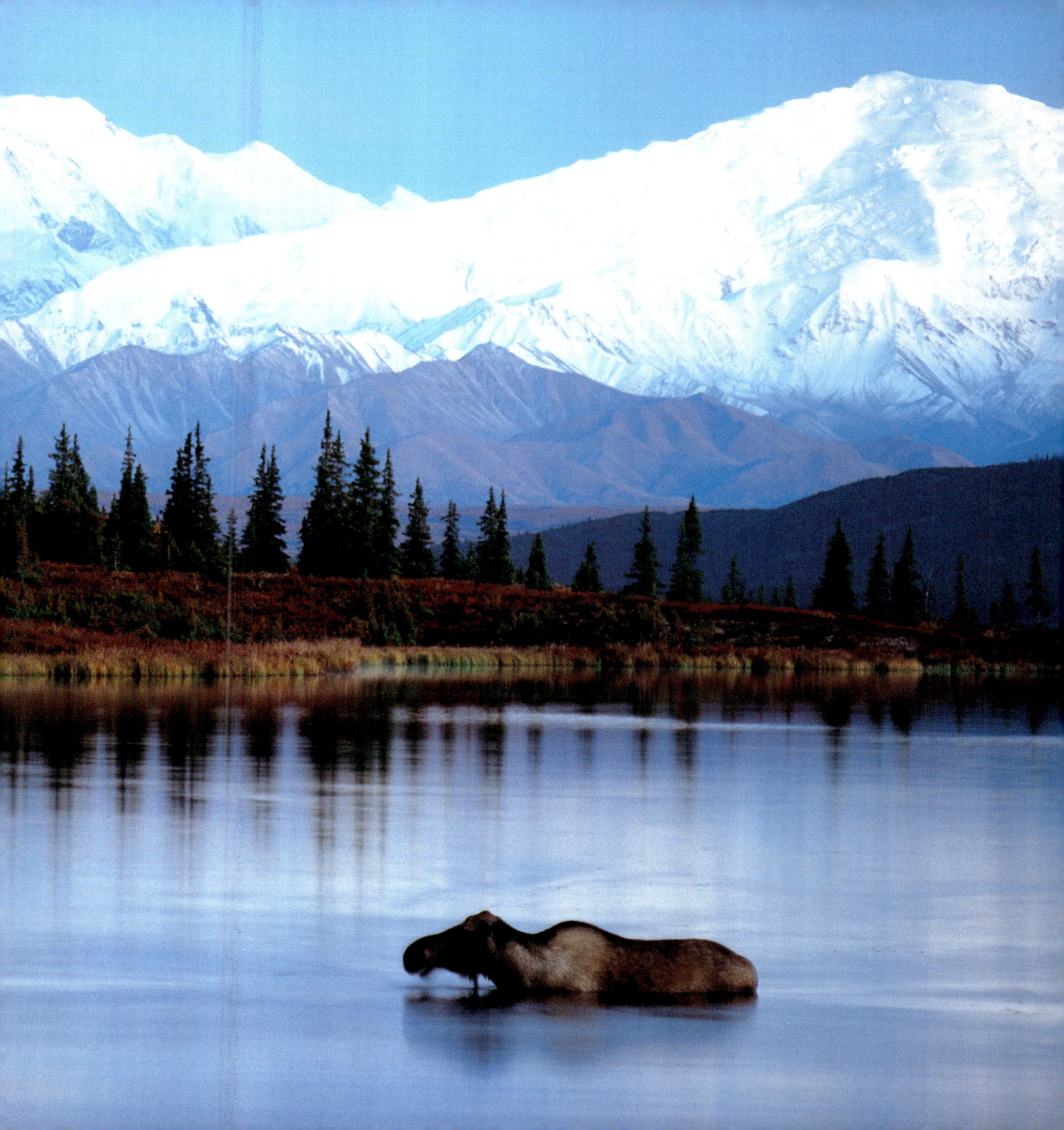

SUMMER 1995

journal entry

"Everything has an out-of-my-head, into-my-heart flavor to it. Not that the head doesn't have a function. It's just that processed information has to leave the logical functions of the brain and enter into the heart for anything meaningful to happen. It's the same with photography. It takes a brain to operate a camera, but it takes a heart to capture a photograph."

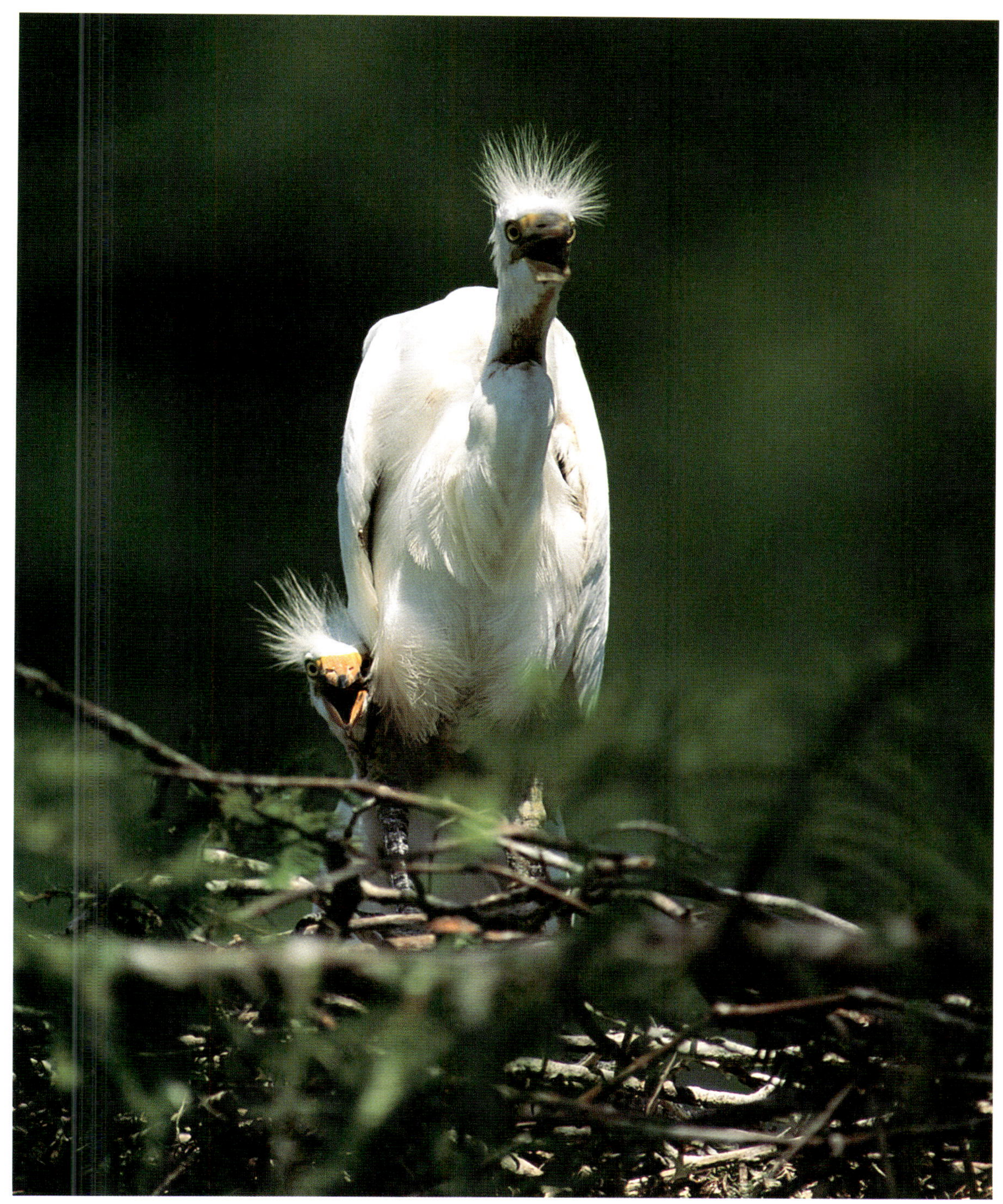

YOUNG EGRETS, MISSISSIPPI, JUNE 1993

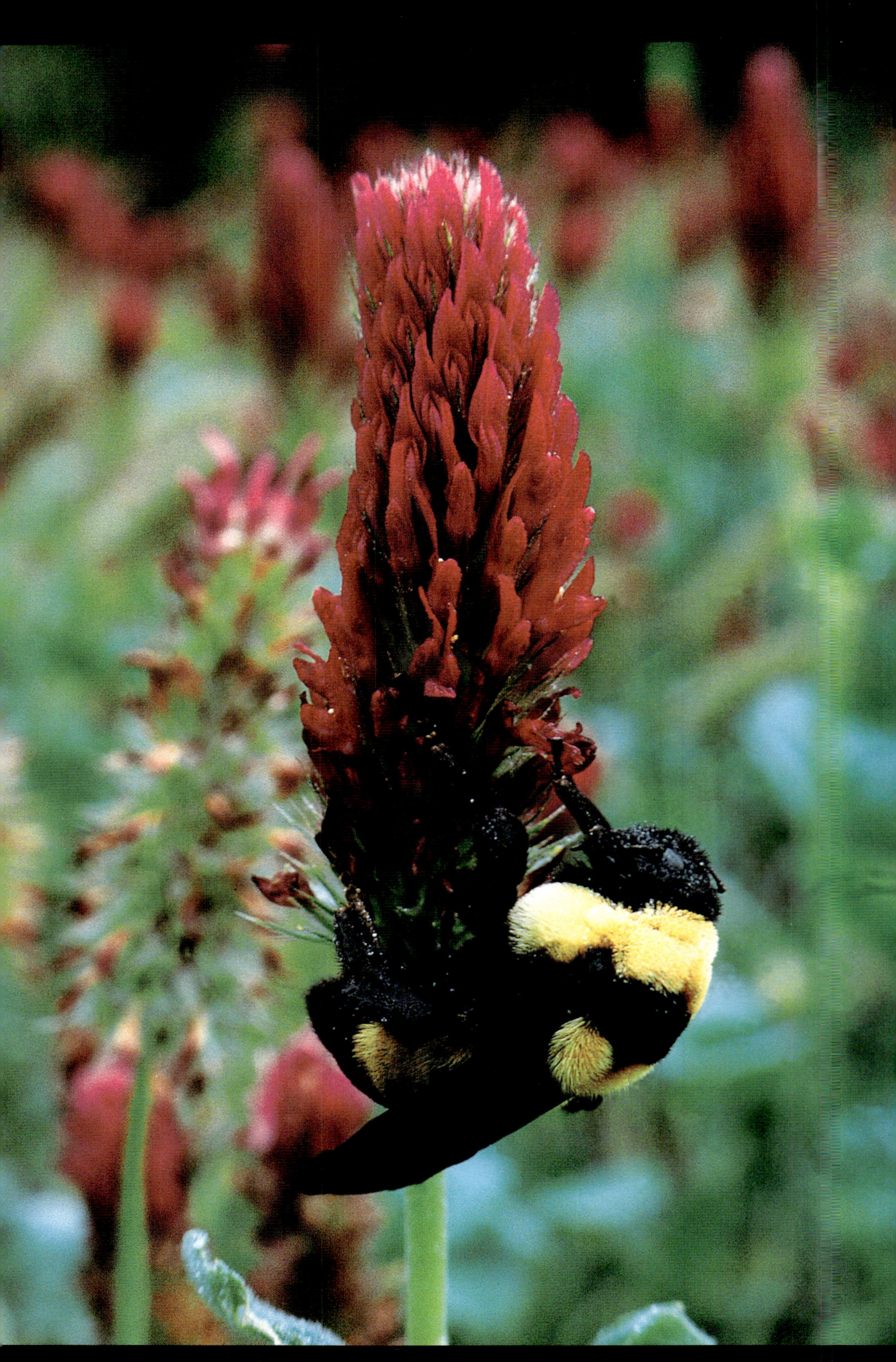

BUMBLE BEE ON CRIMSON CLOVER, MISSISSIPPI, APRIL 1988

My heart was heavy. If you've ever experienced the same feeling, you know it's more than just a cliché. It was truly a physical sensation, a painful weight that robbed me of motivation.

When we're in doubt or pain, we're often advised to "follow our hearts." But how can you follow a heart too full, too heavy, too broken, or too troubled to lead?

GULL AT MORNING TIDE, MAINE, JUNE 1994

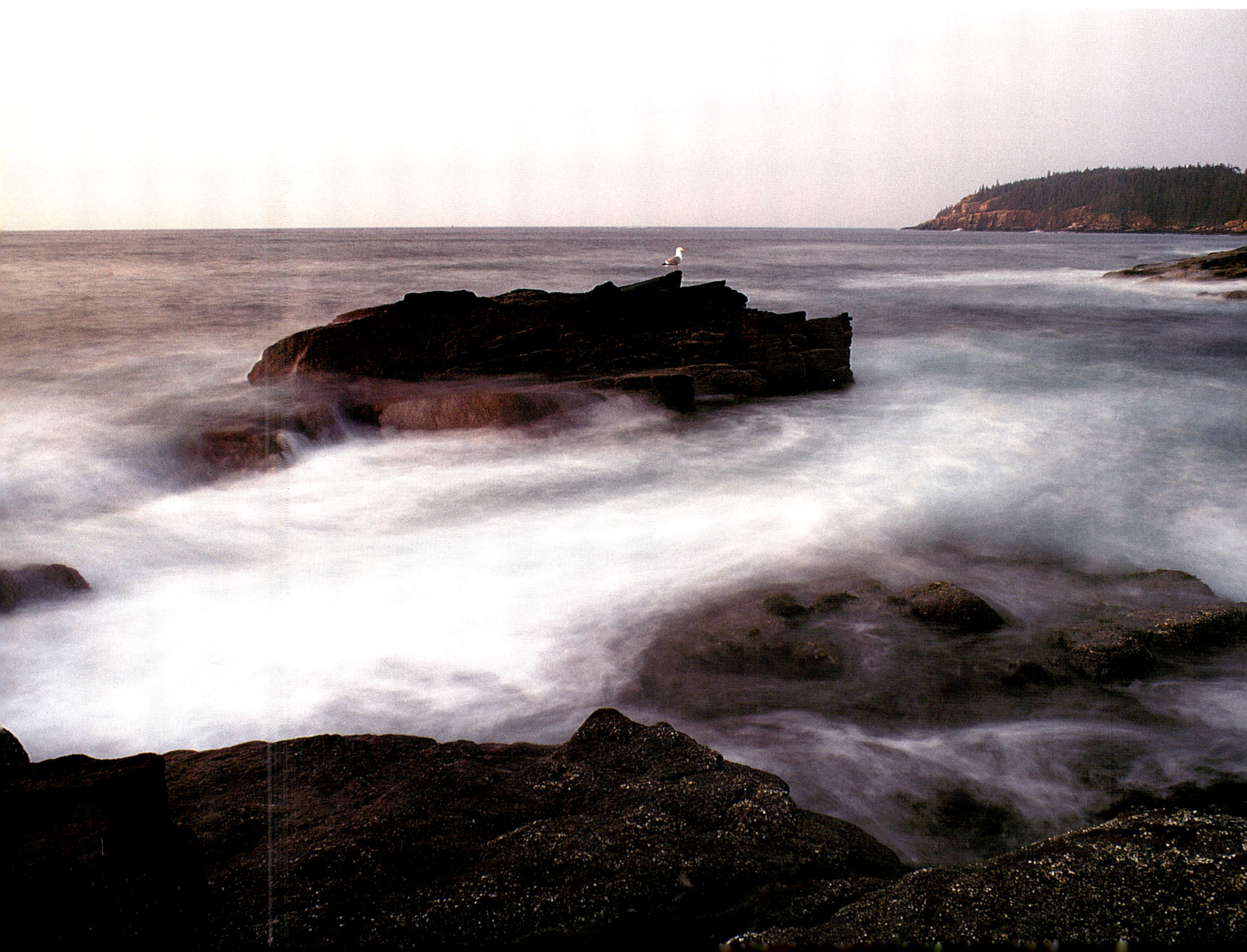

"What do you do when your heart is so full it feels as though it's about to burst? Sleepless nights abound. Tossing and turning going on in your head. The creation, it is so unbelievable. Functional complexity from disorder by chance? It is applied in our minds with our limitations. Like absolute darkness or absolute light, we do not really comprehend these things. The finite mind, we must get beyond it."

In times of crisis, some people seek noise, activity, and distraction. Others crave solitude. I probably don't need to tell you that I fall into the second category.

"I often go inside myself. Down into the recesses of my heart, asking questions that keep me from getting too comfortable, too resigned. I guess I just like digging for reality more than most people, searching out the things in life that really matter. Confronting myself can be painful, but the constant wrestling keeps me in shape for the next trial."

It didn't happen overnight, but the long, quiet days and intense conversations with God returned a little of the peace to my soul. Nature filled my heart with wonder and awe, gradually crowding out enough of the pain for me to wake up to the beauty of the world around me, and the realization that the familiar cliché is true. Life really does go on.

"'Life isn't fair' is a chant of humanity. Yes, it is fair. It rains and shines on the just and the unjust. We must take what comes."

SNOWY EGRET IN RAIN, MISSISSIPPI, MAY 1995

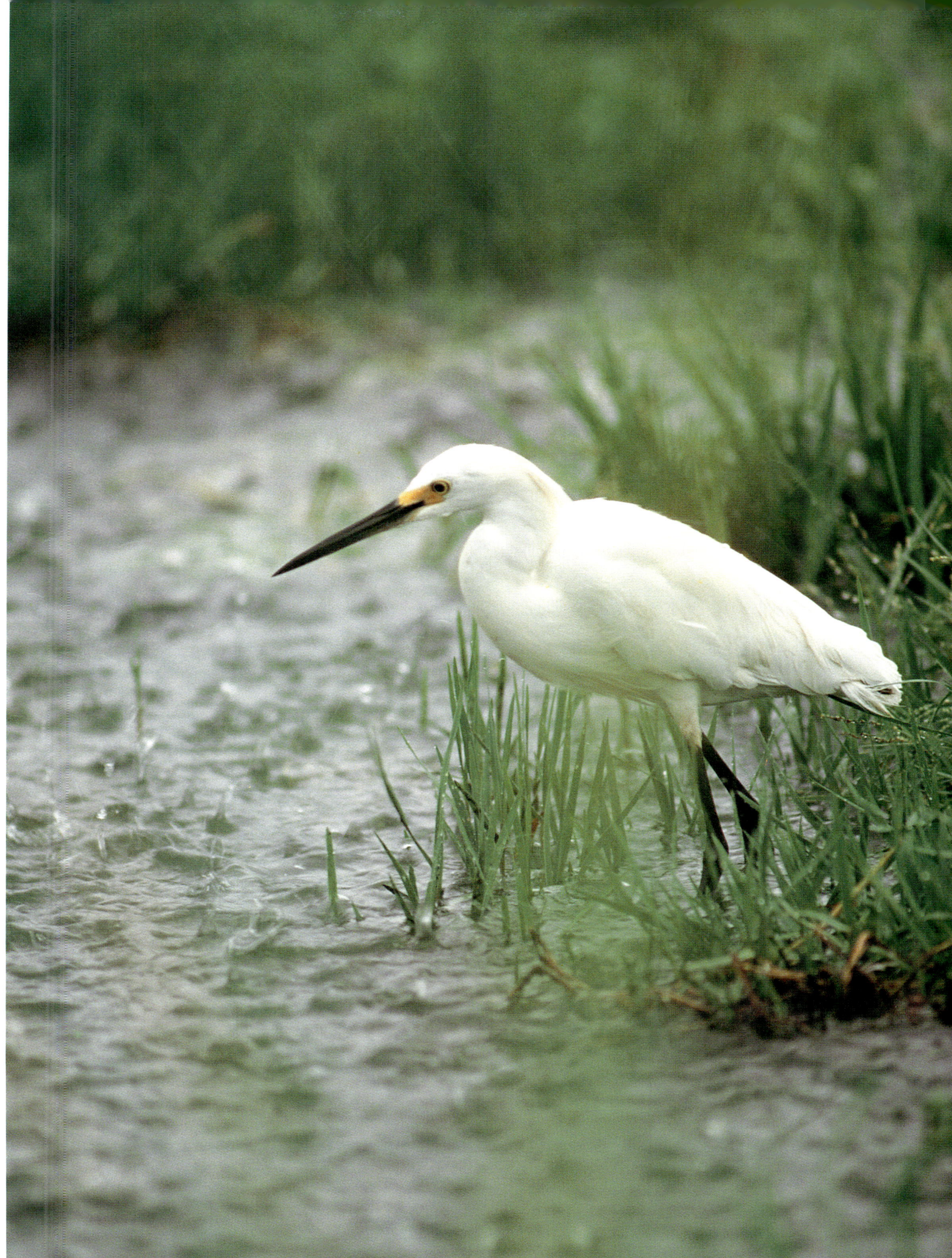

Eventually, keeping up the pain becomes tiresome.

At first, you revel in it. Heartache may not be the most pleasant companion, but you can sure count on it to be there when everyone and everything else seems to have deserted you.

But sooner or later, the pain becomes just another chore. Eventually, you make a conscious decision to let go and look to the future, or you suddenly realize you've already done it unawares.

Either way, the time comes when you stop looking back at what you've lost, and start looking ahead, toward the light.

LAKE TAHOE, CALIFORNIA, AUGUST 1995

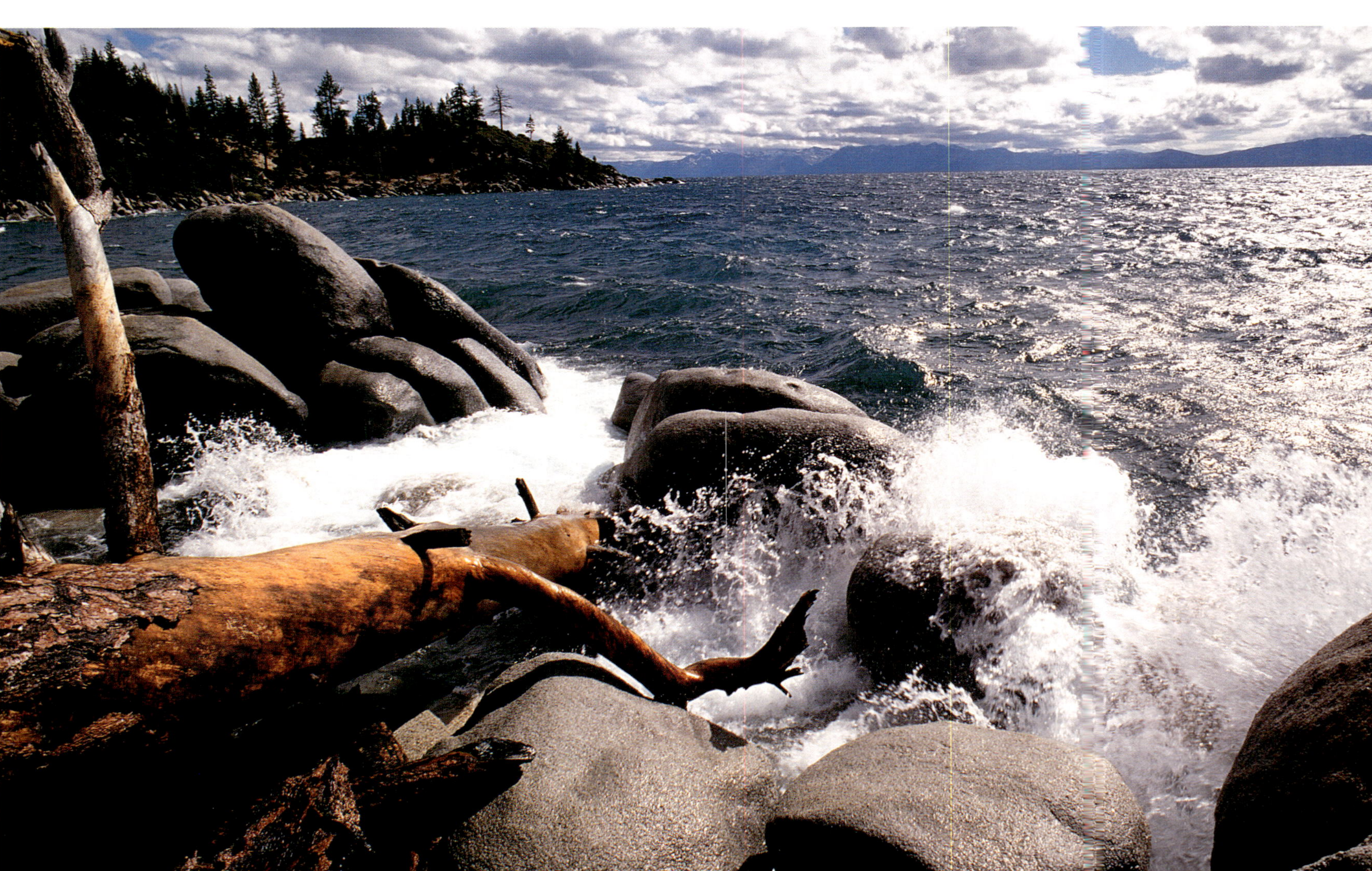

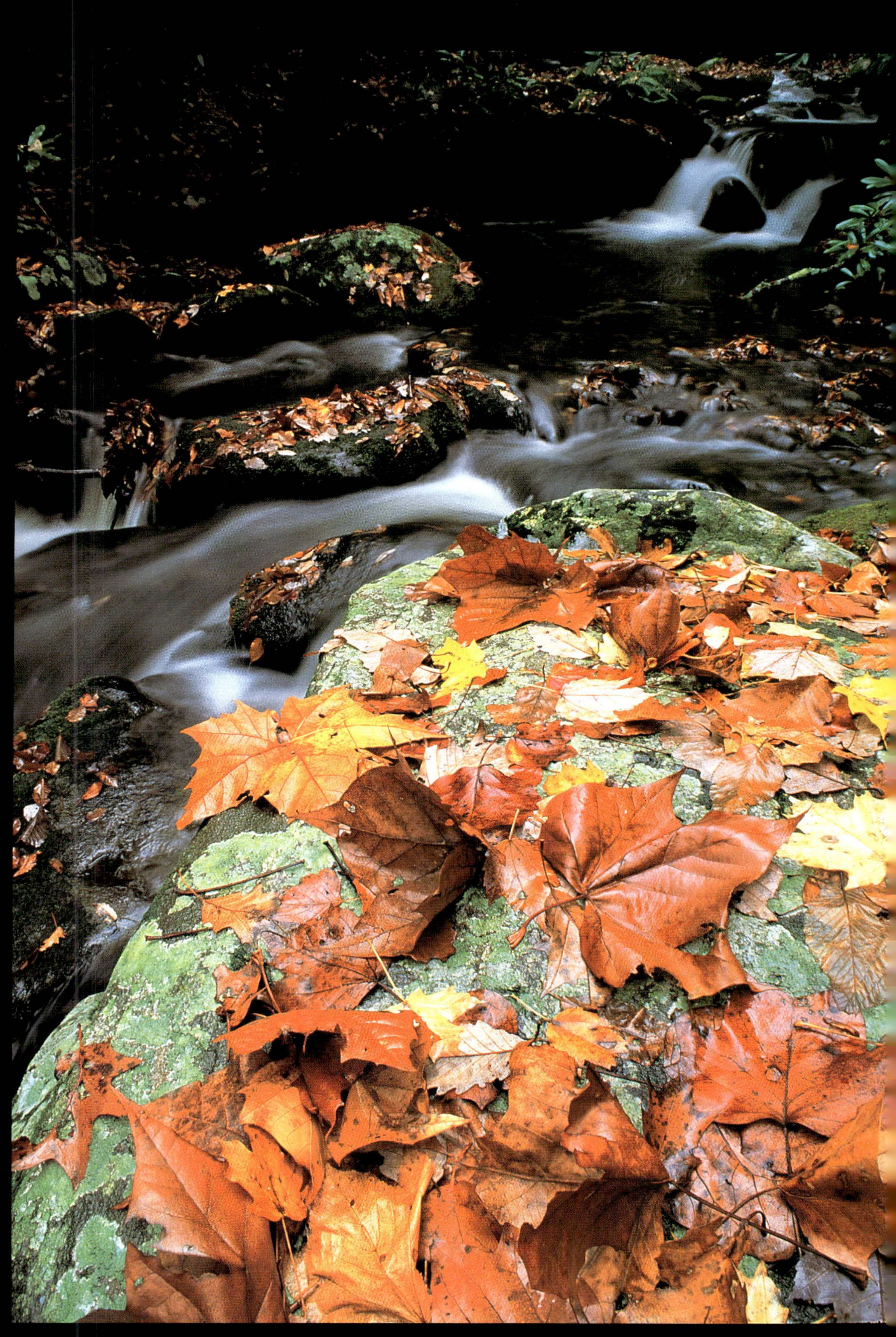

FALL COLOR AND STREAM, TENNESSEE, NOVEMBER 1992

"There is a difference between emotional tears and touched hearts. Emotional tears dry and will leave. Touched hearts will continue."

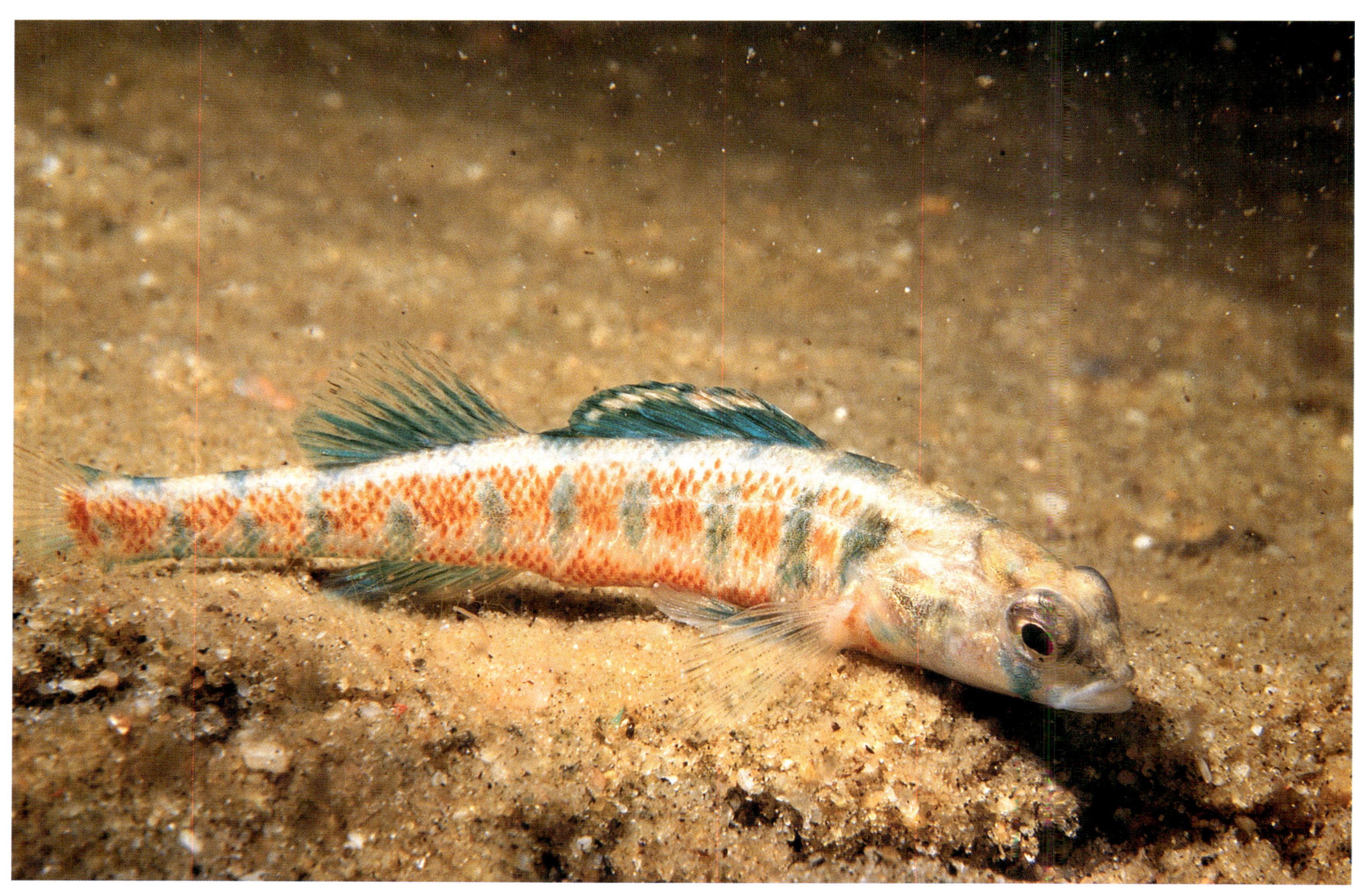

IOWA DARTER FEEDING, QUEBEC, JULY 1995

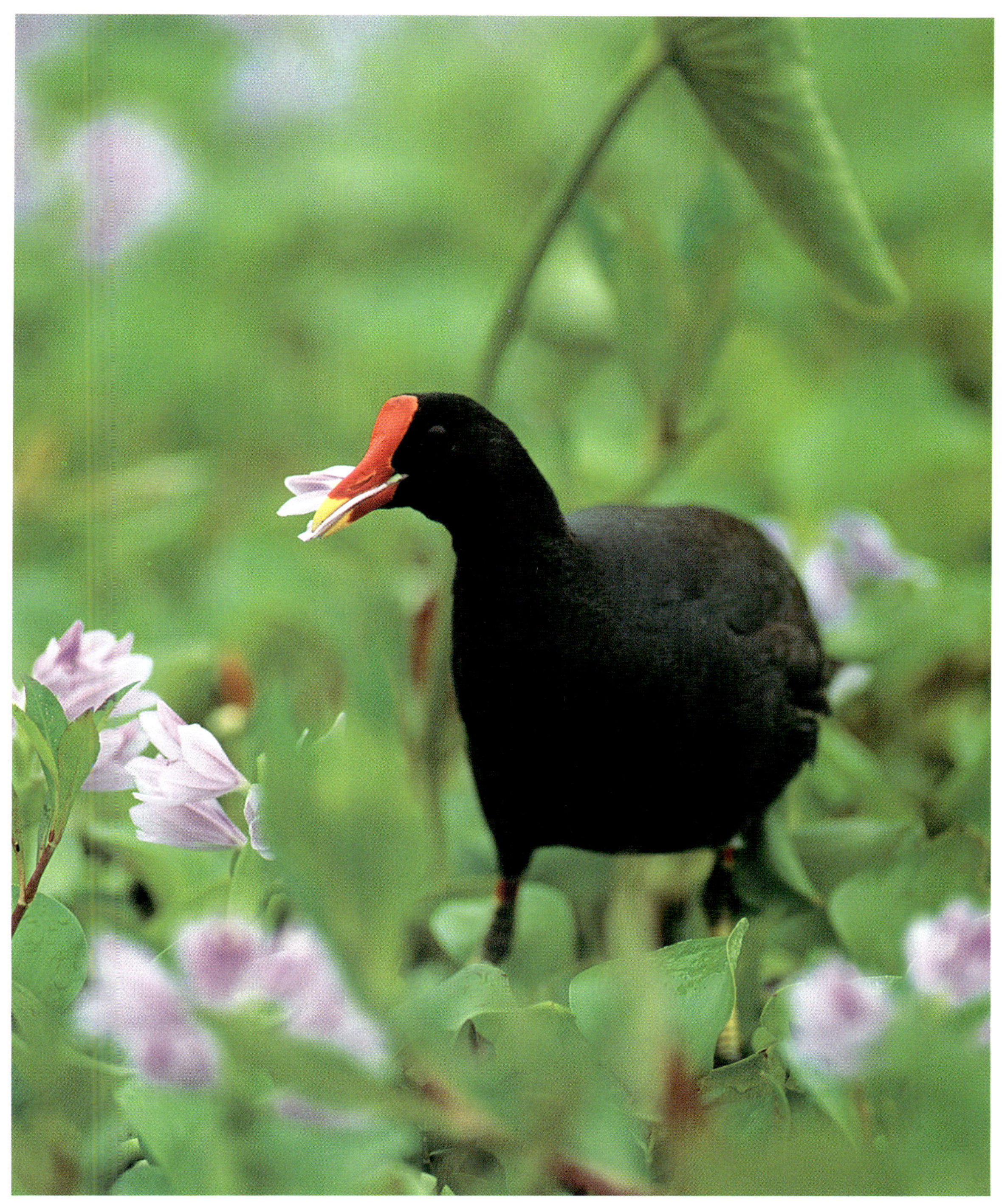

COMMON MOORHEN EATING WATER HYACINTH, MISSISSIPPI, JULY 1991

GRIZZLY BEAR CATCHING SALMON, ALASKA, JUNE 1992

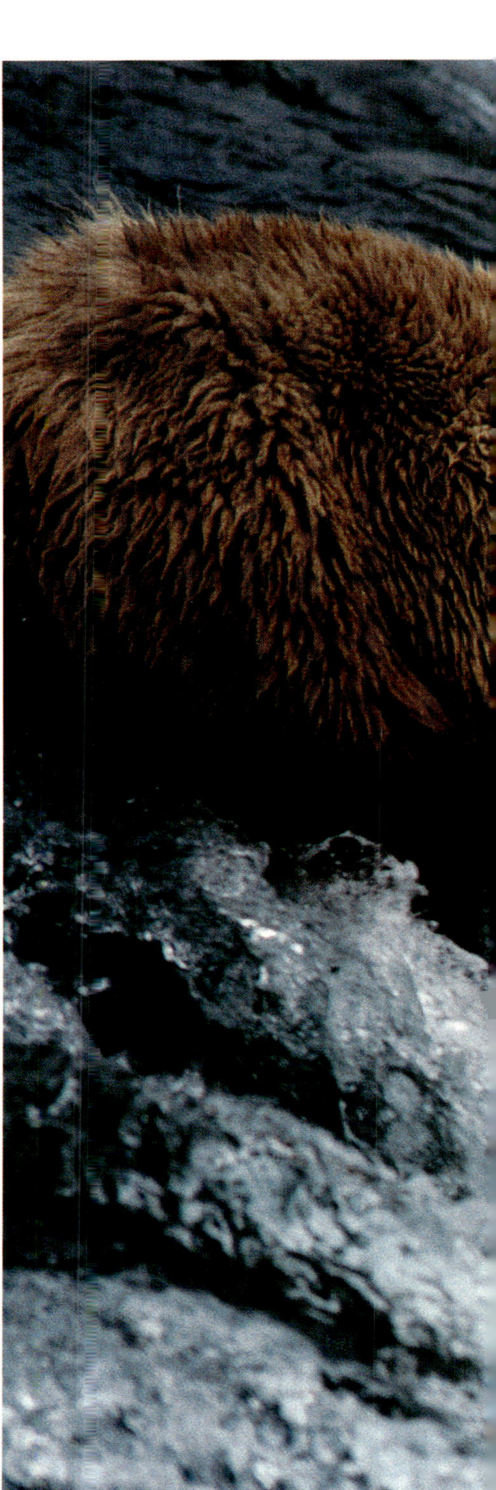

SALMON SKULL, ALASKA, JUNE 1992

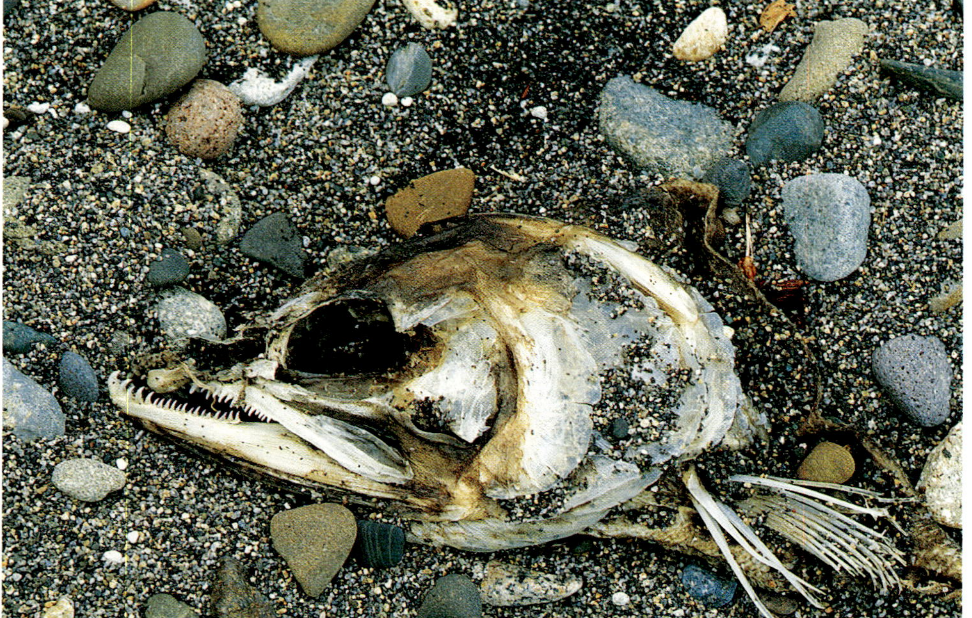

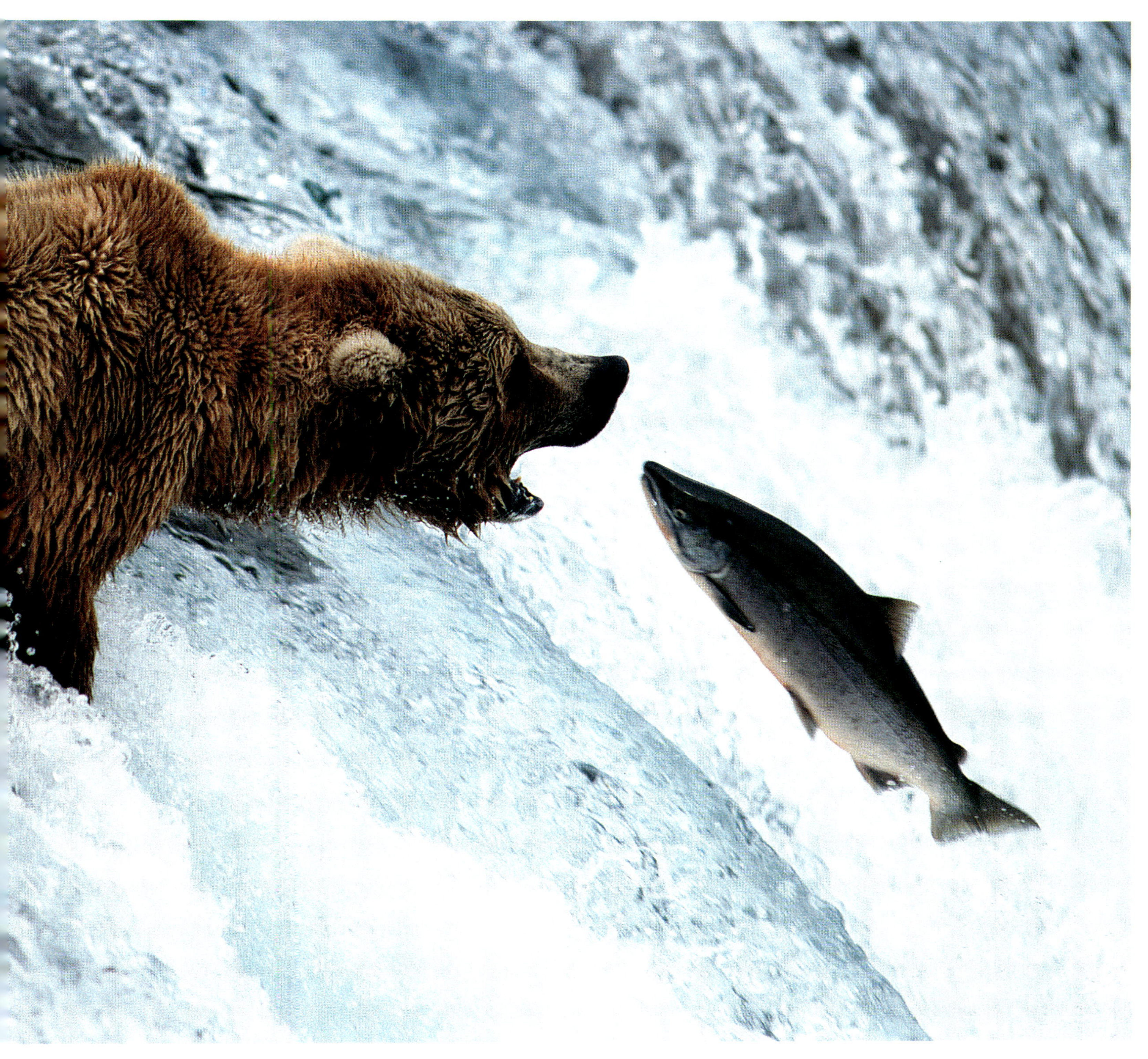

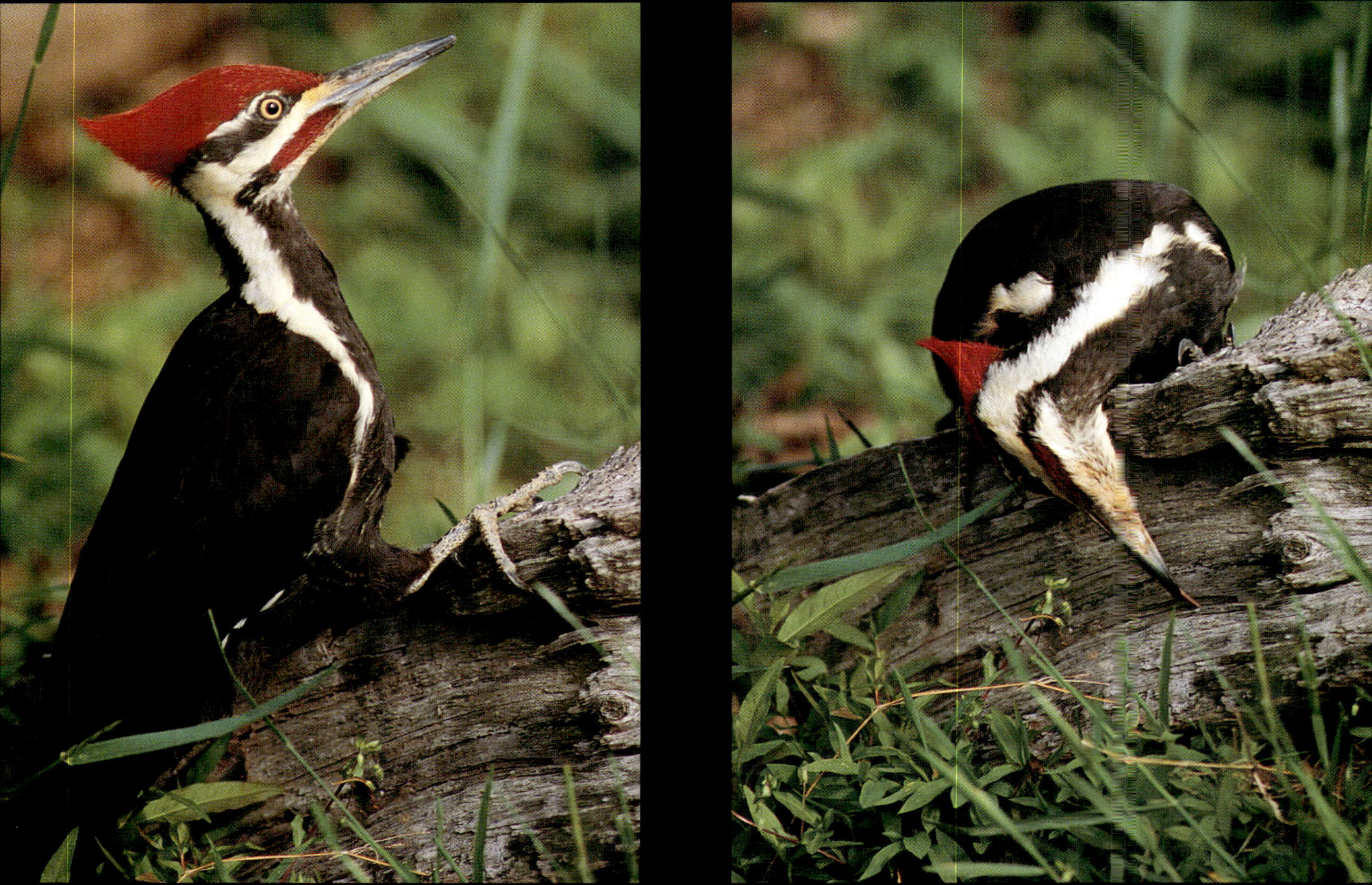

PILEATED WOODPECKER FEEDING, TENNESSEE, MAY 1995

"A fervent heart is what we need. The ardent, impassioned heart the Bible talks about. No flash in the pan or short-lived demonstration of brilliance, but a continuous commitment to those things that are our calling."

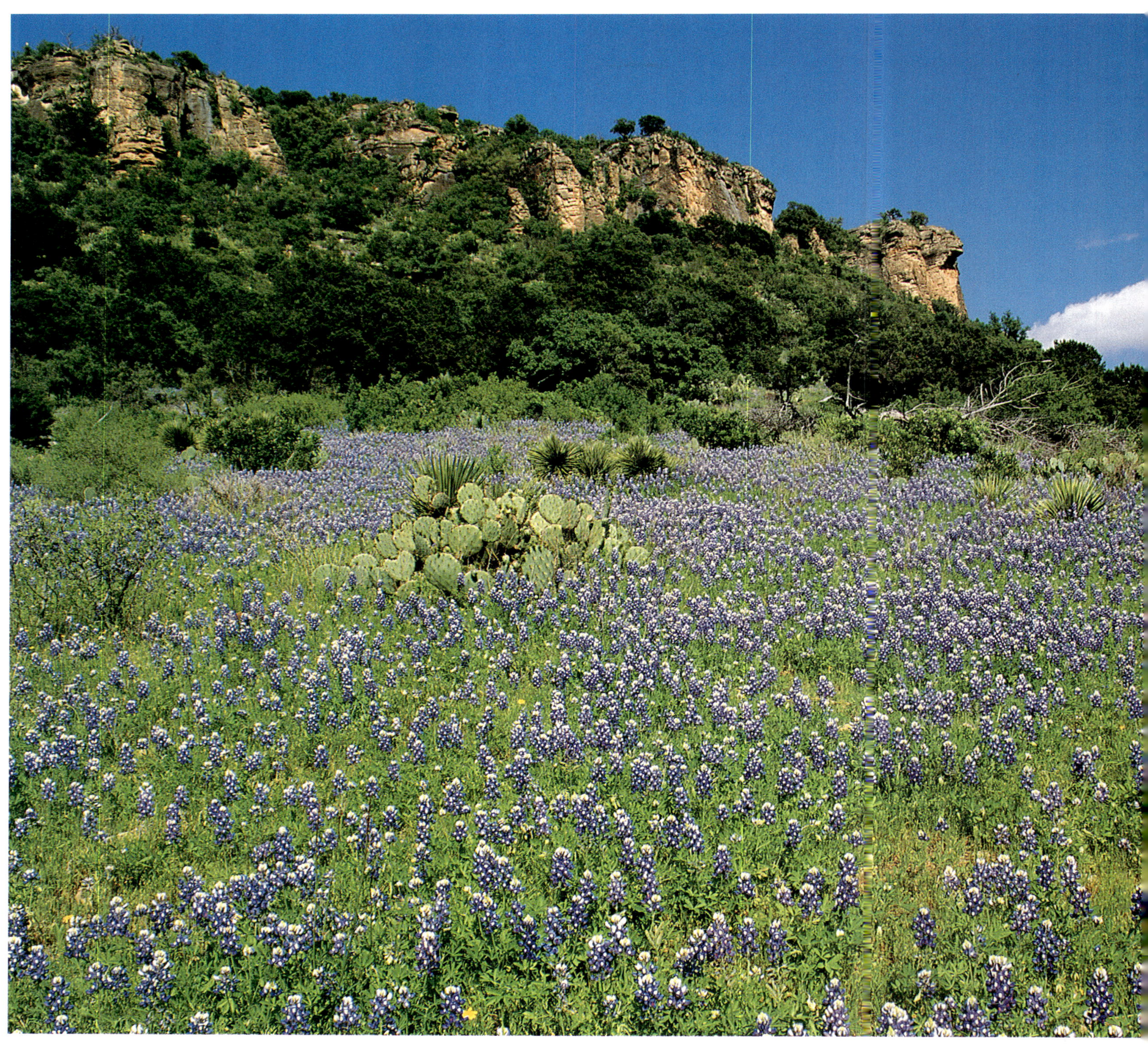

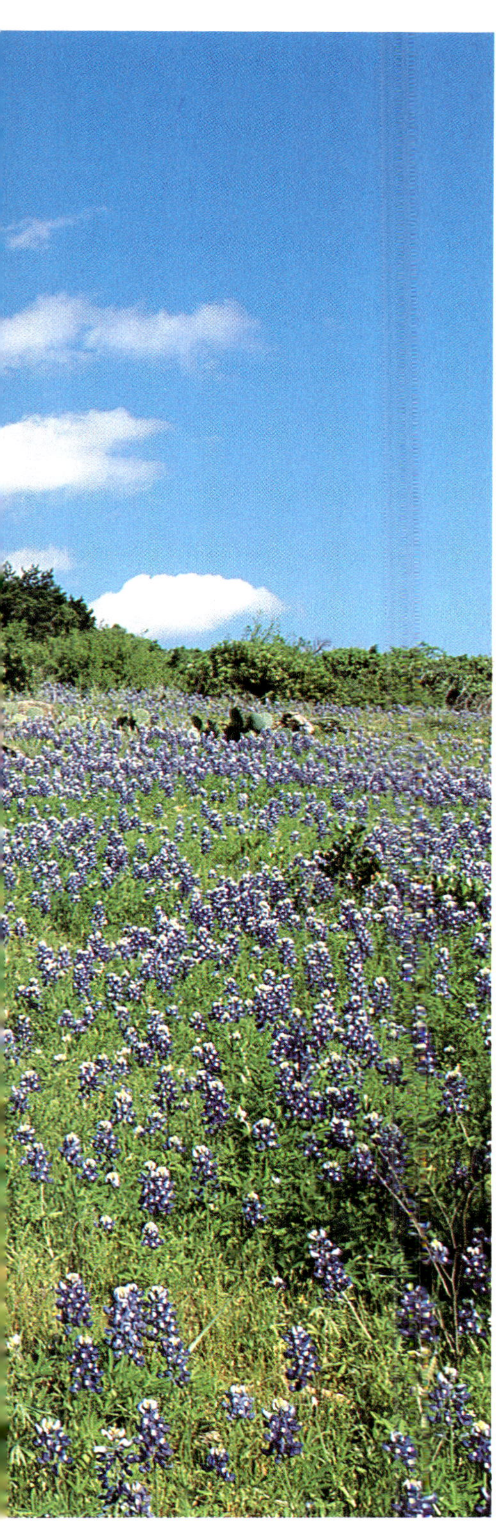

BLUEBONNETS AND CACTI, TEXAS, APRIL 1992

CALIFORNIA QUAIL, NEVADA, AUGUST 1995

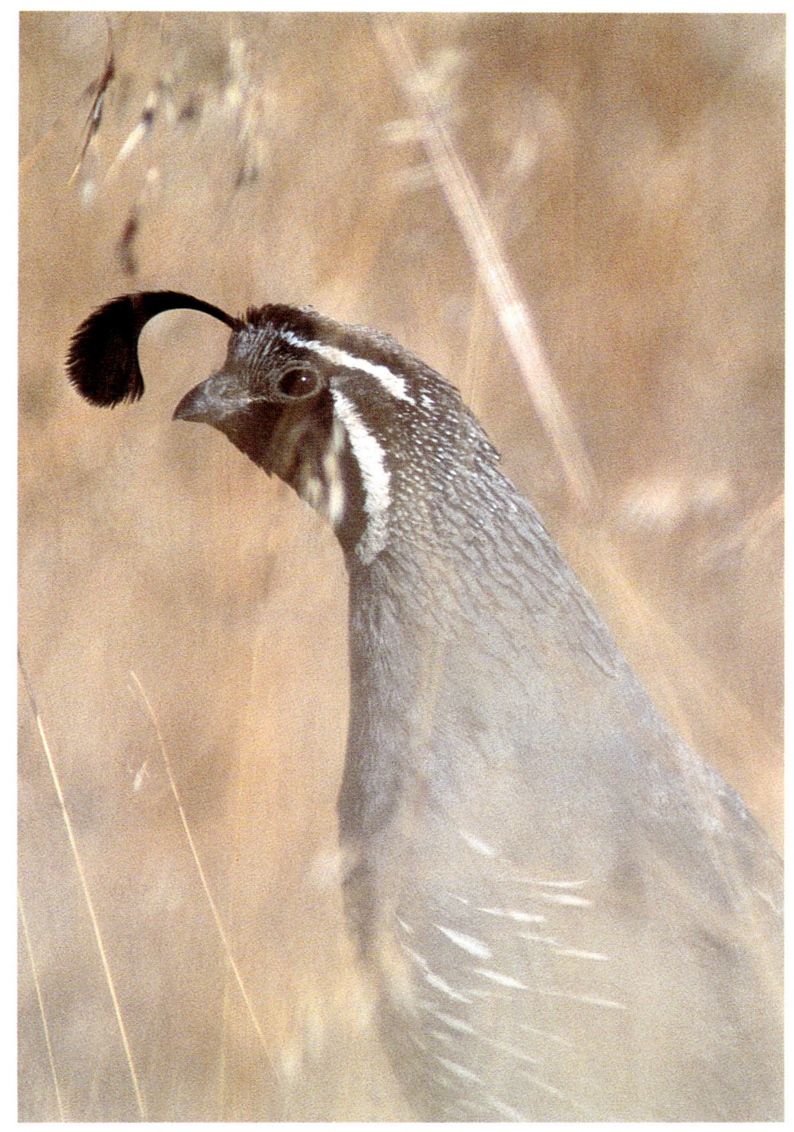

In 1981, I was awakened by the wind, and I discovered it wasn't nature, but nature's designer who was calling. The voice of God was telling me to take a camera, capture images of His creation, and use those images to bring others to Him. The cry of my heart was to see beyond the surface and to answer that call.

"Thank you Lord, for I was blind, but now I see."

In spite of everything that had changed over the years, capturing those images was still my assignment.

OLD FAITHFUL IN FULL MOON, WYOMING, SEPTEMBER 1990

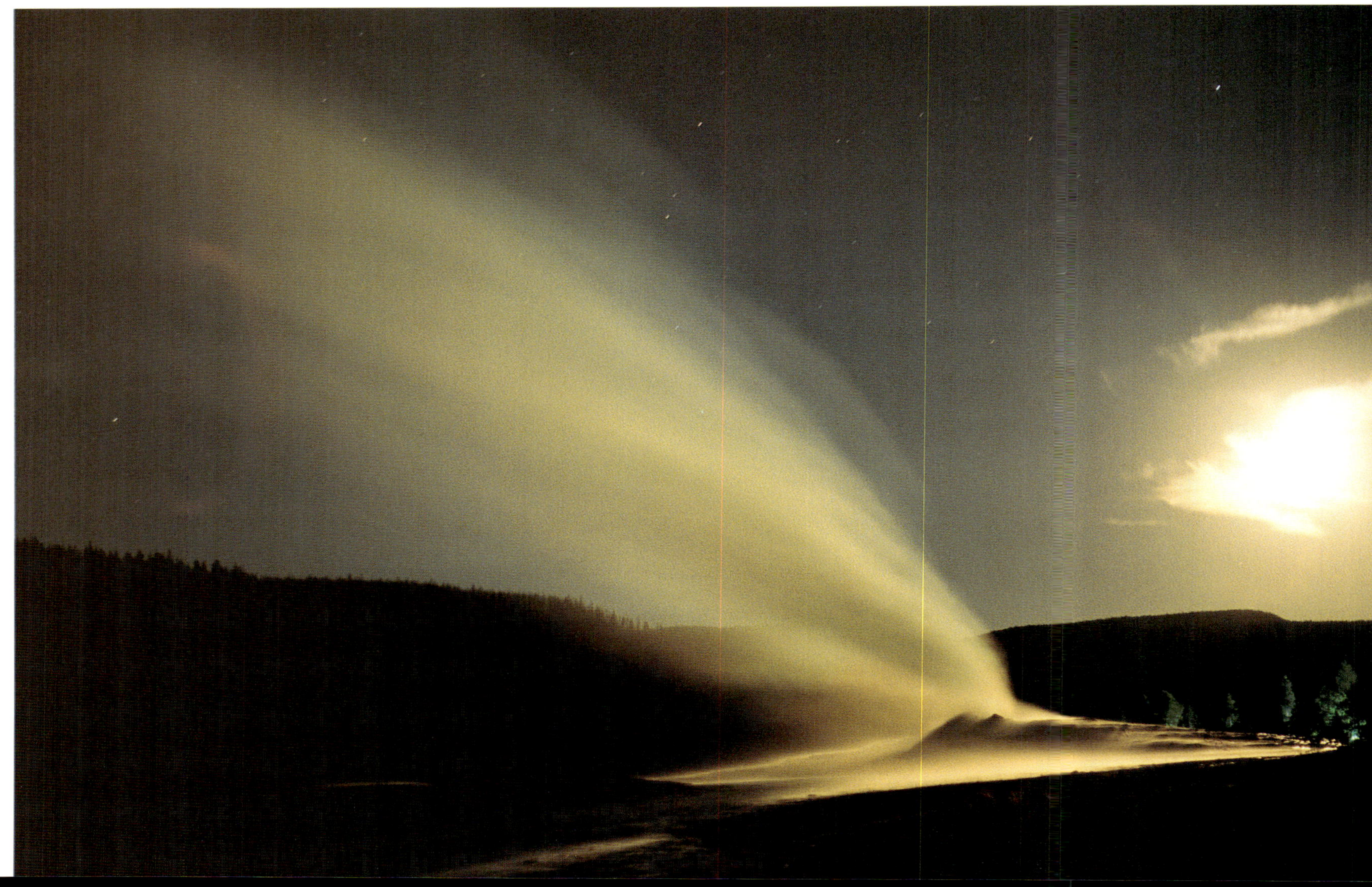

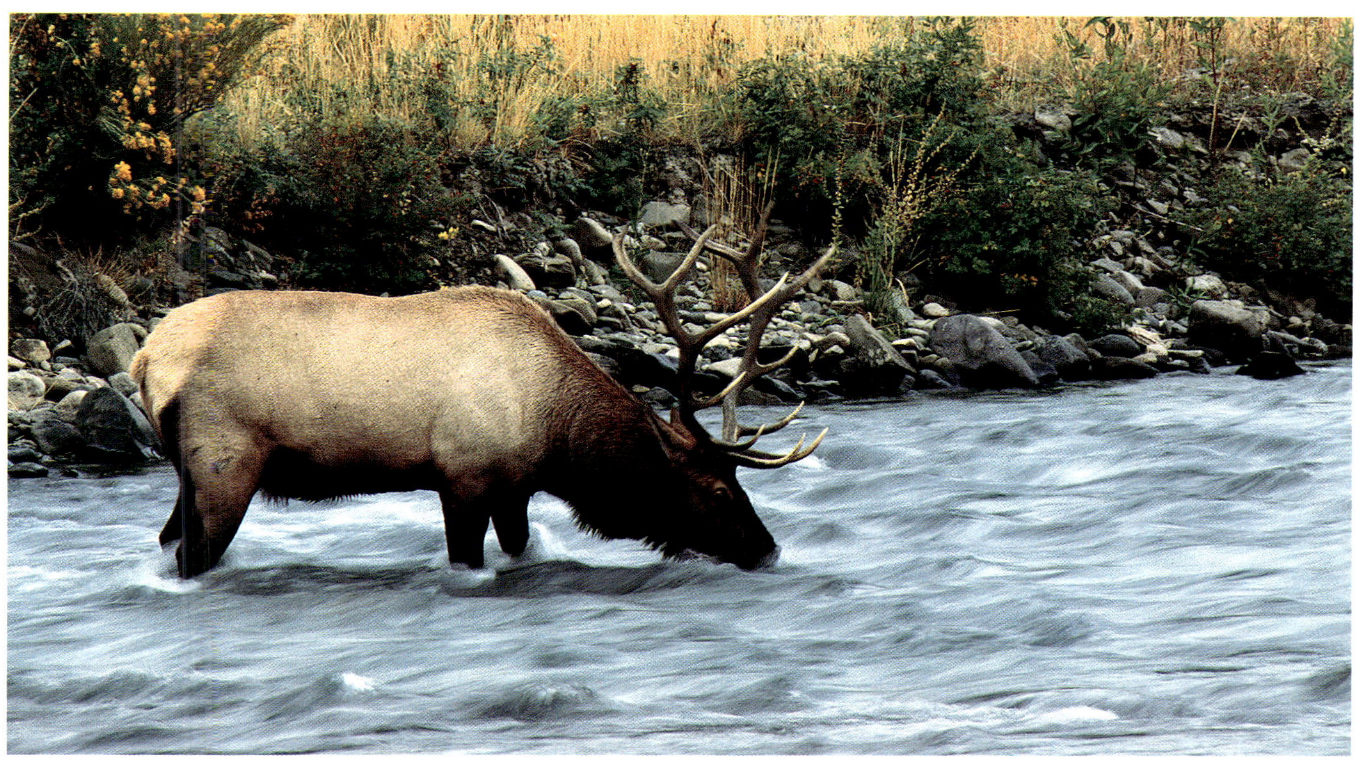

ELK IN STREAM, MONTANA, SEPTEMBER 1990

You will only truly succeed at those things which consume you and are worthy of filling your heart completely. Joy is evidence of that completeness.

My circumstances may have changed, but I still loved wildlife photography. It was my calling, and I was once again prepared to pursue it with a fervent heart.

"Wonderful photographs do exist, they just don't come very often, the really good ones I'm talking about. Those that capture the very essence of nature and radiant beauty. Wondrous moments when perfect light touches and unveils not only a breathtaking image, but that intangible quality that separates the men from the boys."

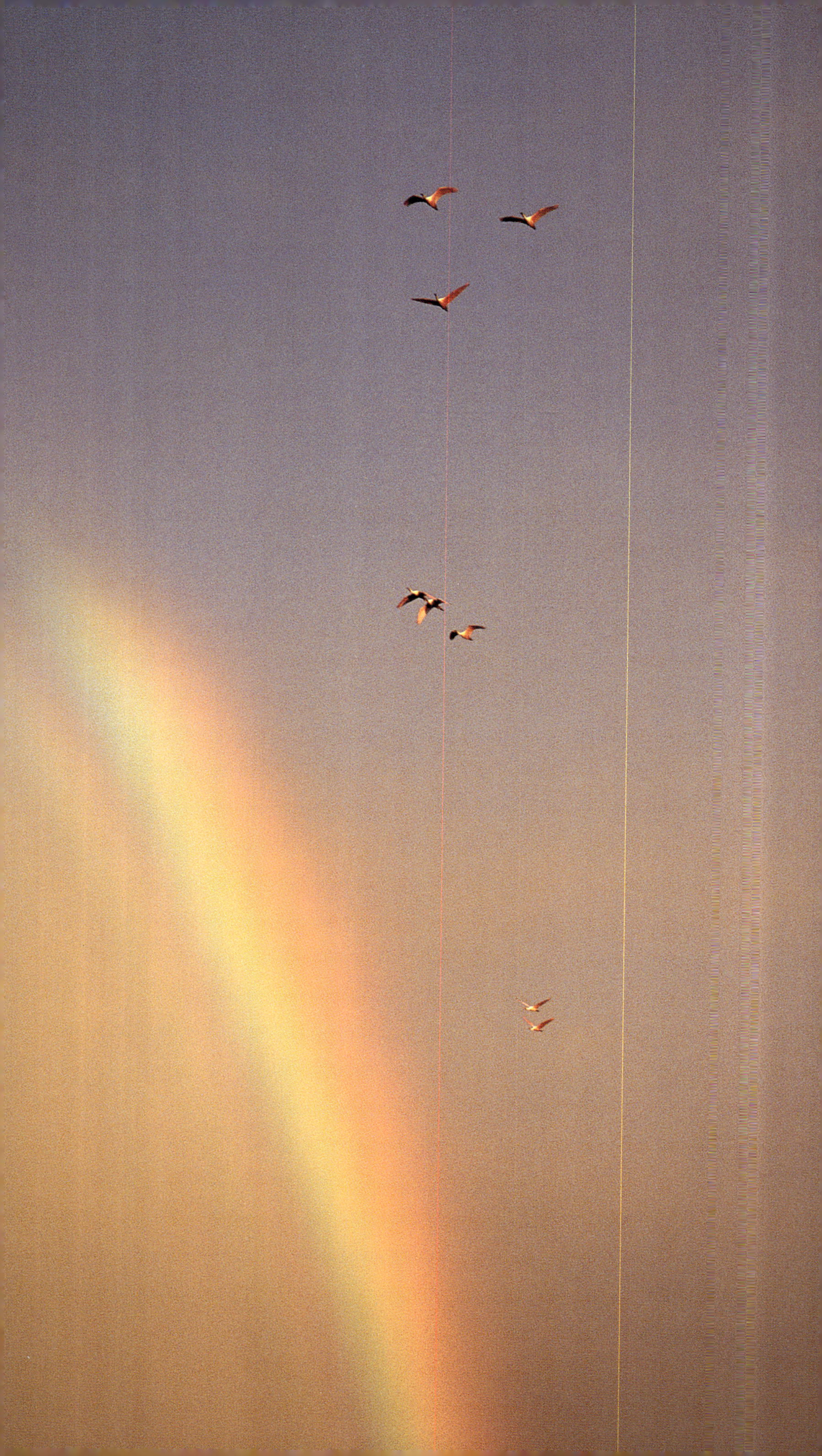

My desire was back. The drive to capture the best image, to make people smile in delight or gasp in wonder, the desire to please God with my efforts.

The real proof of such desire lies in its pursuit. Once again, I was ready to chase the wind.

"The perfect image is something that eludes me. That perfect moment when it all works. Taking pictures is the 'education,' the photograph is the 'enlightenment.' I've accomplished this only a few times, never was it planned or expected. The harder I work for it, the more elusive it becomes."

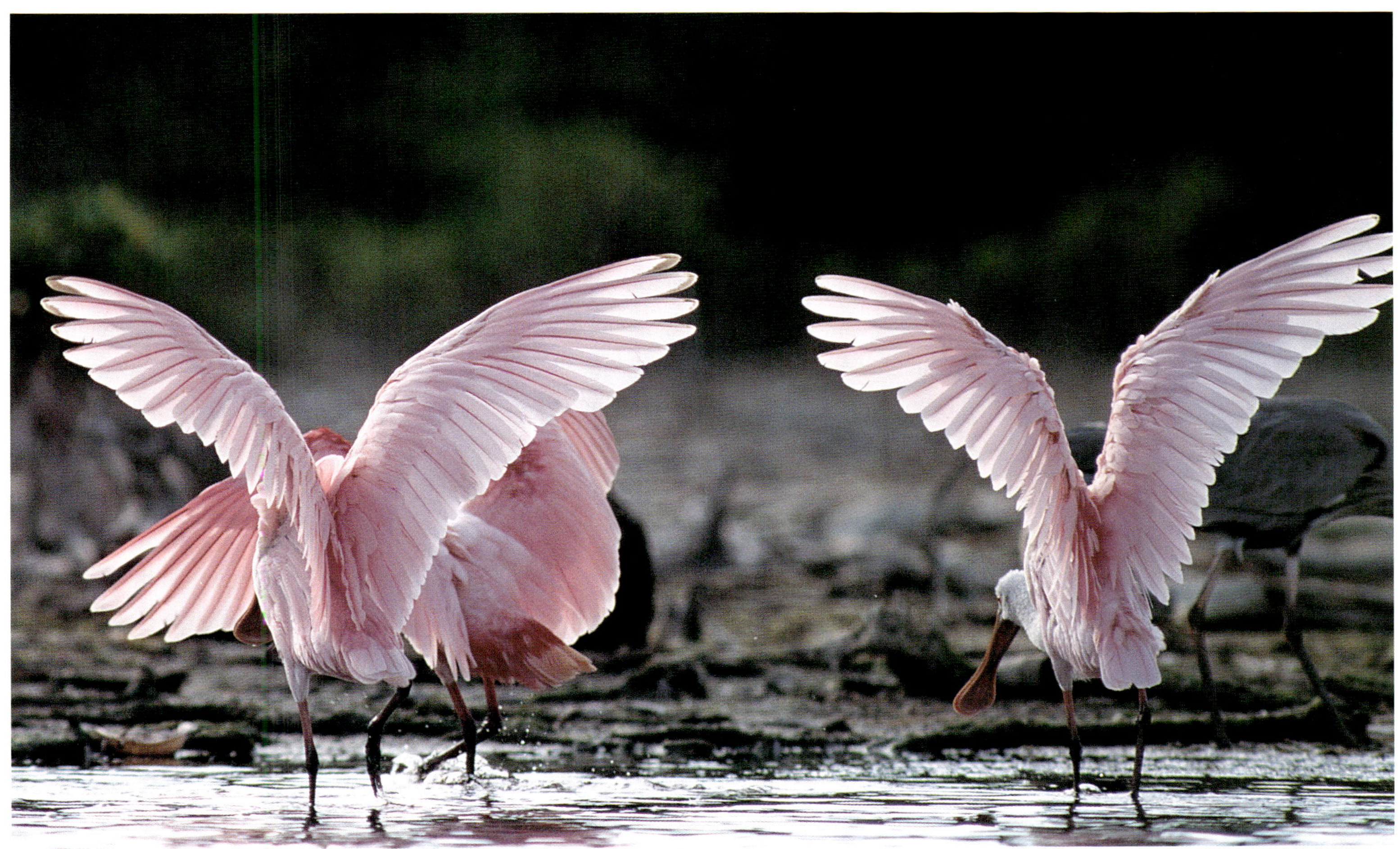

ROSEATE SPOONBILLS STRETCHING, FLORIDA, JANUARY 1994

ROSEATE SPOONBILLS IN RAINBOW, FLORIDA, JANUARY 1994

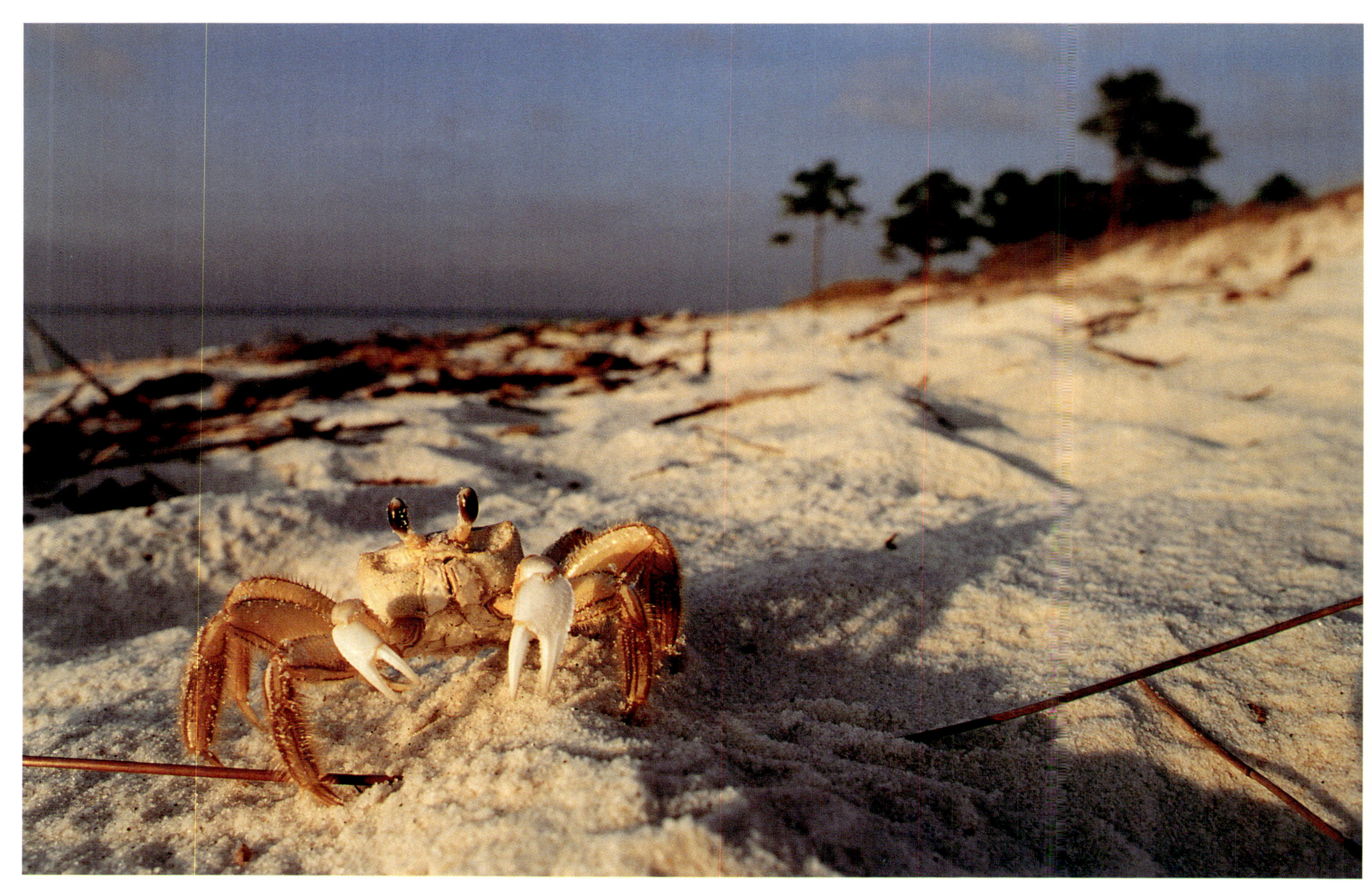

GHOST CRAB ON BEACH, MISSISSIPPI, MARCH 1991

BROWN PELICANS IN SUNSET, FLORIDA, MARCH 1997

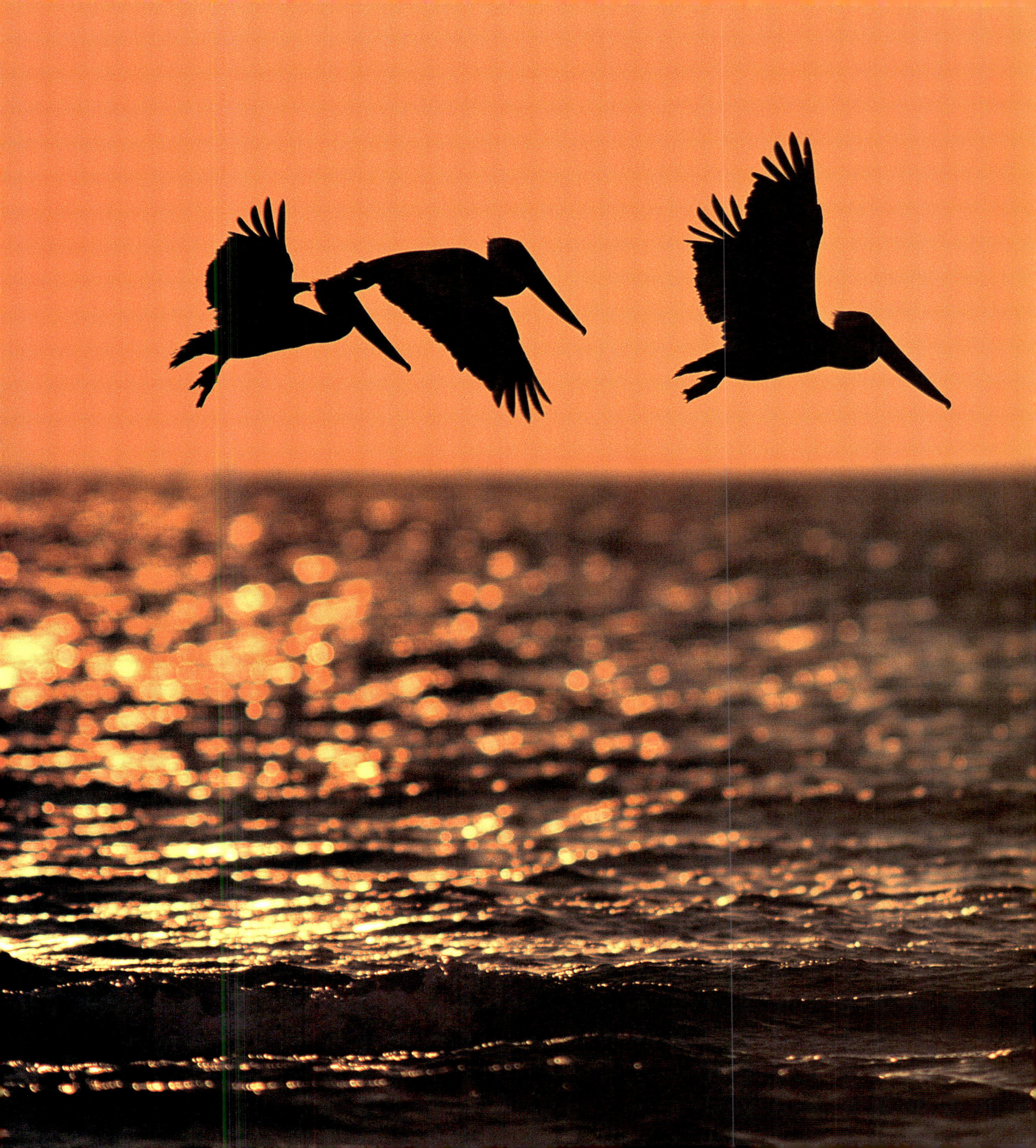

"My boys' well-being is all there is in my mind at times – wanting them to have life in such abundance that I constantly seek things for their interest in my own life. Life is full of adventure and laughter as well as very serious. I want them to see it all. They never know from visit to visit what's in store for them, and that's the beauty of it all."

I often wonder what my three sons will remember when they look back upon their childhoods. I'm sure there will be fond recollections of fishing trips and hiking expeditions, campfires and pet snakes, and assorted adventures in the wilderness.

But what will they *really* gain from their father's unorthodox career? Are there values I can instill in them specifically because I made this career choice? Are they missing out on things they would learn if I were a policeman, or a banker, or a doctor? Am I missing opportunities to teach them something meaningful through my life's work?

"I love adventure and new discoveries of all sorts, expanding my vision and knowledge. The boys see and love this, too. Our time together is precious.

"Their interest in the outdoors is always a mystery to me. I'm not sure if they are simply drawn to it or if they are influenced by my own love, closeness, and understanding of it."

WHITE-TAILED DEER IN VELVET, MISSISSIPPI, AUGUST 1993

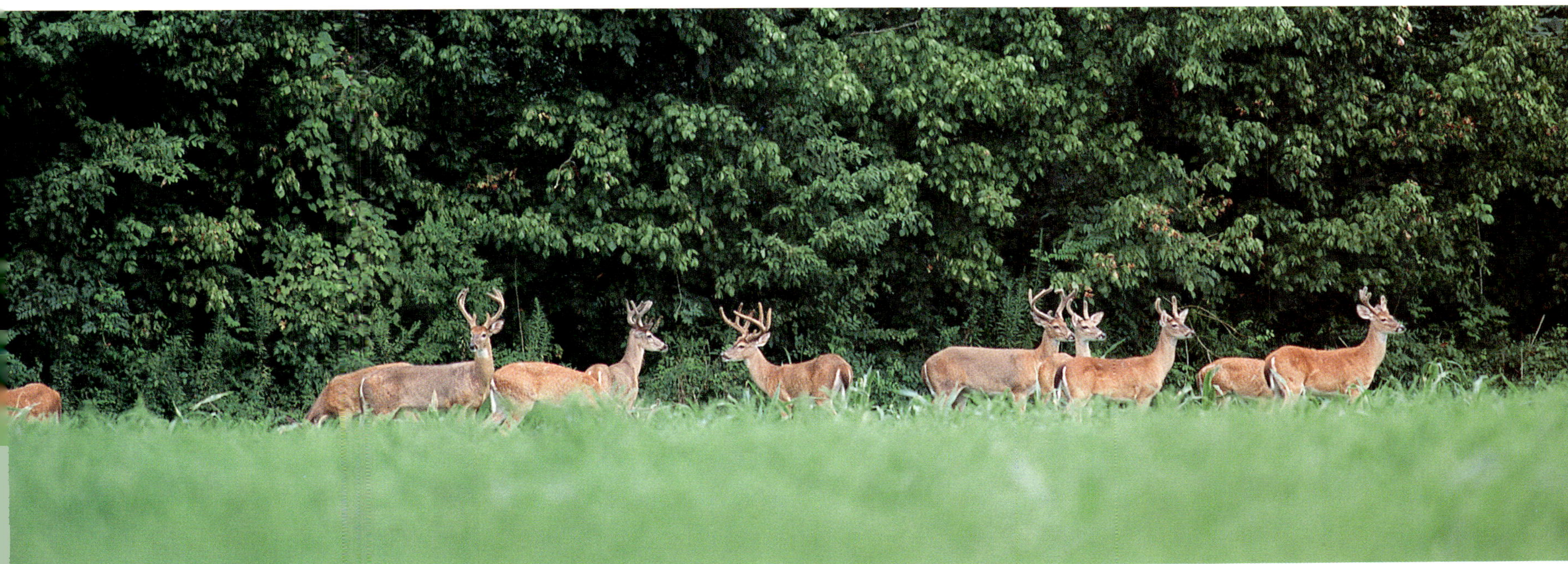

BULLFROG IN BREEDING COLOR, QUEBEC, JULY 1996

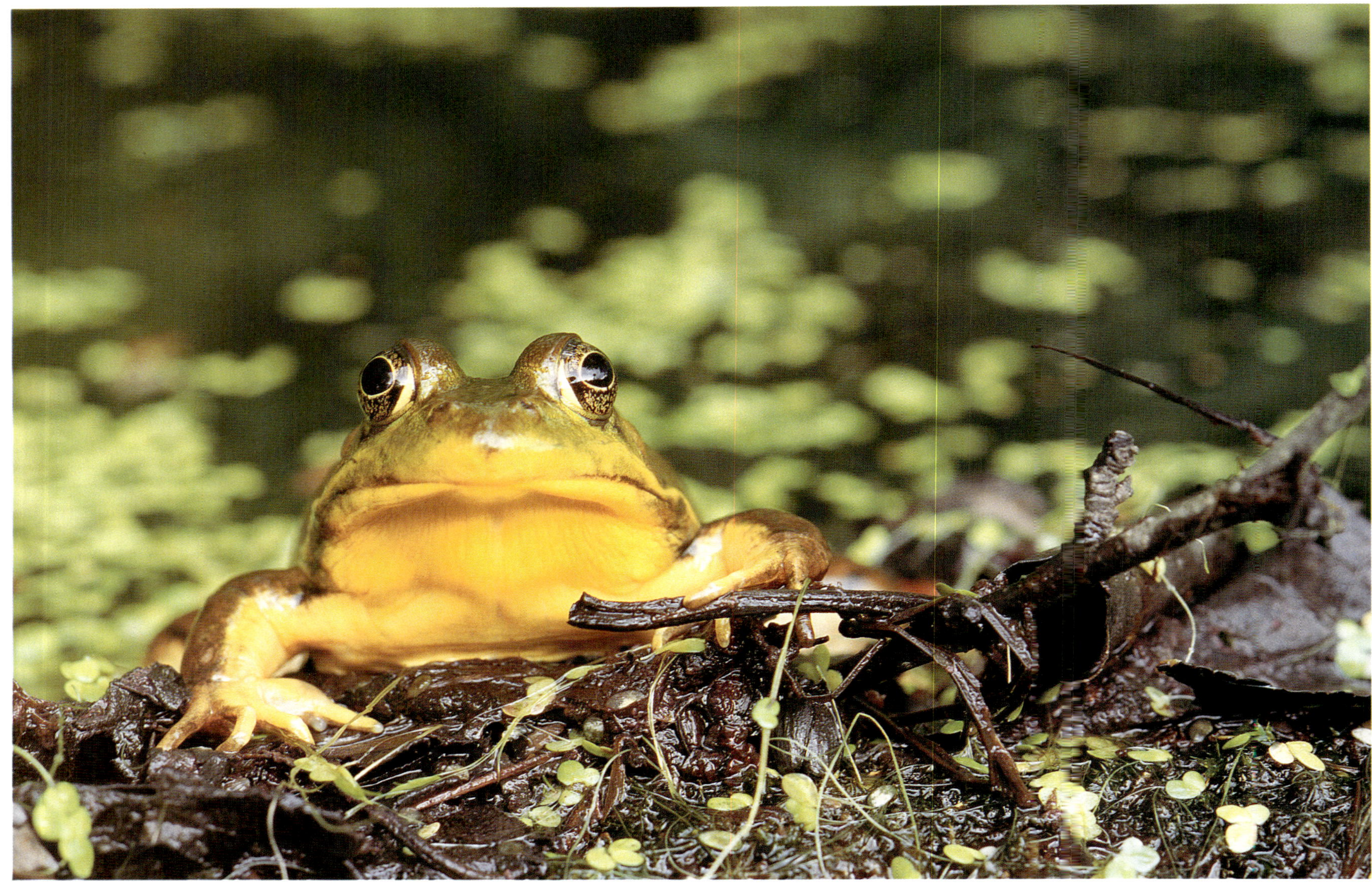

When they were eleven, nine, and four years old, I took my sons to a lily pad-laden cove in Quebec for an afternoon of catching frogs.

Late in the day, the oldest turned to me with a look of joy and said, "You know, I could do this every day!"

What a smile bloomed in my heart! My desire for the boys was this very thing – that they would find pleasure in the natural world which was enormous, yet built on something as small as a frog. It was something I had loved as a child, and maybe someday my child's child would love it, too.

The pace of the Creator again fills the mind and heart. Nature keeps us all on the same playing field.

"I don't want it to always be perfect for them – always catching lots of fish, always bright and sunny. No, I want them to experience the fullness of creation. Good. Bad. Reality. *Nature is surely that."*

I know that God called me to become a wildlife photographer. In the early years of my career, I saw that calling as His ultimate instruction to me. Then my sons were born. Now I know that God has a calling for those three boys, and it's a more important calling than my own. My assignment as a photographer is important not only in my own life, but as part of God's plan for my sons.

"I want the boys to have it all. Not things or possessions, but all the 'colors of life.' I also want them demonstrated in my own life so they can see it in action. That would be the greatest teaching of all, for them to see it lived in front of them, and then live it themselves. Their futures will ultimately be their own responsibility, but it will not be their excuse that their dad was a bad influence."

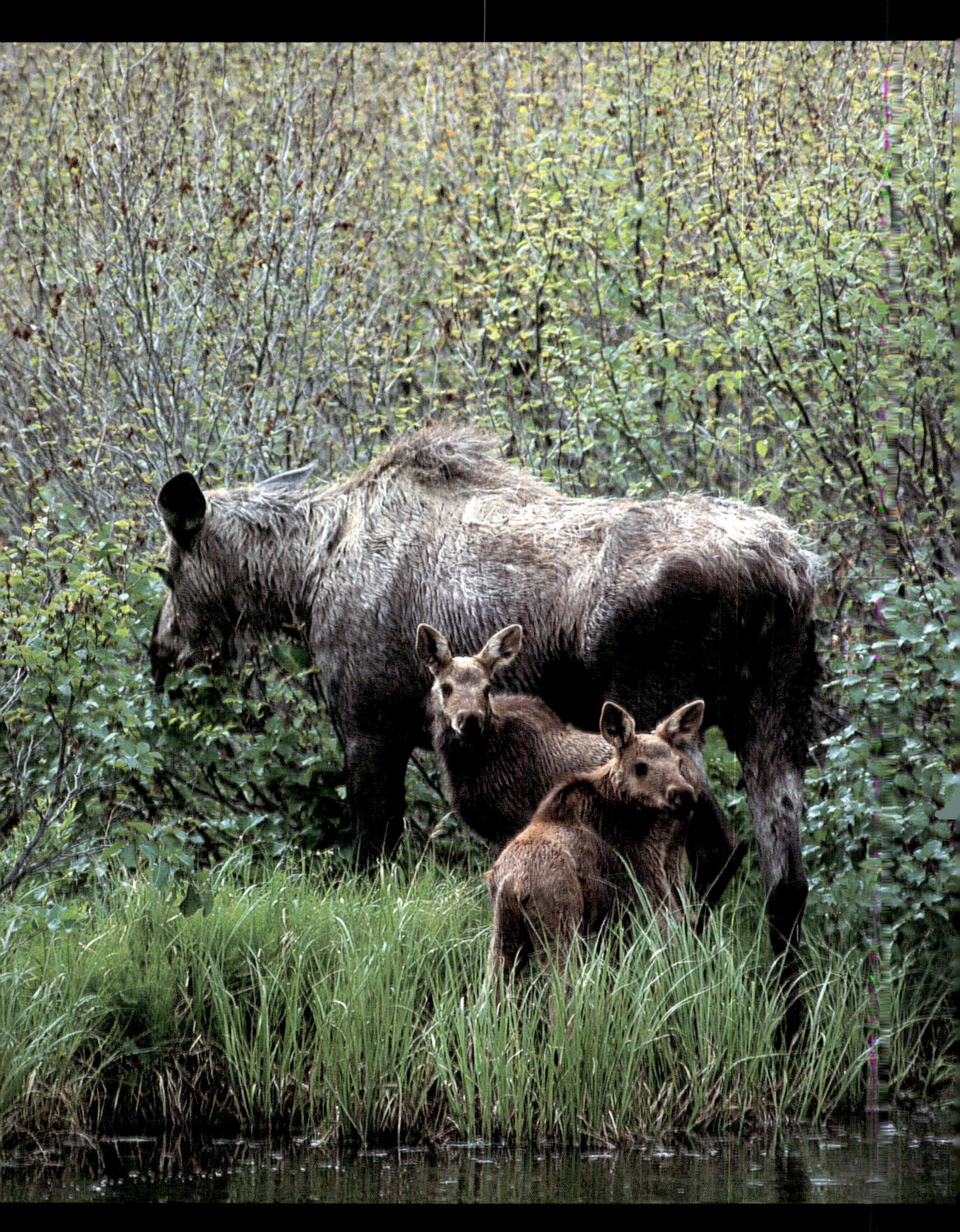

MOOSE AND YOUNG, ALASKA, JUNE 1992

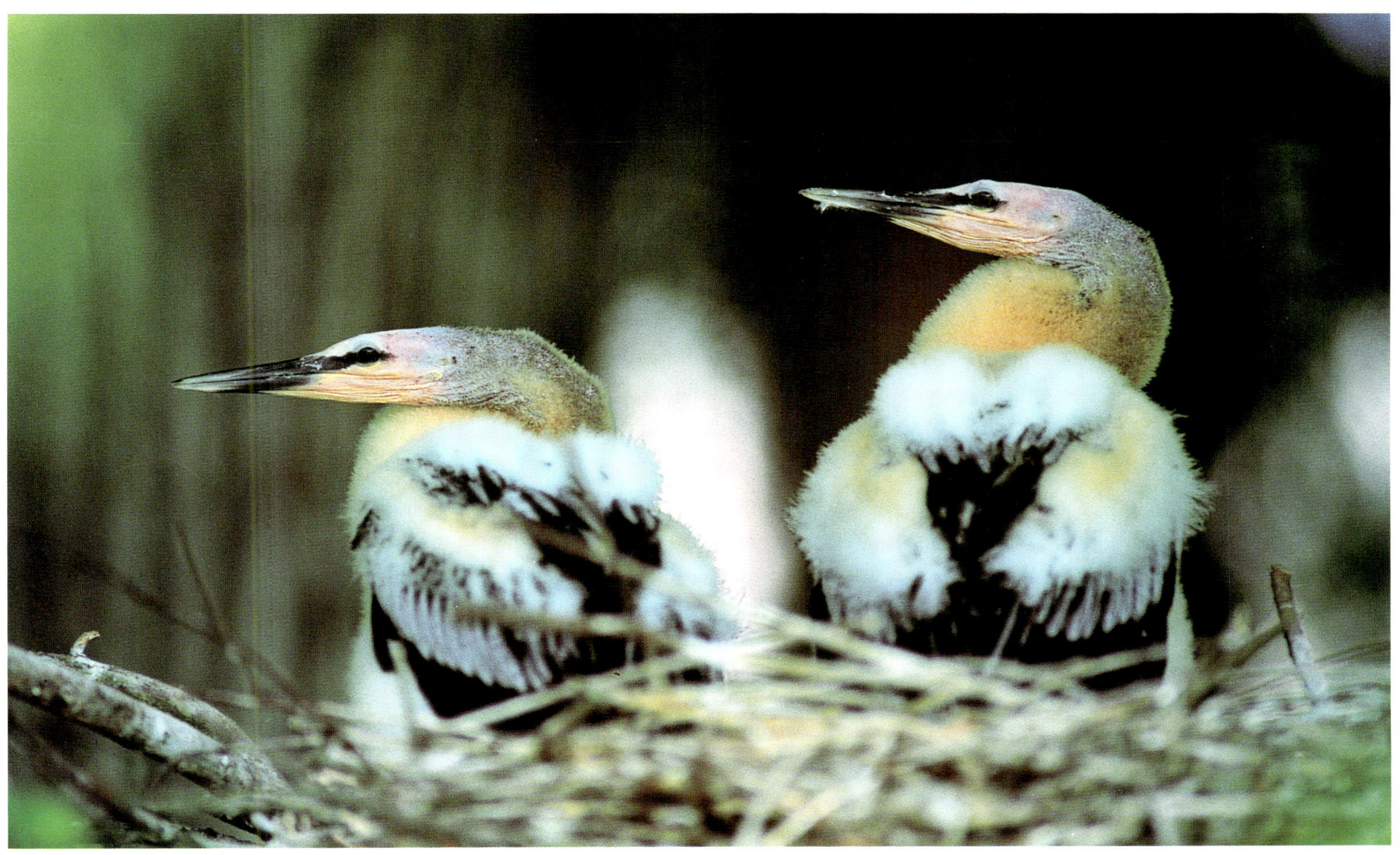

YOUNG ANHINGAS, MISSISSIPPI, JUNE 1993

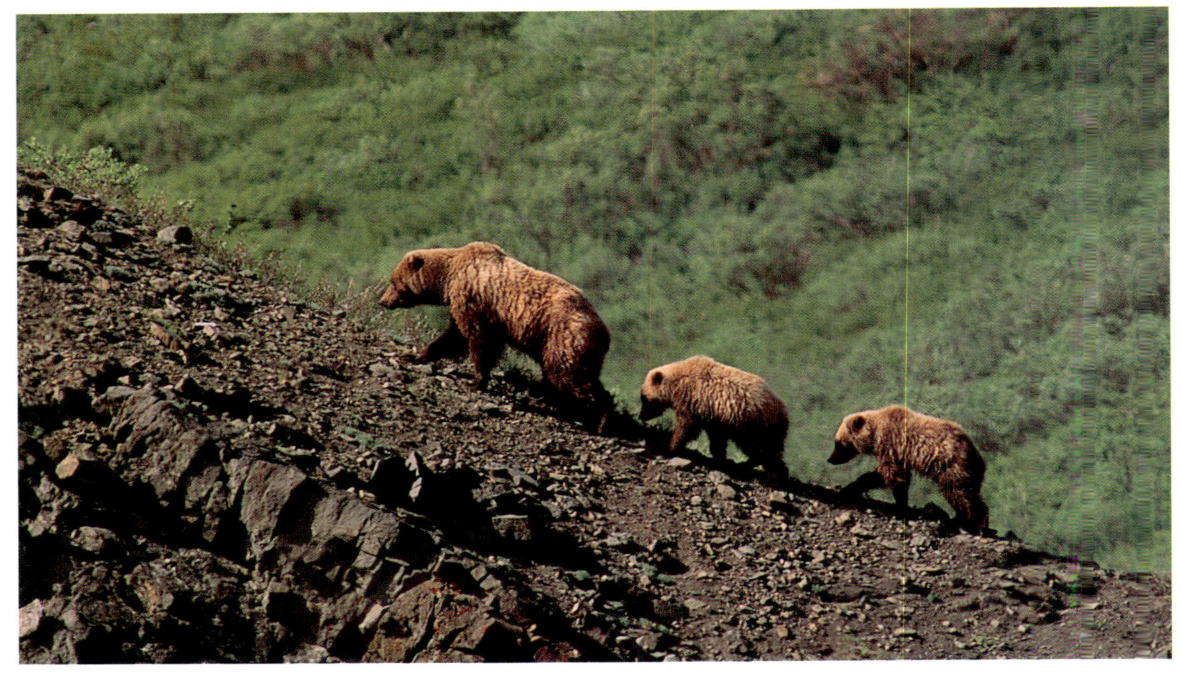

GRIZZLY BEAR AND CUBS, ALASKA, JUNE 1992

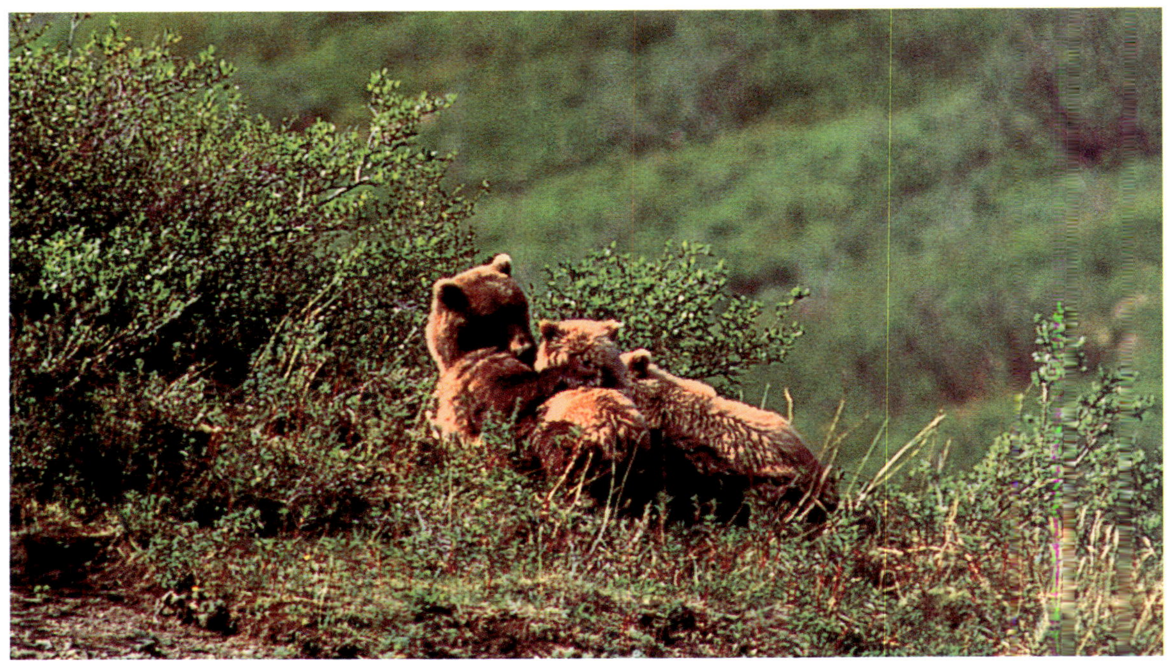

GRIZZLY BEAR NURSING CUBS, ALASKA, JUNE 1992

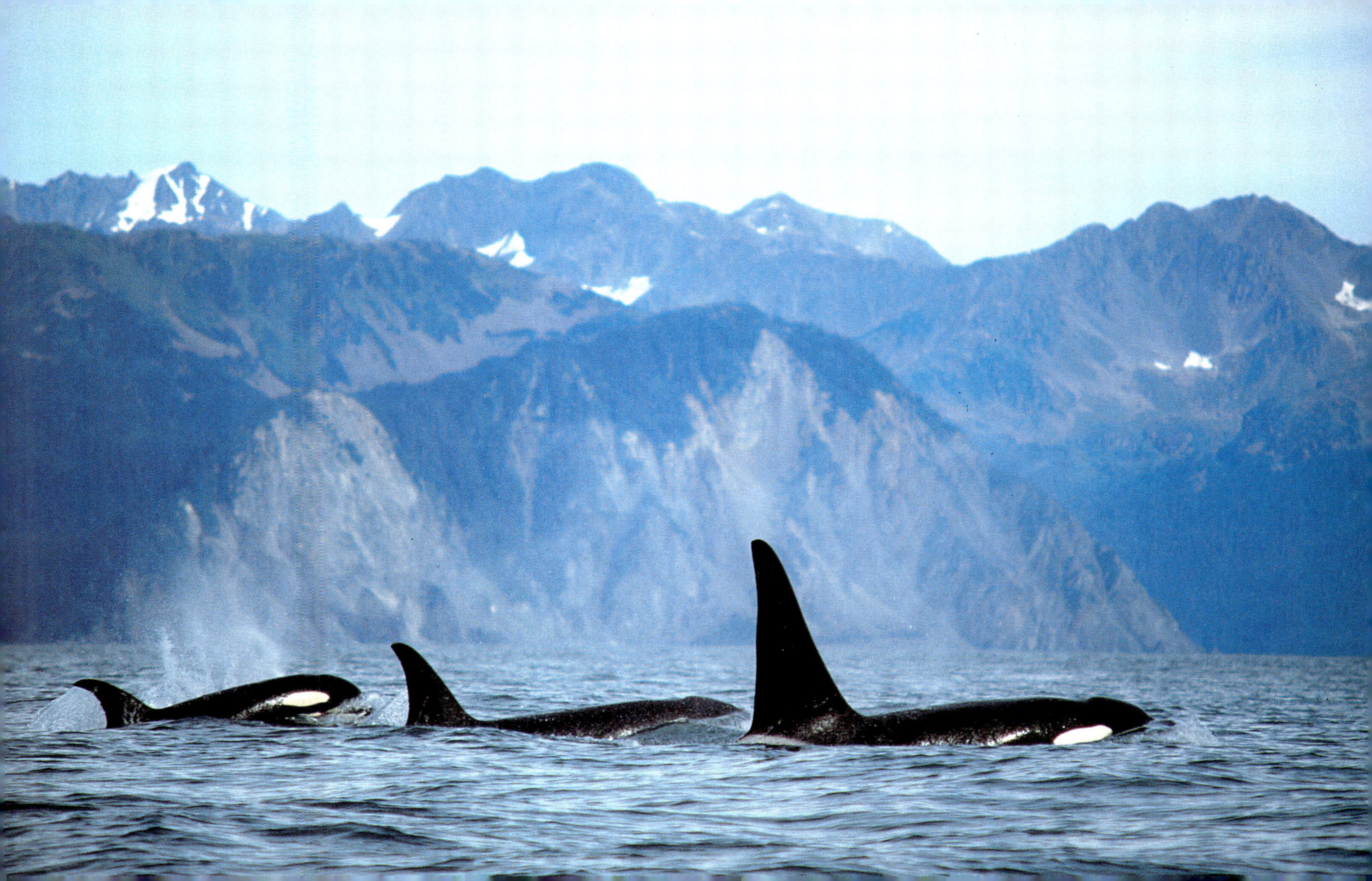

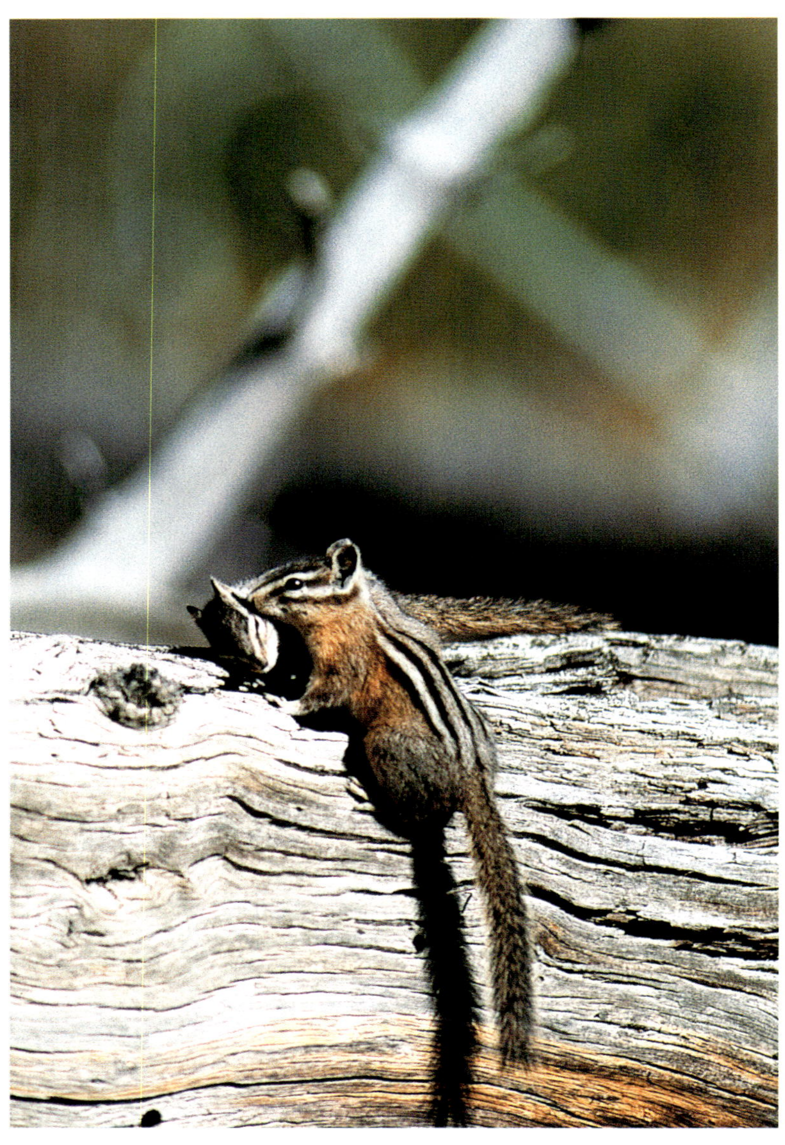

CHIPMUNKS, MONTANA, SEPTEMBER 1990

WHITE PELICANS, FLORIDA, MARCH 1997

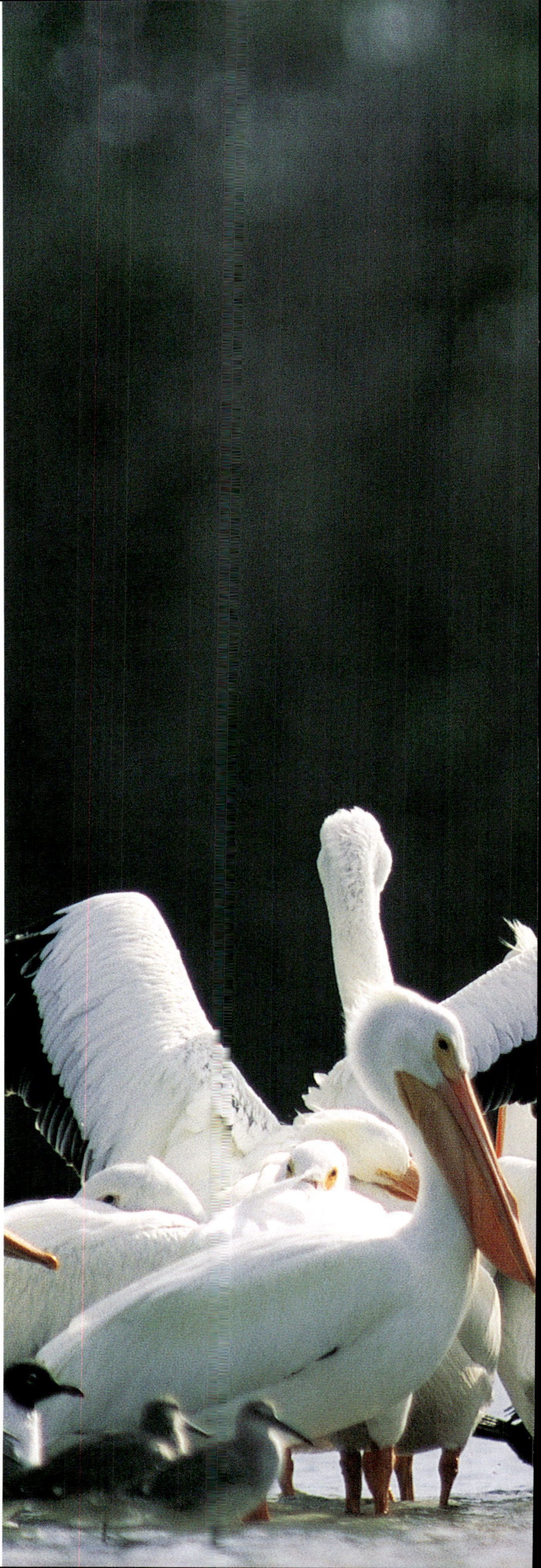

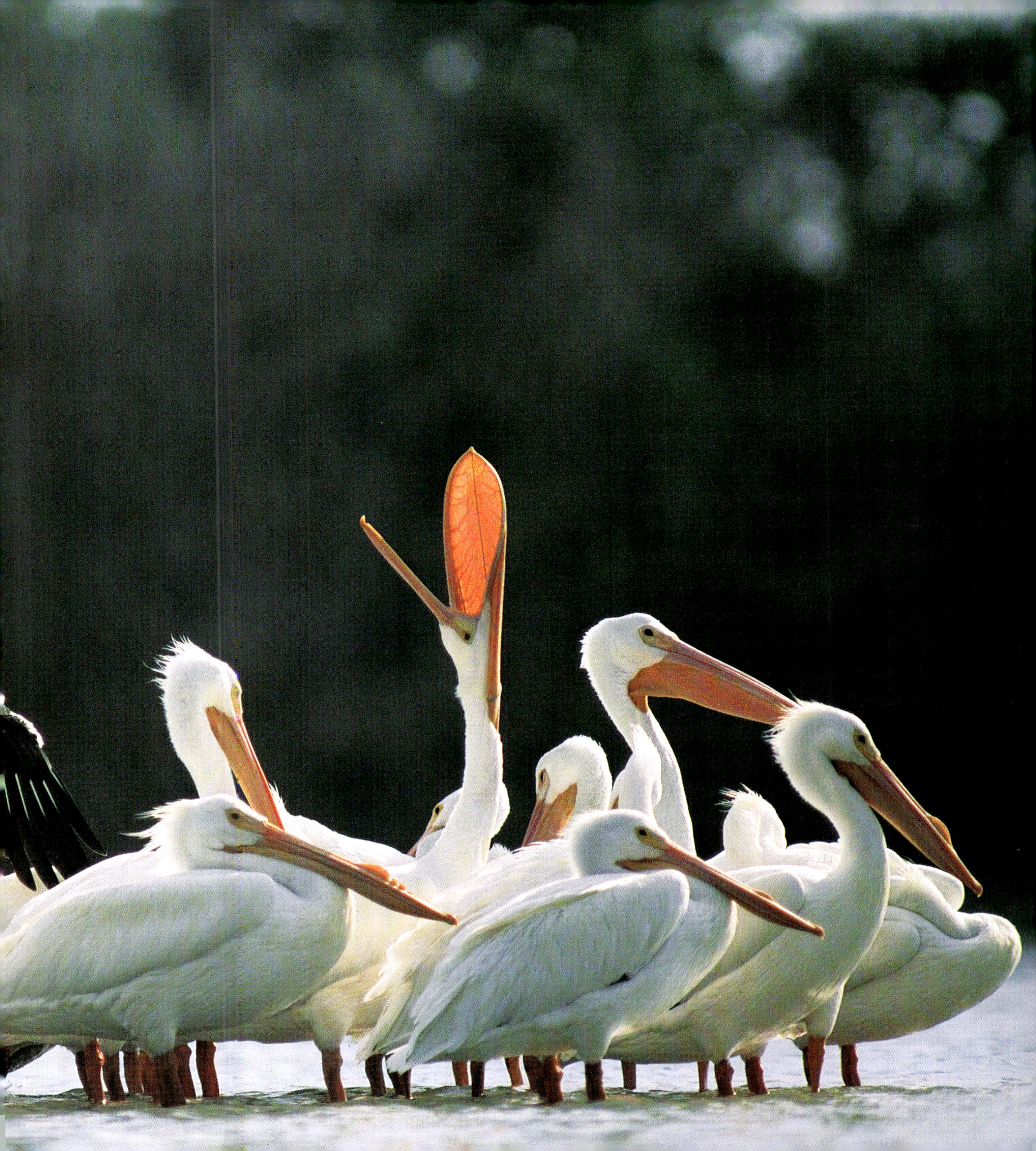

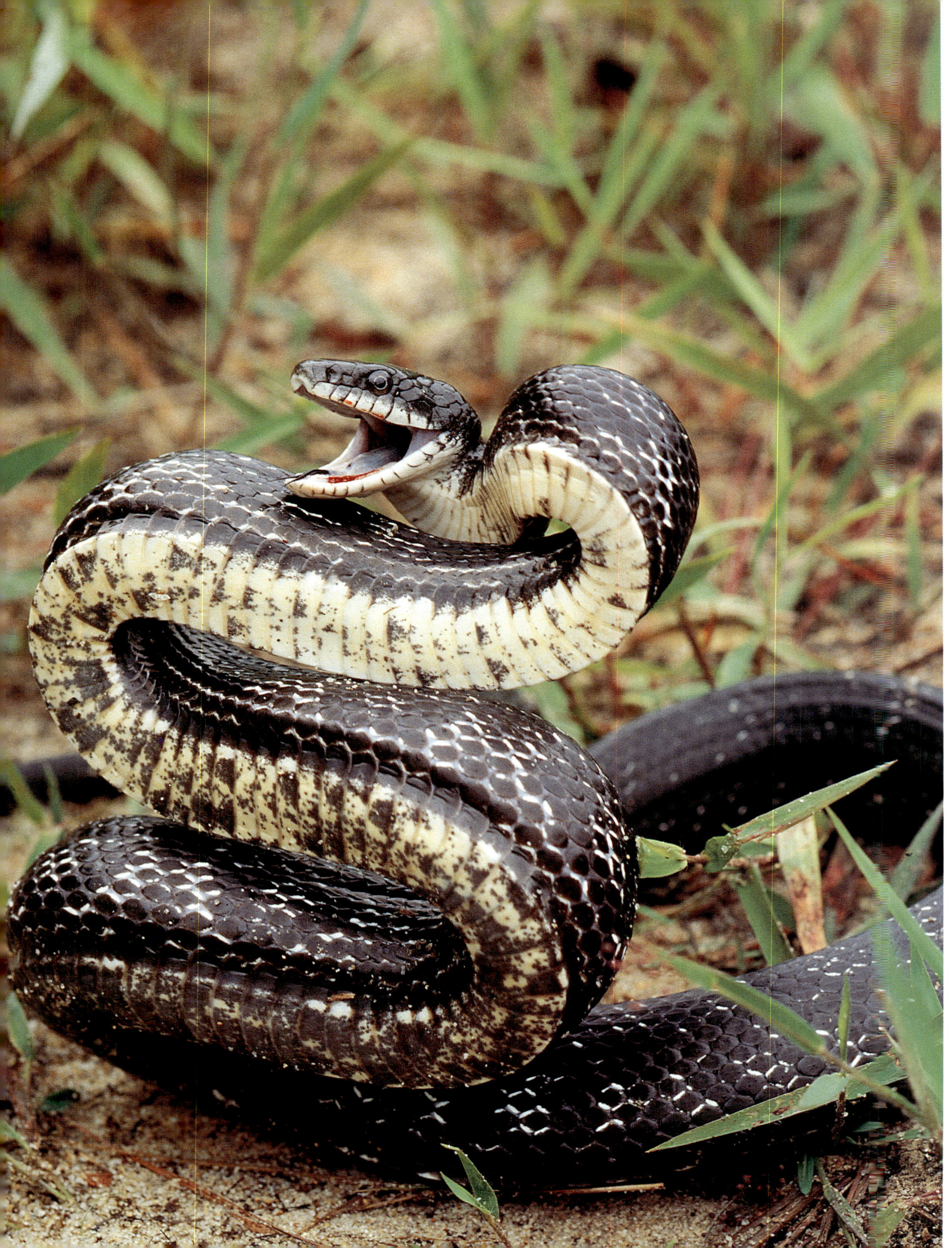

KINGSNAKE,
DELAWARE,
MAY 1996

"People always ask me if I'm afraid of snakes. I tell them 'No, I'm afraid of people.' I can tell when a snake is going to strike and I know why. With people, I don't have a clue."

I may have found solace hiding in the wilderness with my sons, but I couldn't stay there forever.

Returning to "civilization" involved more than simply driving back into the city. After my many months of intense introspection, relating to other people on anything more than a cursory level would require a mental and emotional adjustment as well.

"I shoot in solitude most of the time, choosing to go away from the movement of people. Always choosing, it seems, the road less traveled."

You'd probably never guess it if you met me in person, but I see myself as an introvert. It's not that I don't like people, I'm just very cautious and extremely sensitive – maybe overly sensitive.

A friend in Alaska summed it up in his own journal, writing, "Steve takes his work very seriously, not wanting his concentration disturbed. He is not rude, but he is not by any means gregarious."

"My heart has been wounded more than once, and I suspect that it's never quite healed. I'm puzzled – it seems I can give *love from my heart, but have a very hard time* receiving it. *I want to increase the boundaries of my heart, but find it so difficult.*

"I suspect by protecting it, I've never really let the healing balm of light come through. I feel like an apple without an eye."

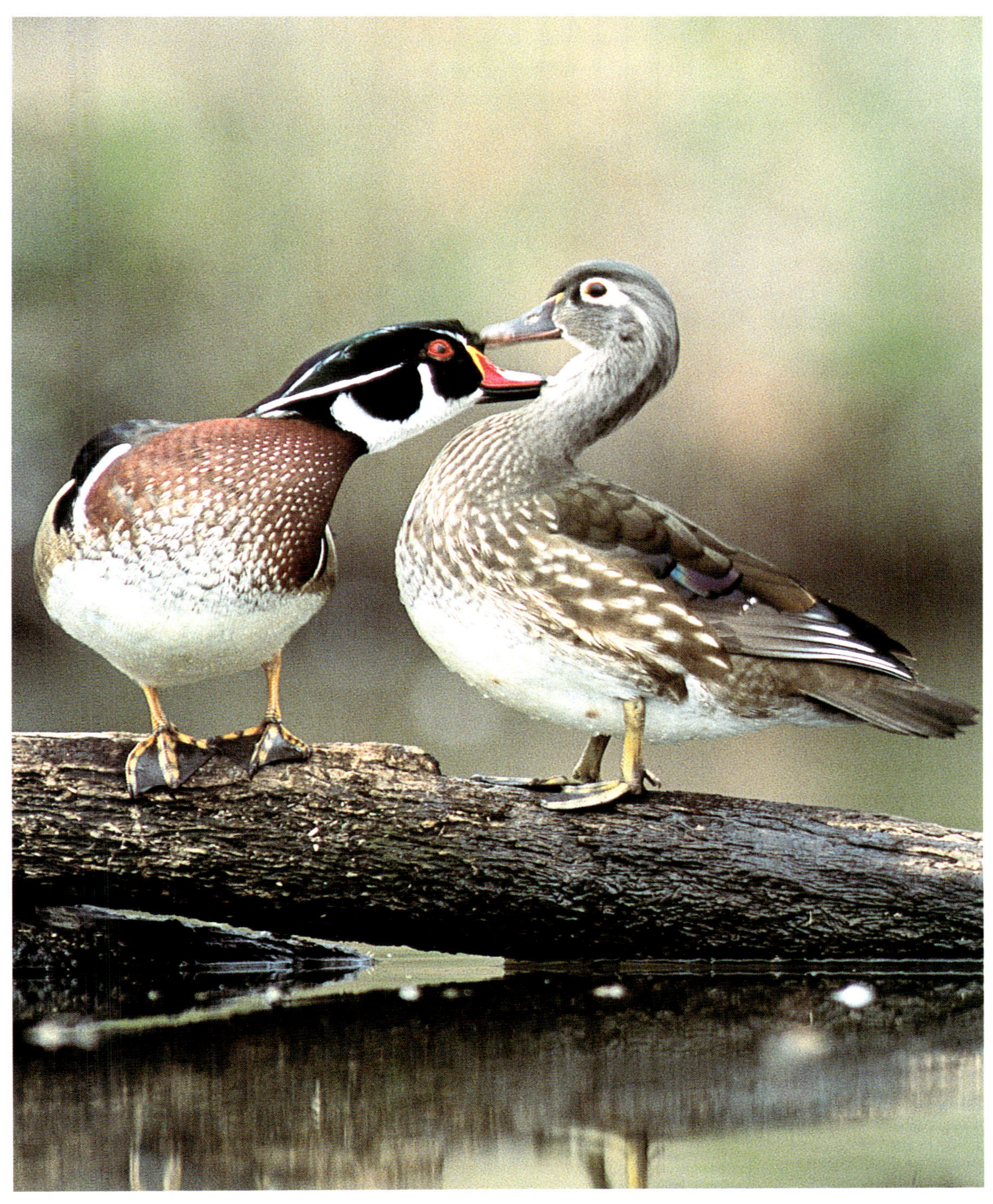

WOOD DUCKS PREENING, MISSISSIPPI, JANUARY 1993

Having a sensitive spirit may have its drawbacks, but I believe it's absolutely necessary to the work I do. The images I'm most proud of capture more than just beautiful scenery or animals in action. There's a *feeling* in them, an intangible quality that comes from giving in to that sensitivity, letting it guide my eyes and hands as I compose, react, and....

Those are the images that touch people.

"I pray that people will see what I see – the world enlightened. Of course, enlightenment flows from the Lord of all creation. When people are moved by my work, it isn't me. If ever the Lord were pushed away, the enlightenment would vanish and all my efforts would become temporary."

STELLAR SEA LIONS, ALASKA, AUGUST 1996

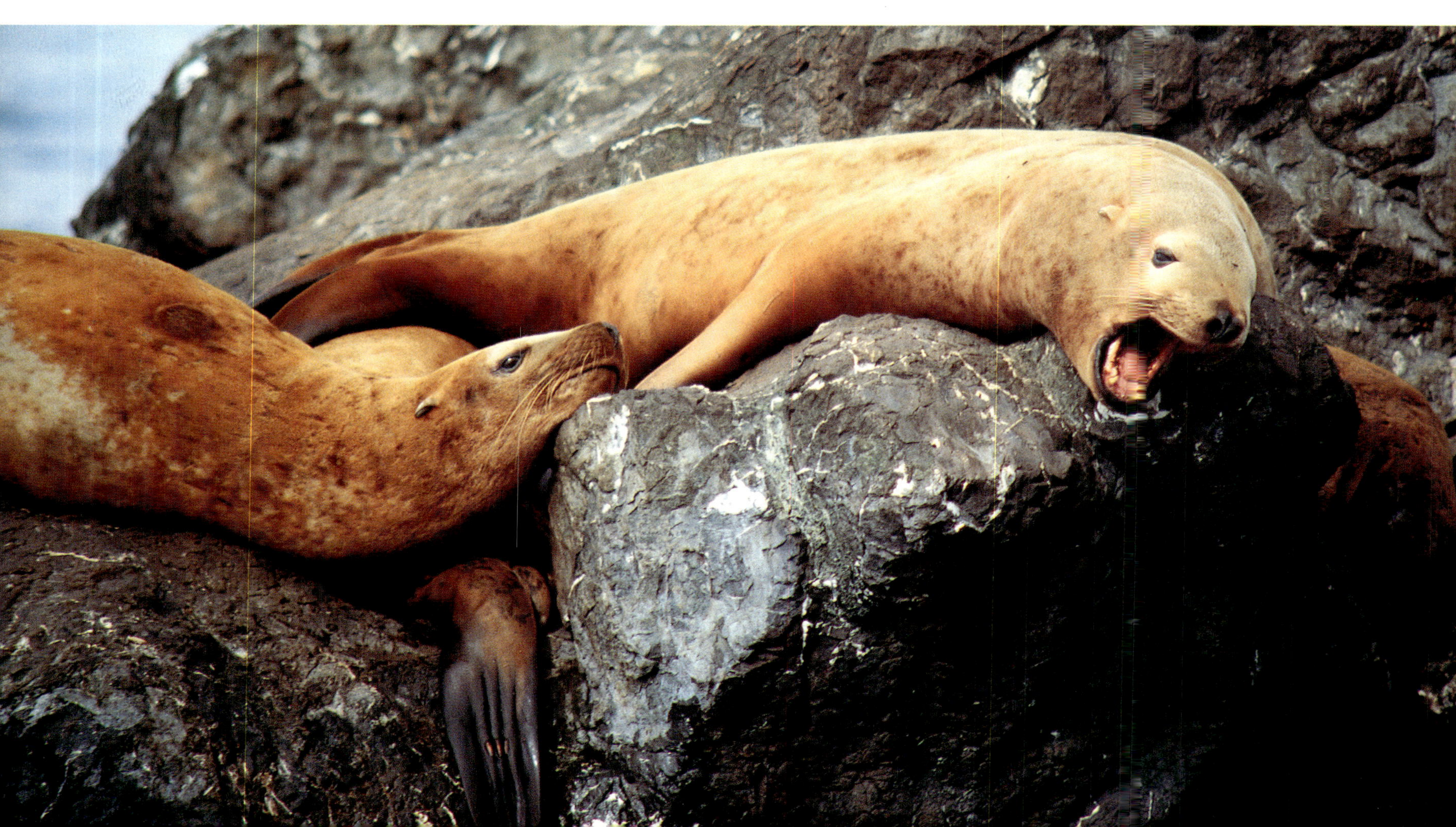

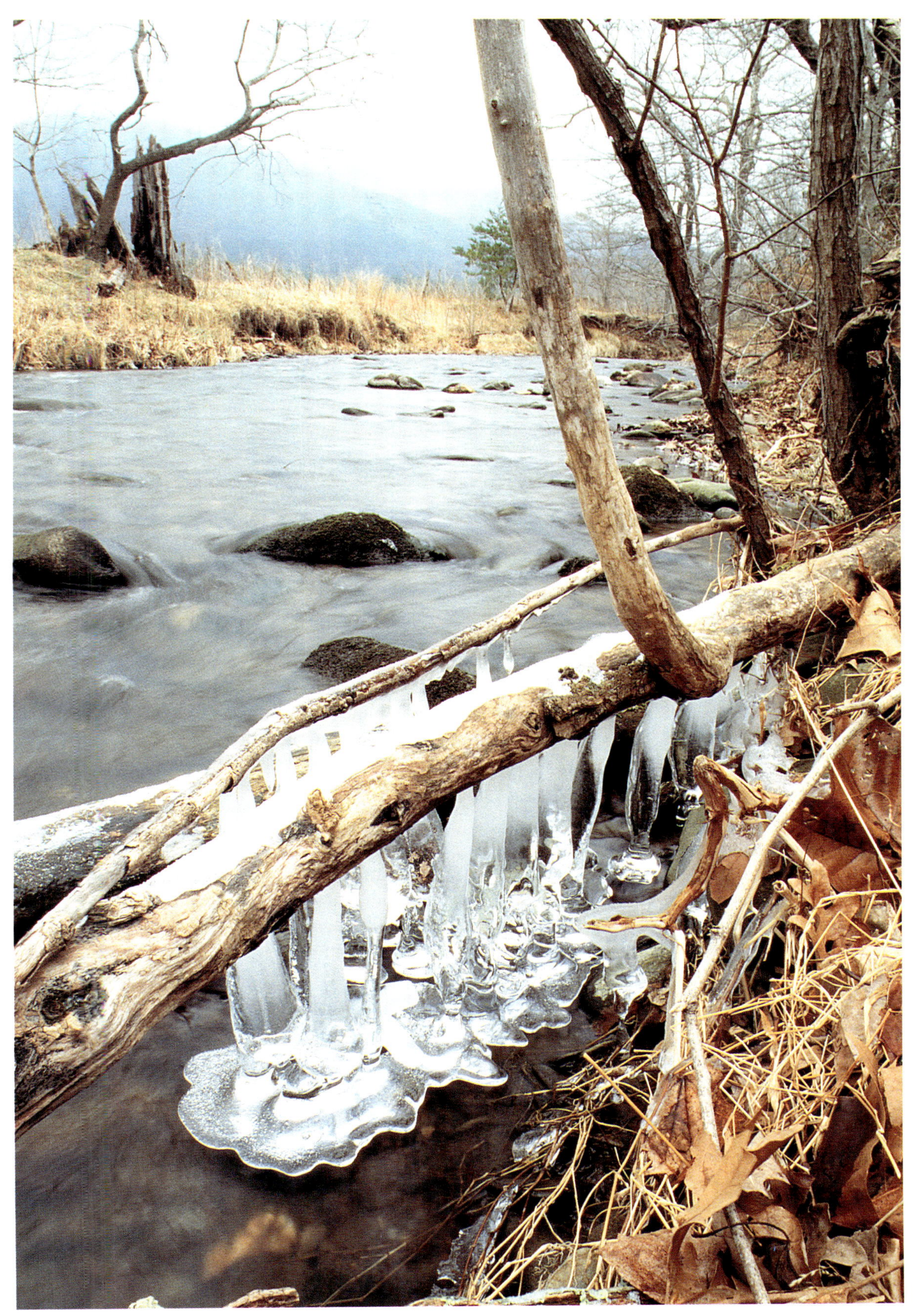

ABRAMS CREEK IN ICE, TENNESSEE, DECEMBER 1995

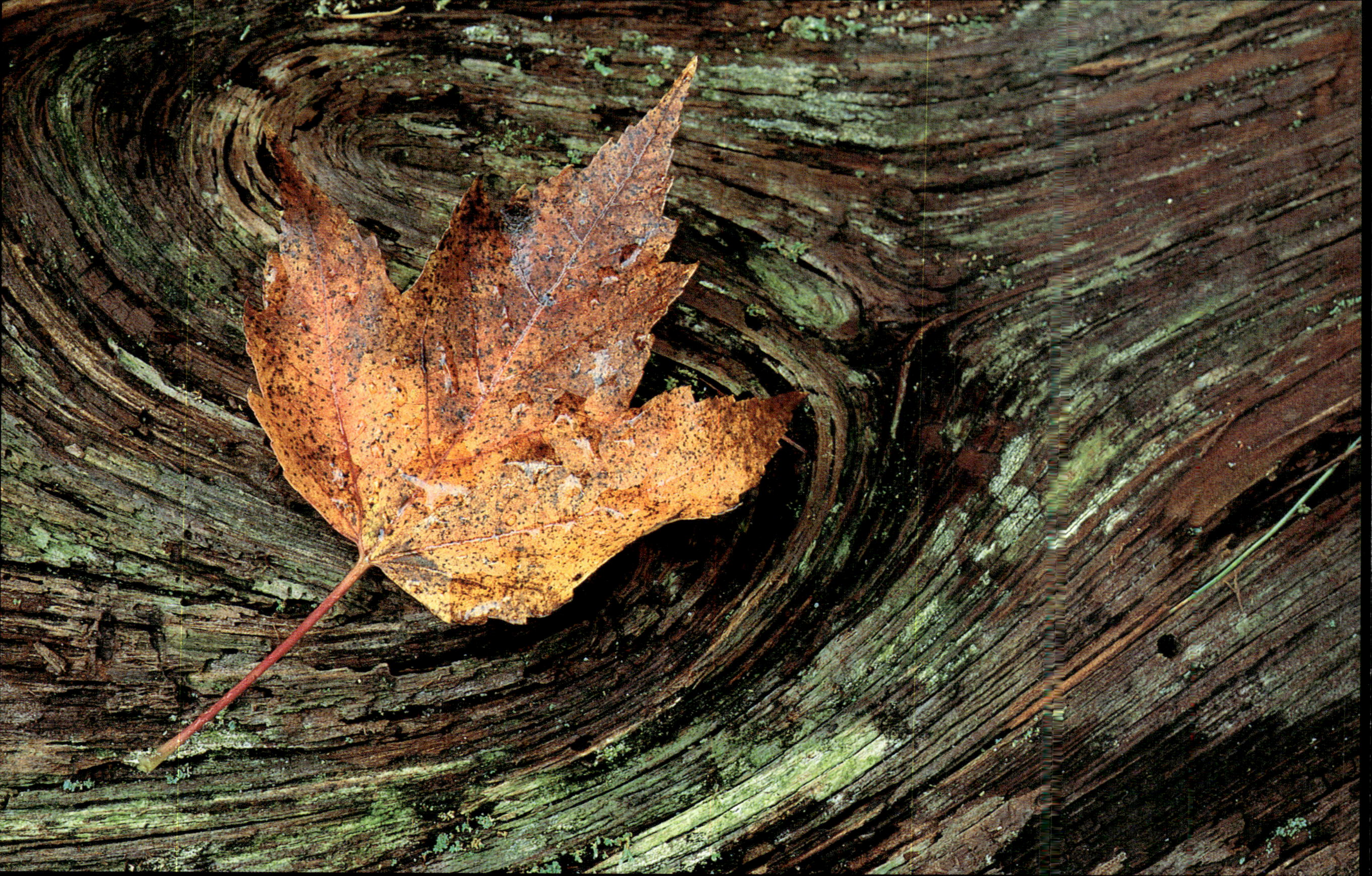

My favorite Bible verse, II Corinthians 4:18, says it best. "Look not at the things which are seen, but the things which are unseen. The things which are seen are temporary, but the things which are unseen are eternal."

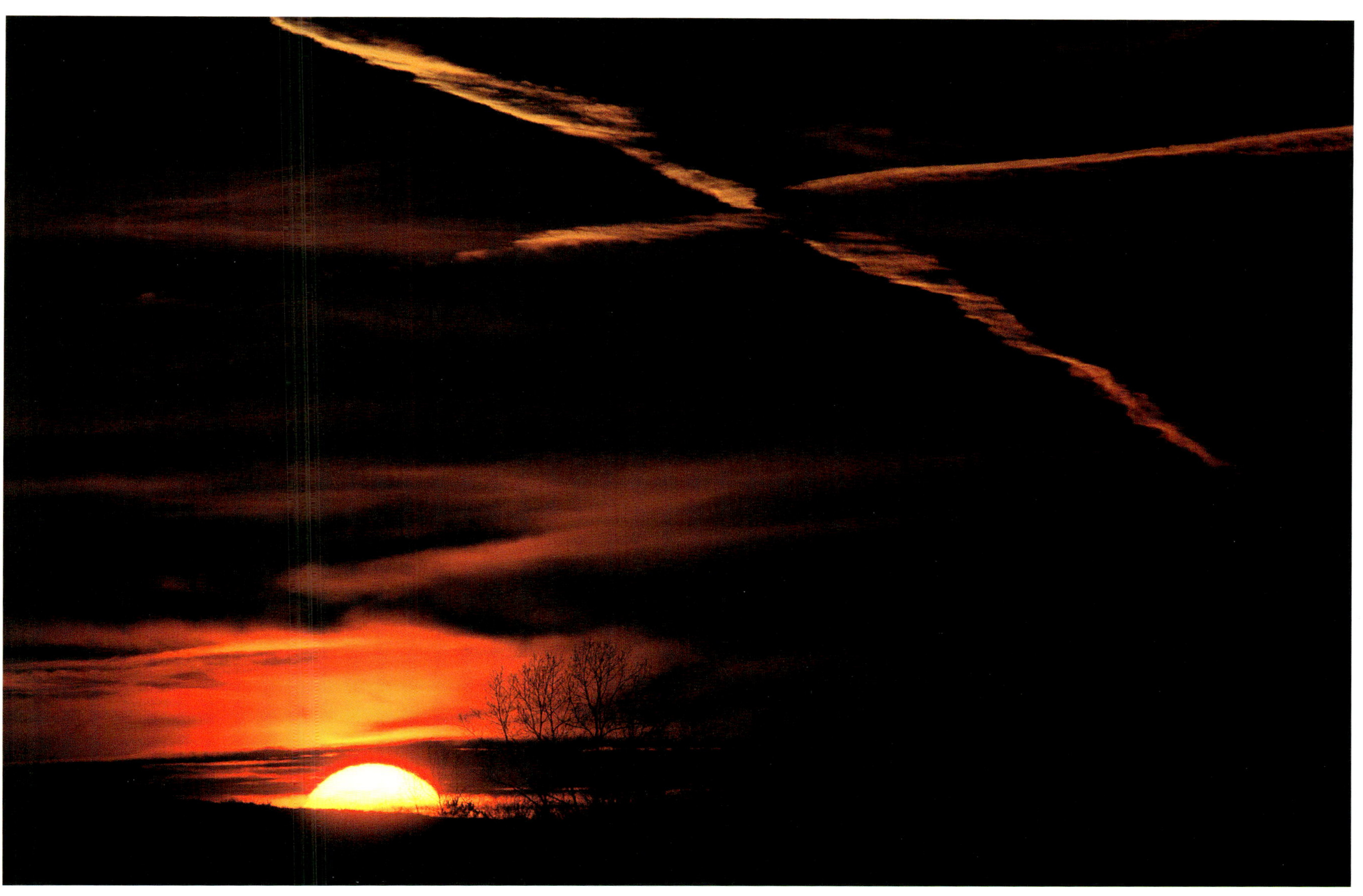

CROSS AT SUNSET, MISSISSIPPI, FEBRUARY 1986

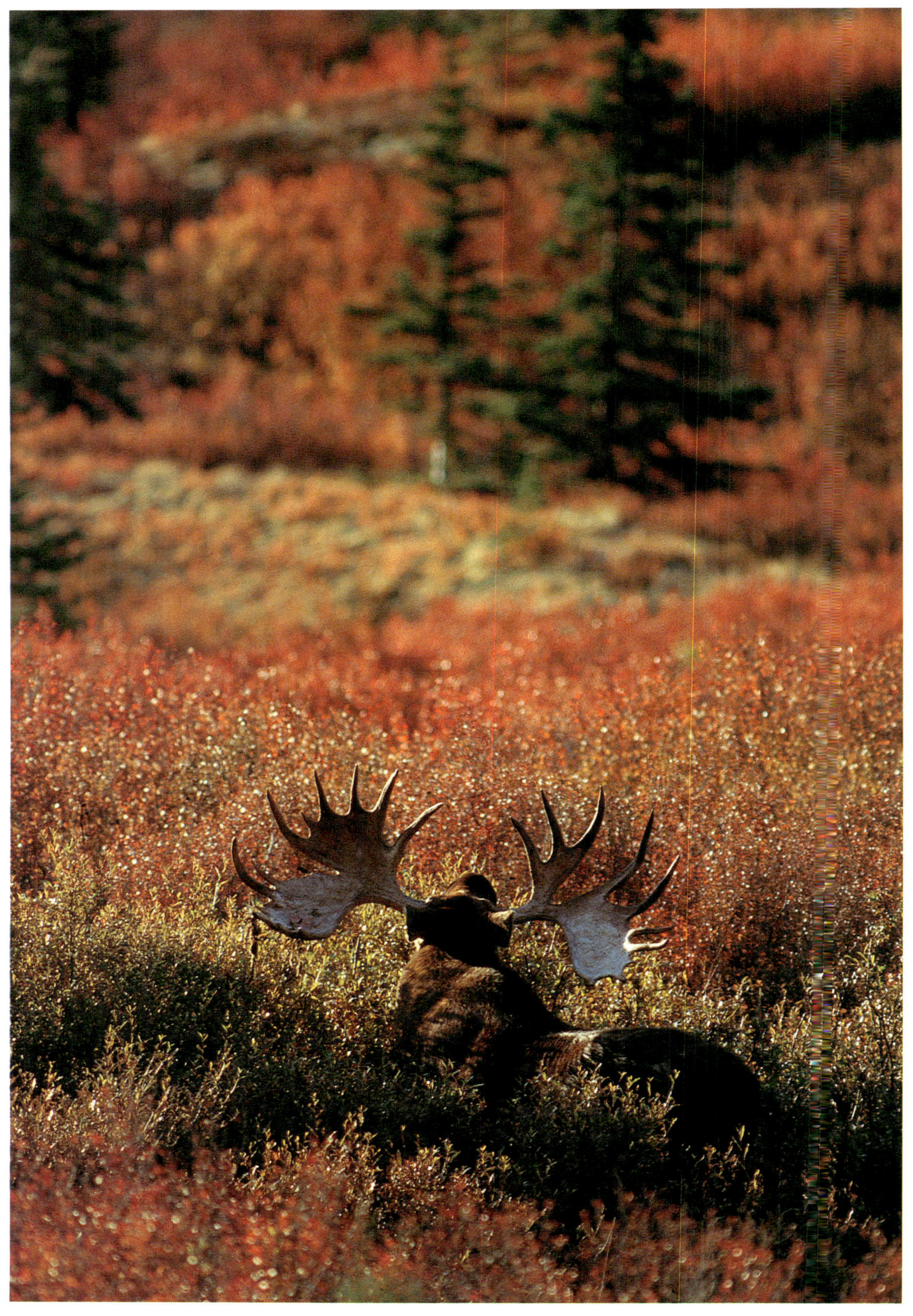

MOOSE IN FALL COLOR, ALASKA, SEPTEMBER 1996

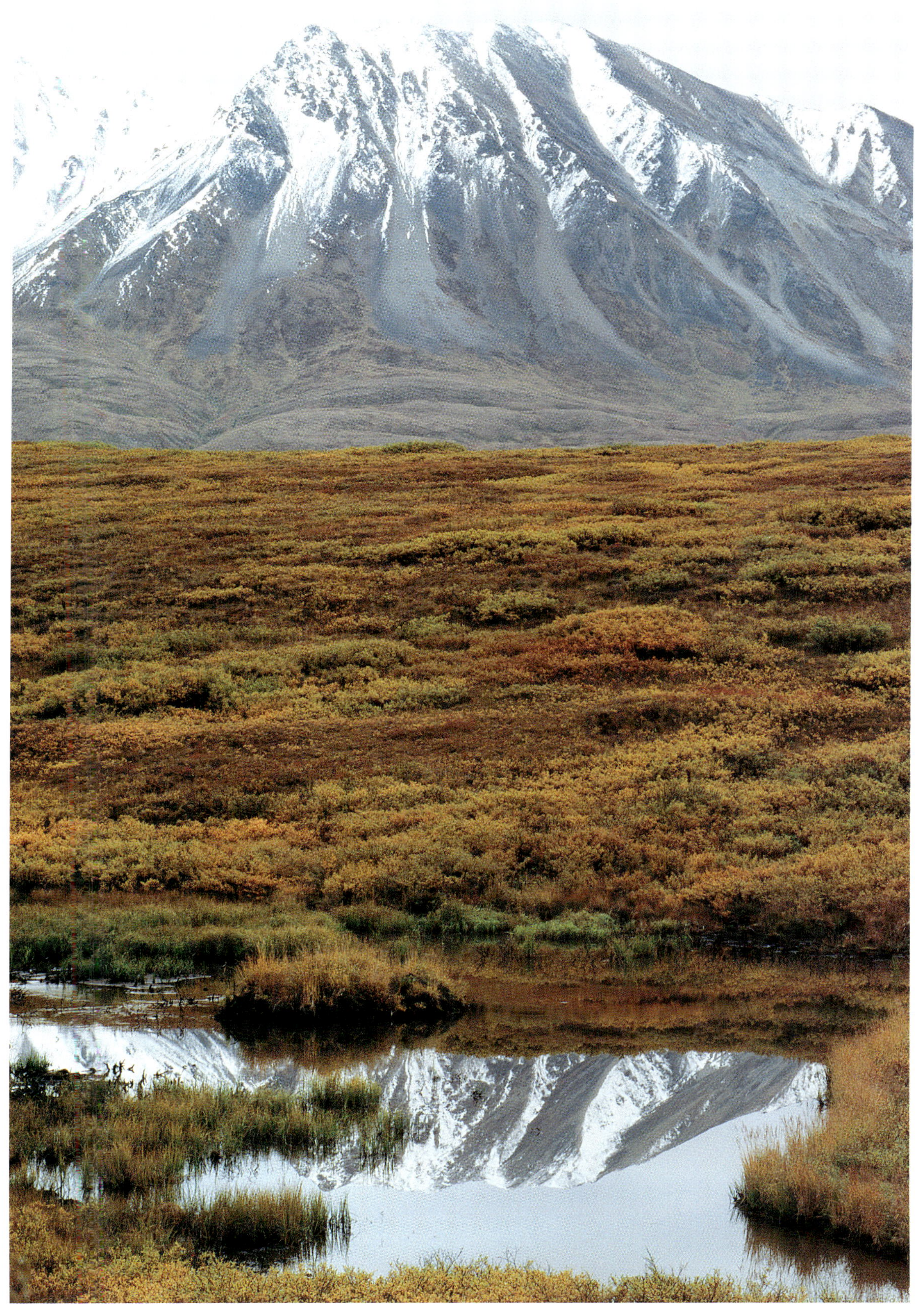

MOUNTAIN AND REFLECTION, ALASKA, SEPTEMBER 1996

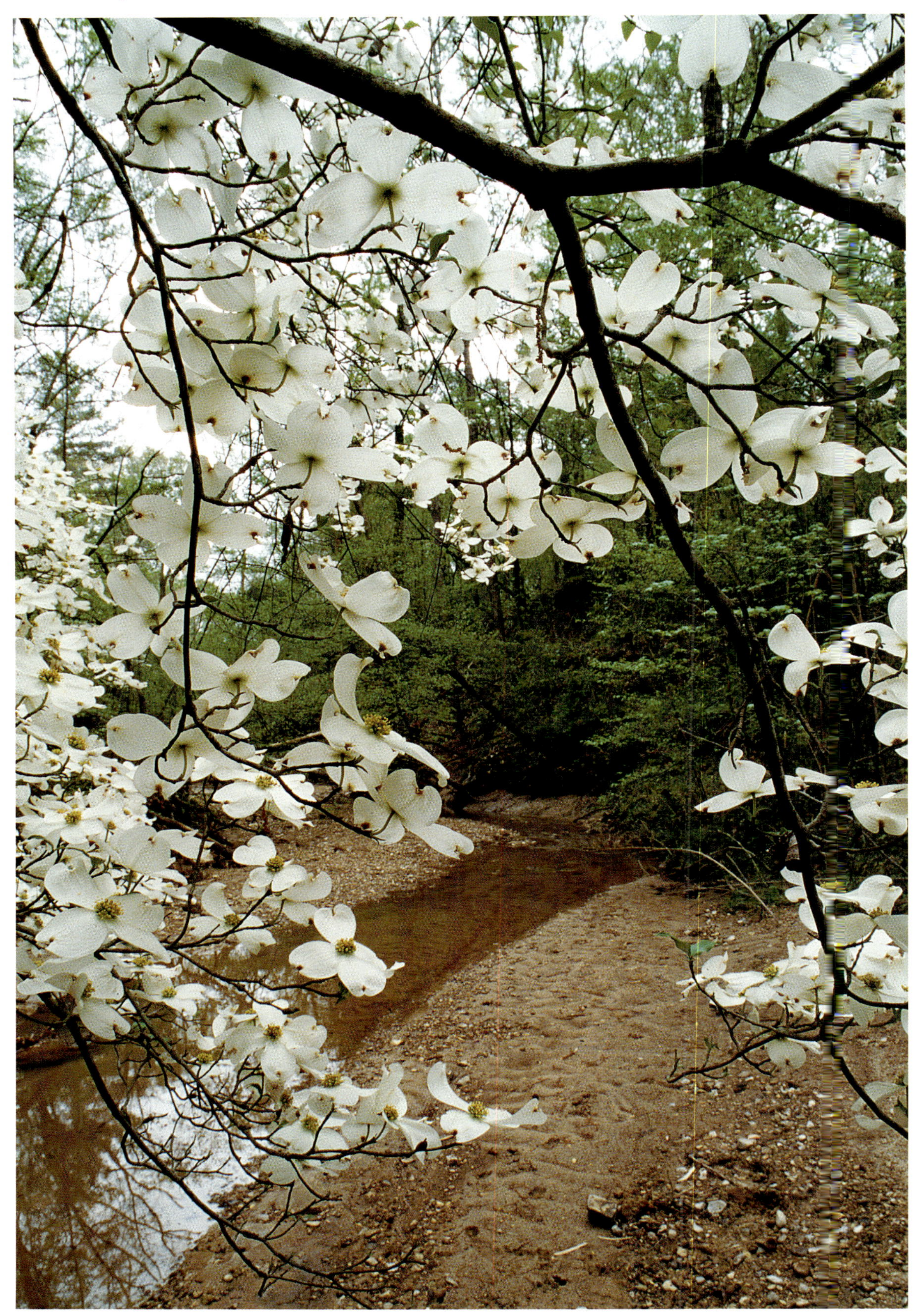

DOGWOODS OVER OWENS CREEK, MISSISSIPPI, MARCH 1993

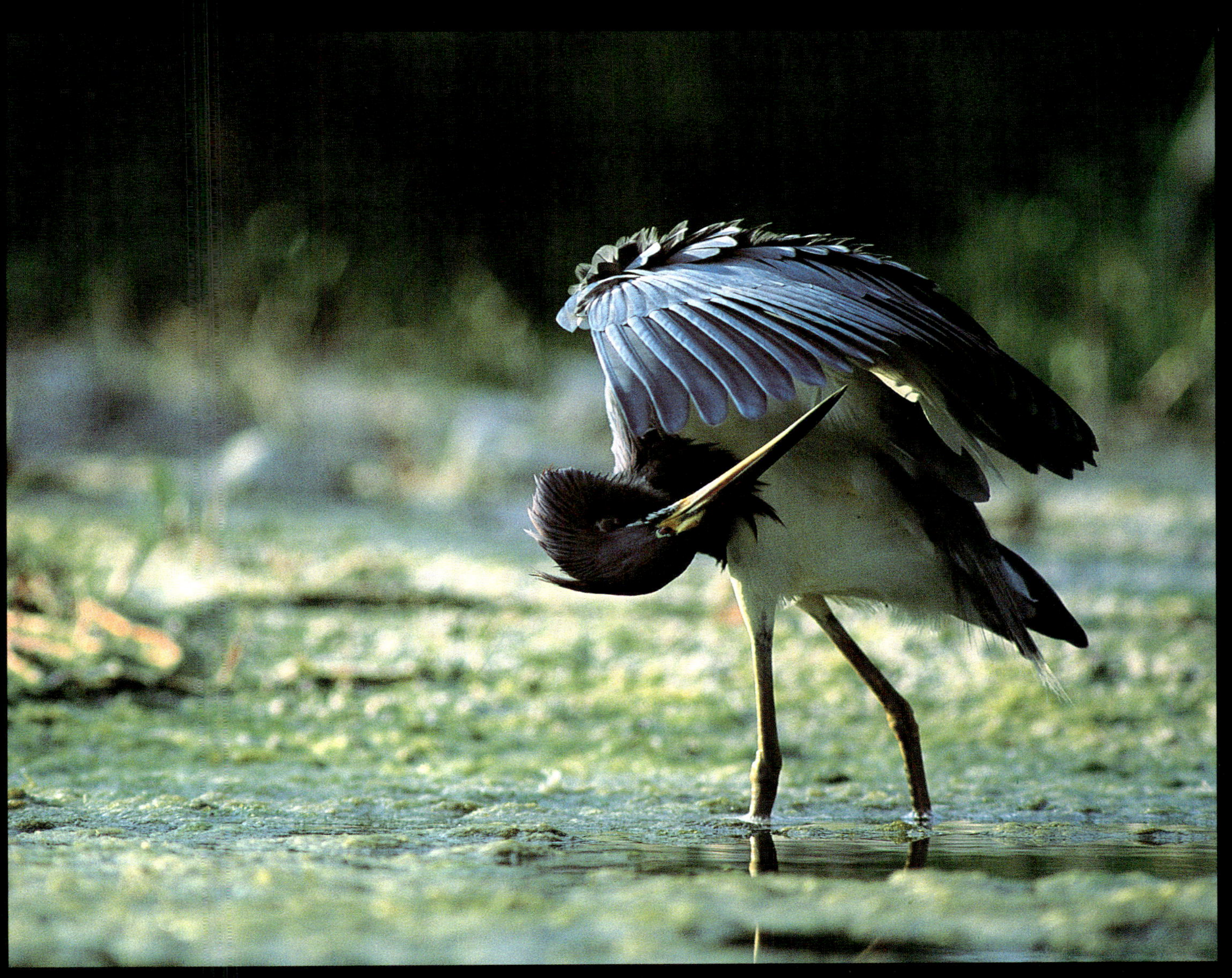

TRICOLORED HERON PREENING, FLORIDA, MARCH 1997

During a trip to Boston, I attended an exhibit of paintings by Winslow Homer. The show was a progressive exhibit, beginning with Homer's earliest works and concluding with his final paintings. From the moment I stepped through the museum doors, I was completely absorbed.

"In this exhibit, I see the growth of an artist. Not merely the explorations of different mediums and subject matter and improved artistic techniques, but the growth of the man himself. Homer painted what he was experiencing in each moment – not just the landscape or the subject matter he was working with, but his emotions, and the stirrings of his own heart.

"Looking at the paintings, I see an intent of purpose and a drive that I empathize with – a compelling energy that reaches far beyond any pat artistic philosophy."

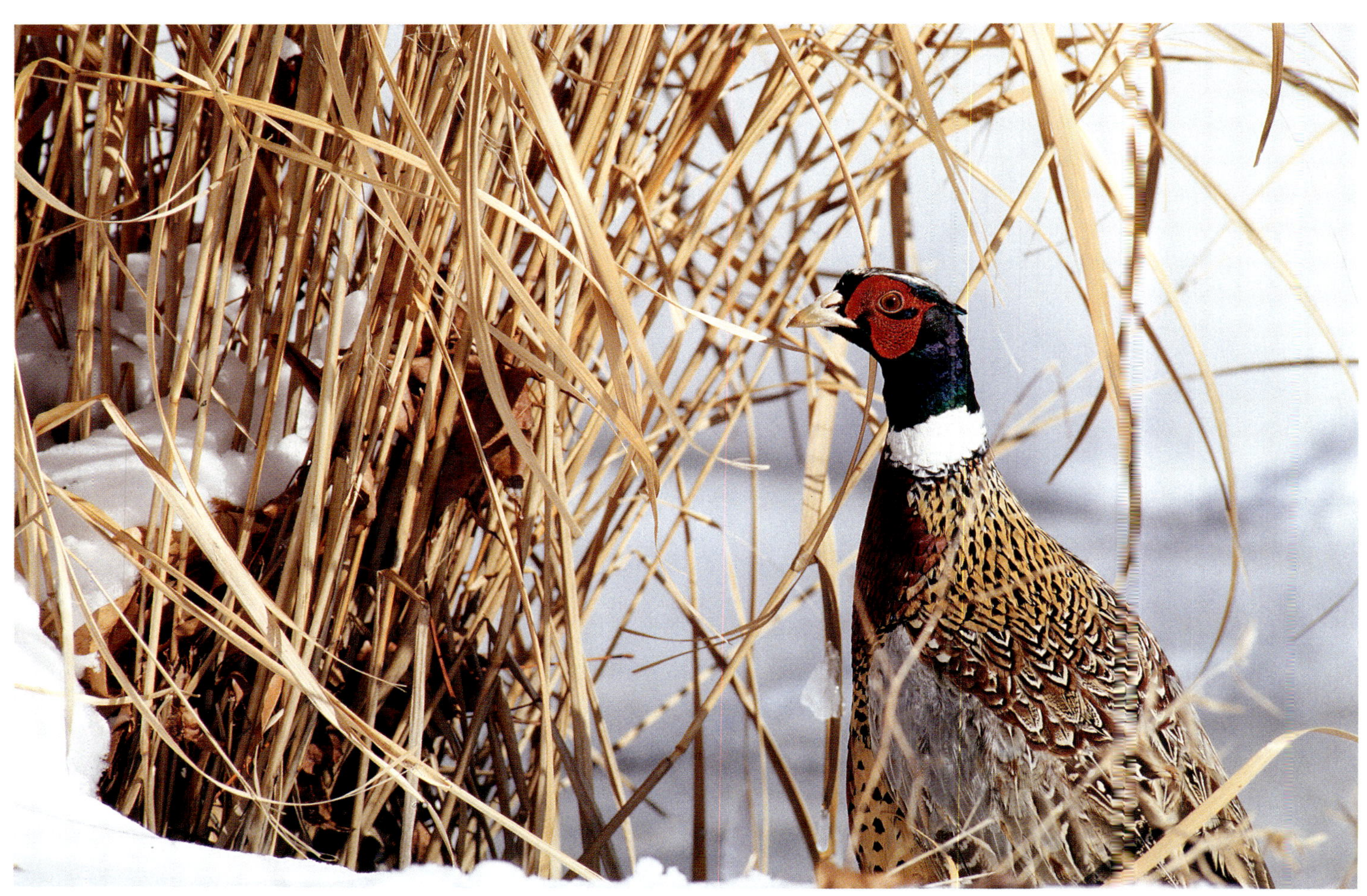

Standing in the museum, I realized a battle was raging inside me. A fever that left me cold. Once again, it was the clash between head and heart. I couldn't "think through" a calling. The issue wasn't what I *wanted* to do, but what I *had* to do. There was no "philosophy" here! Only a burning passion that drove me on.

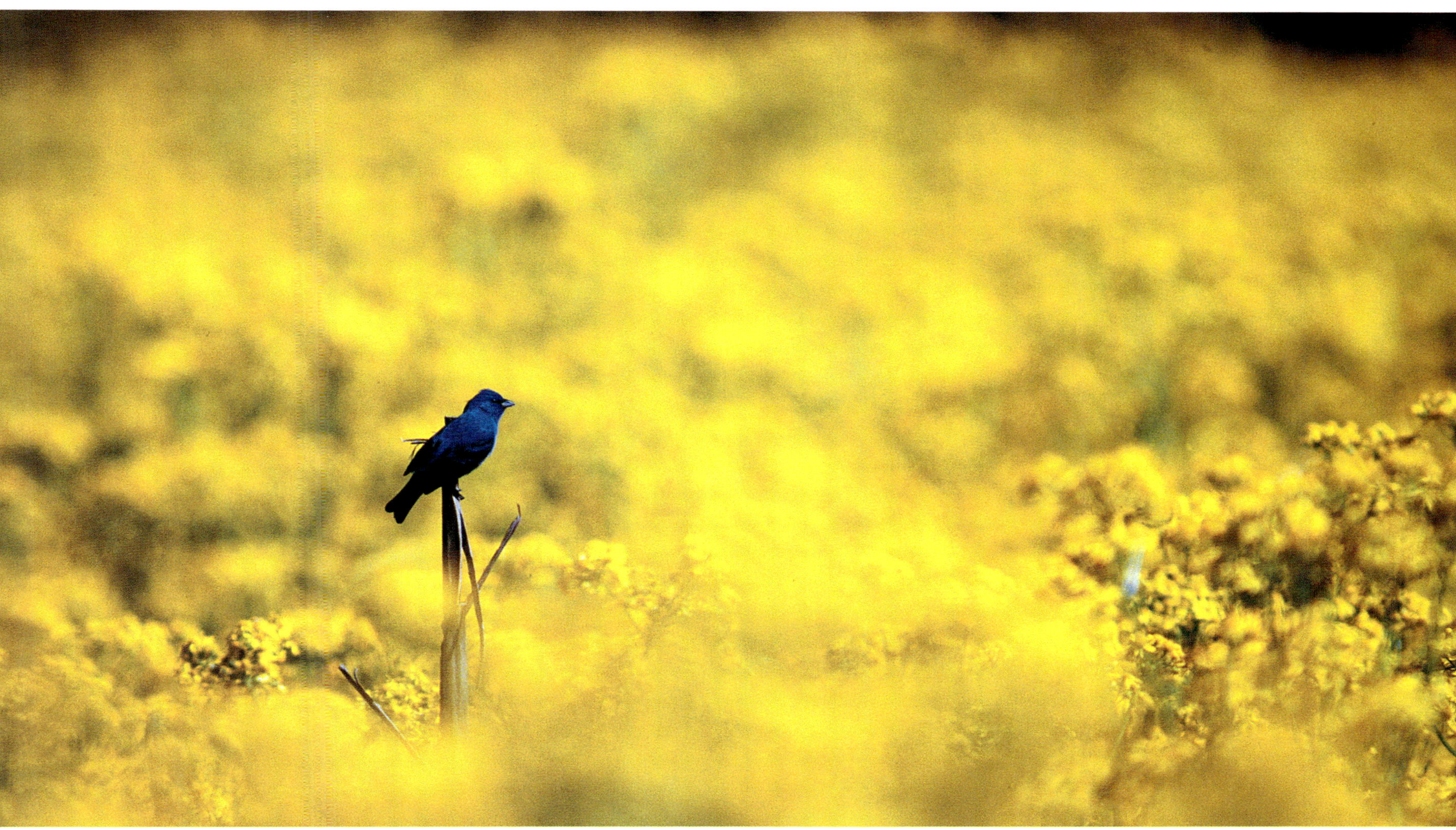

INDIGO BUNTING IN YELLOWTOP, MISSISSIPPI, MAY 1996

RING-NECKED PHEASANT IN SNOW, DELAWARE, JANUARY 1996

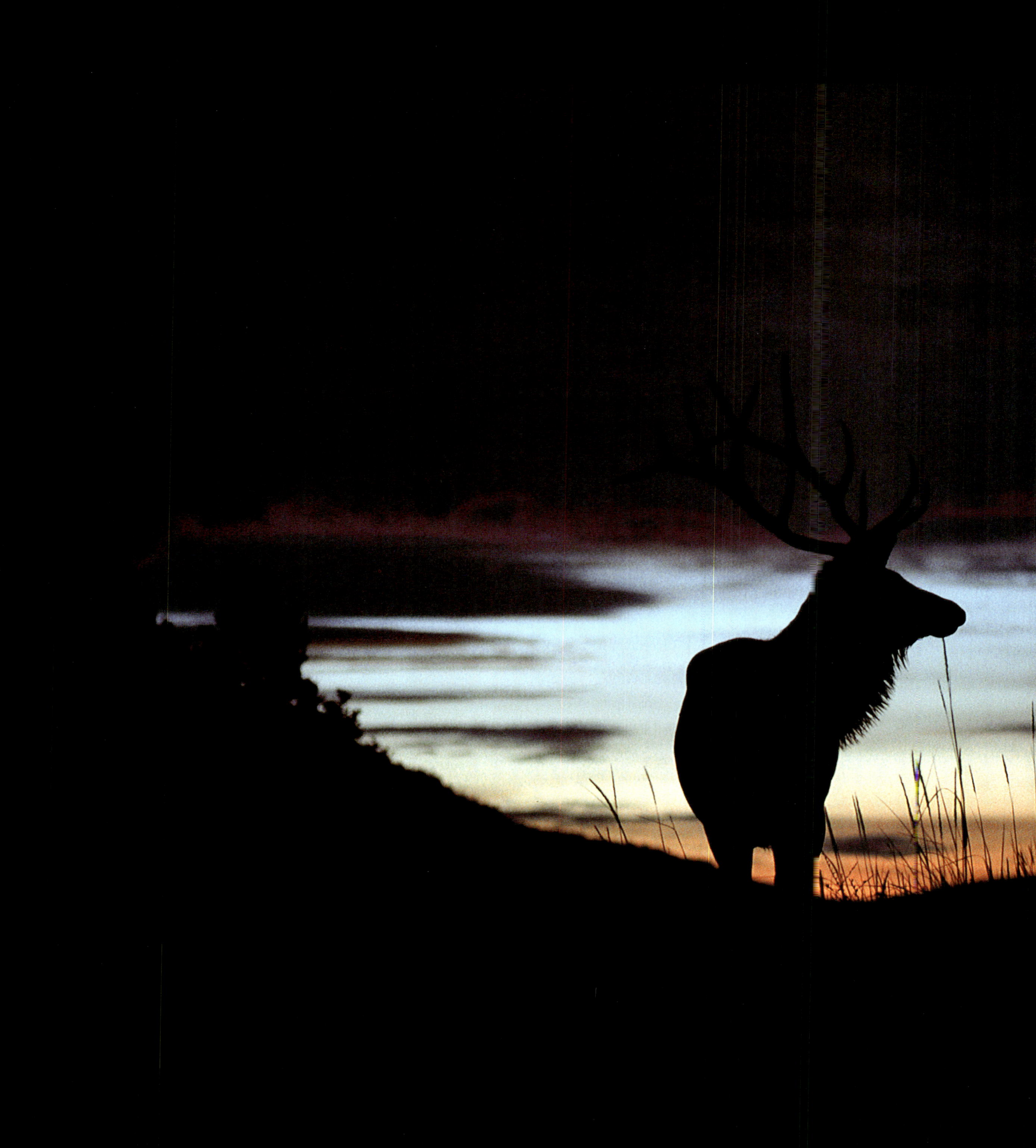

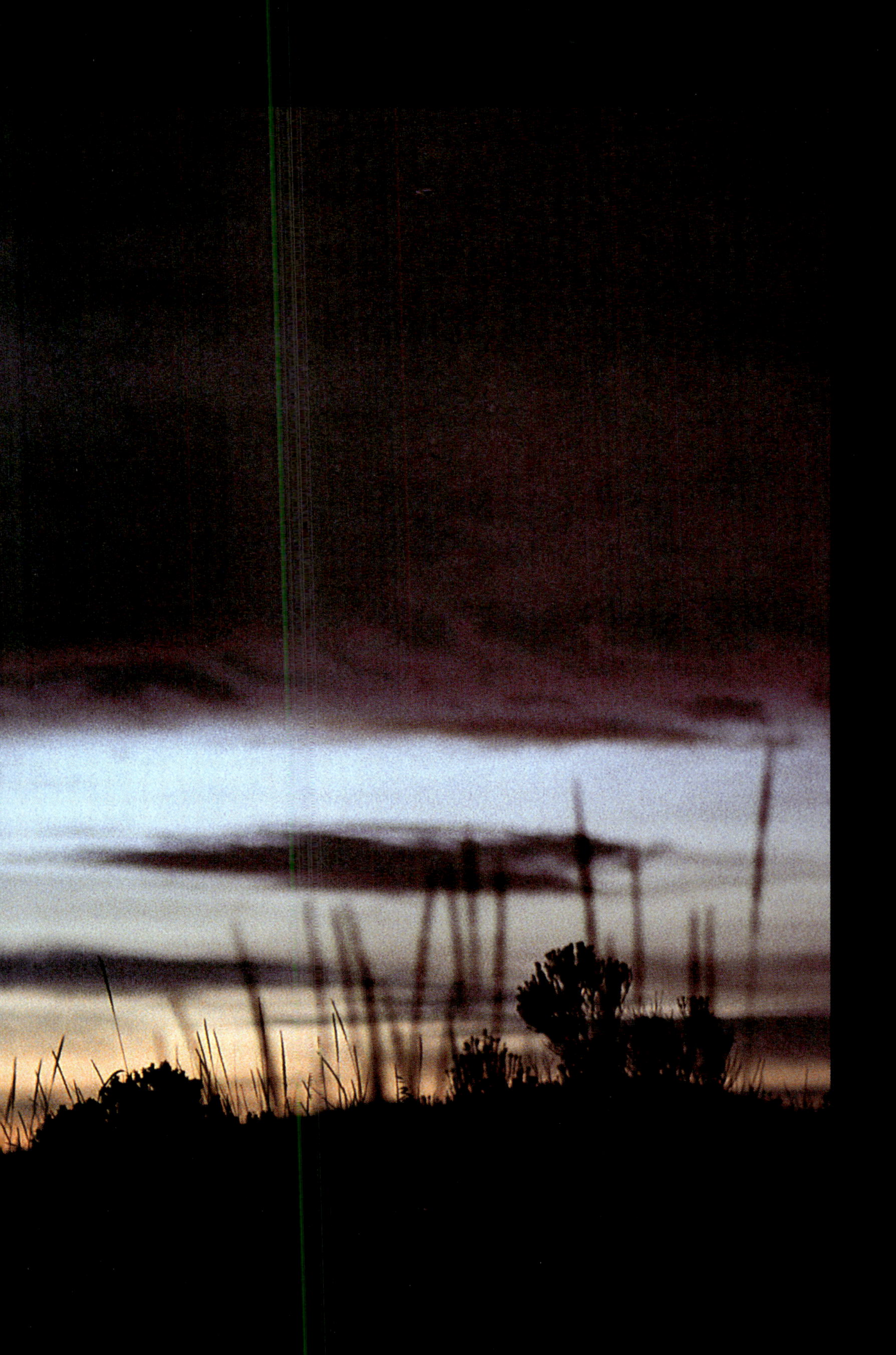

ELK AT SUNRISE, MONTANA, SEPTEMBER 1990

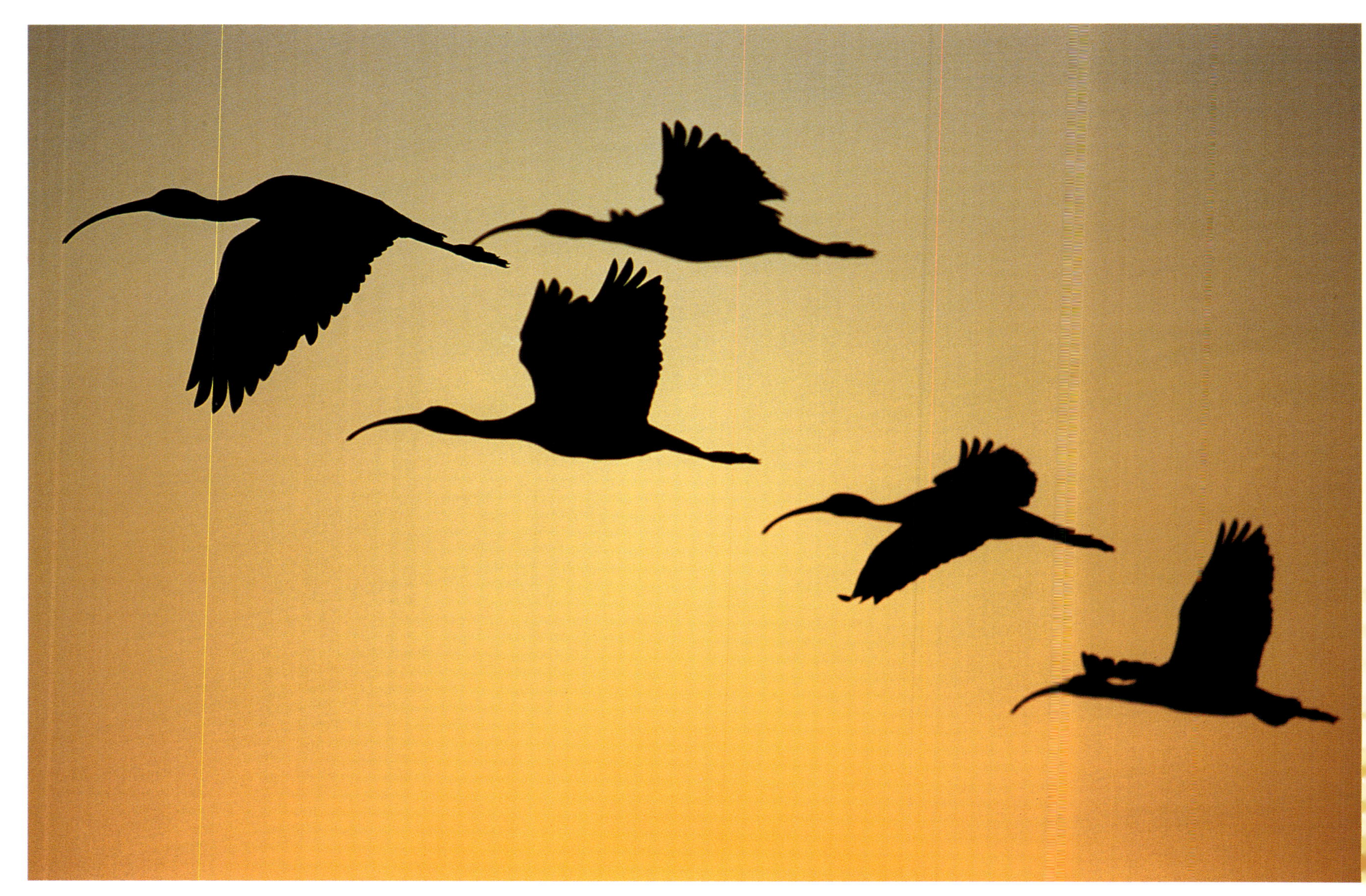

WHITE IBIS AT SUNSET, FLORIDA, JANUARY 1994

"What time is it when it's time to move on?"

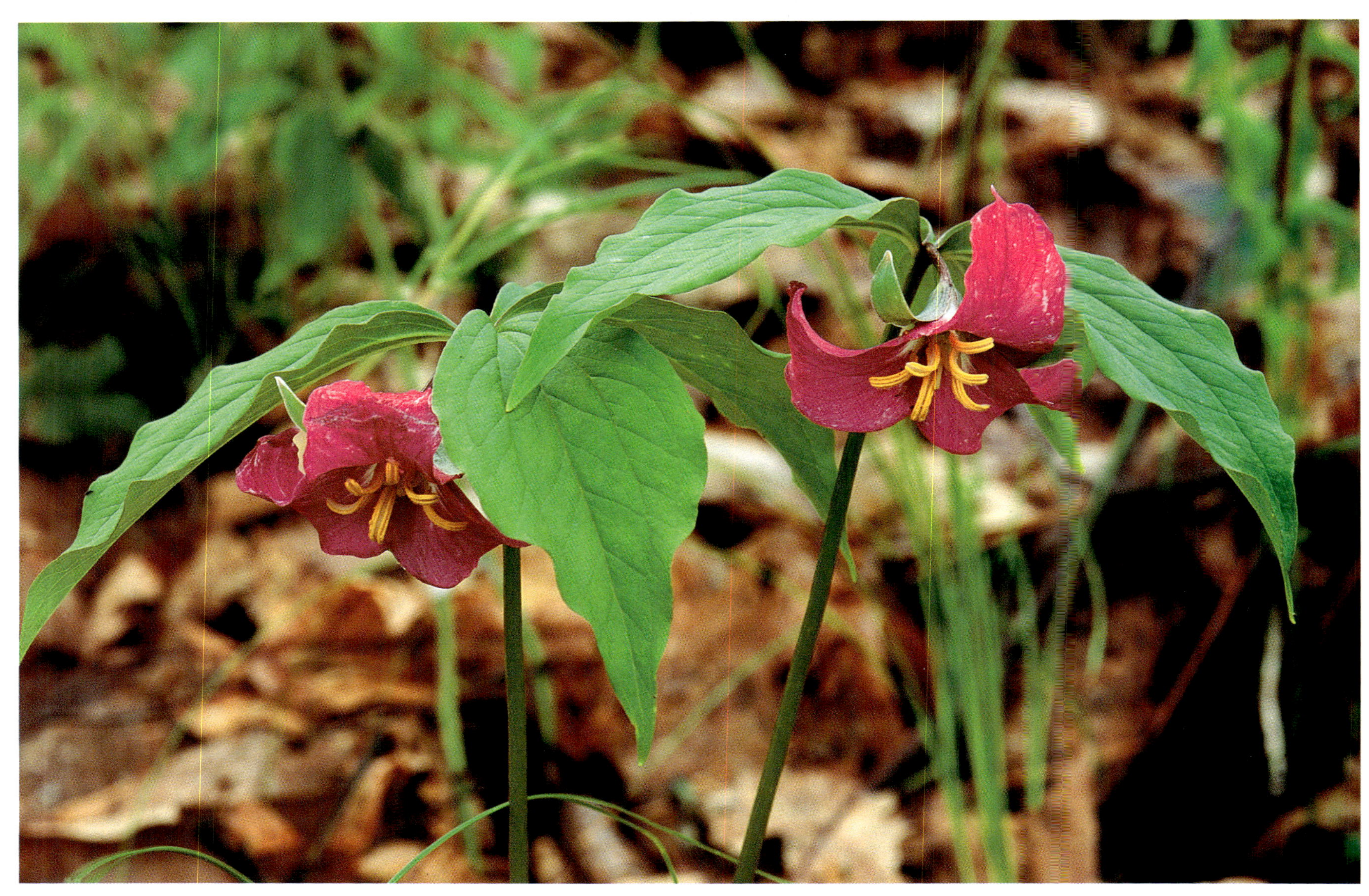

CATESBY'S TRILLIUM, NORTH CAROLINA, NOVEMBER 1992

"There's an itch under my skin I can't scratch. The business is going fine, the boys seem okay, I'm somewhat happy, but something's up. My spirit is obviously being moved to something new.

"I know I'm a slow-to-change person, but when I finally do change, the move is sure and fast. That time is at hand, even though I have no idea where or how. The Lord knows. He is the light unto my path."

"I arrived in my blessed Canada! Boy, am I different. It's the solitude and remoteness I love. The surrounding beauty doesn't hurt either.

"I'm going to relax and seek the Lord the next week or so. Of course, I'll get a little work and fishing in, too. I'm seeking direction and wisdom for the coming periods in my life. I want to be ready for whatever is to take place.

"My prayers are guided by this moving inside, but like the rest of my walk with the Lord, I'll know at 11:59!"

You can only conquer the past by focusing on the future, and the future begins with whatever is in your hands today.

Leaving the past behind was – and still is – hard for me. I find forgiveness easy, forgetting very difficult. Everybody has a "once upon a time." For me, there have been several. But if there's one thing I've learned, it's that yesterday's pain does not lessen tomorrow's potential.

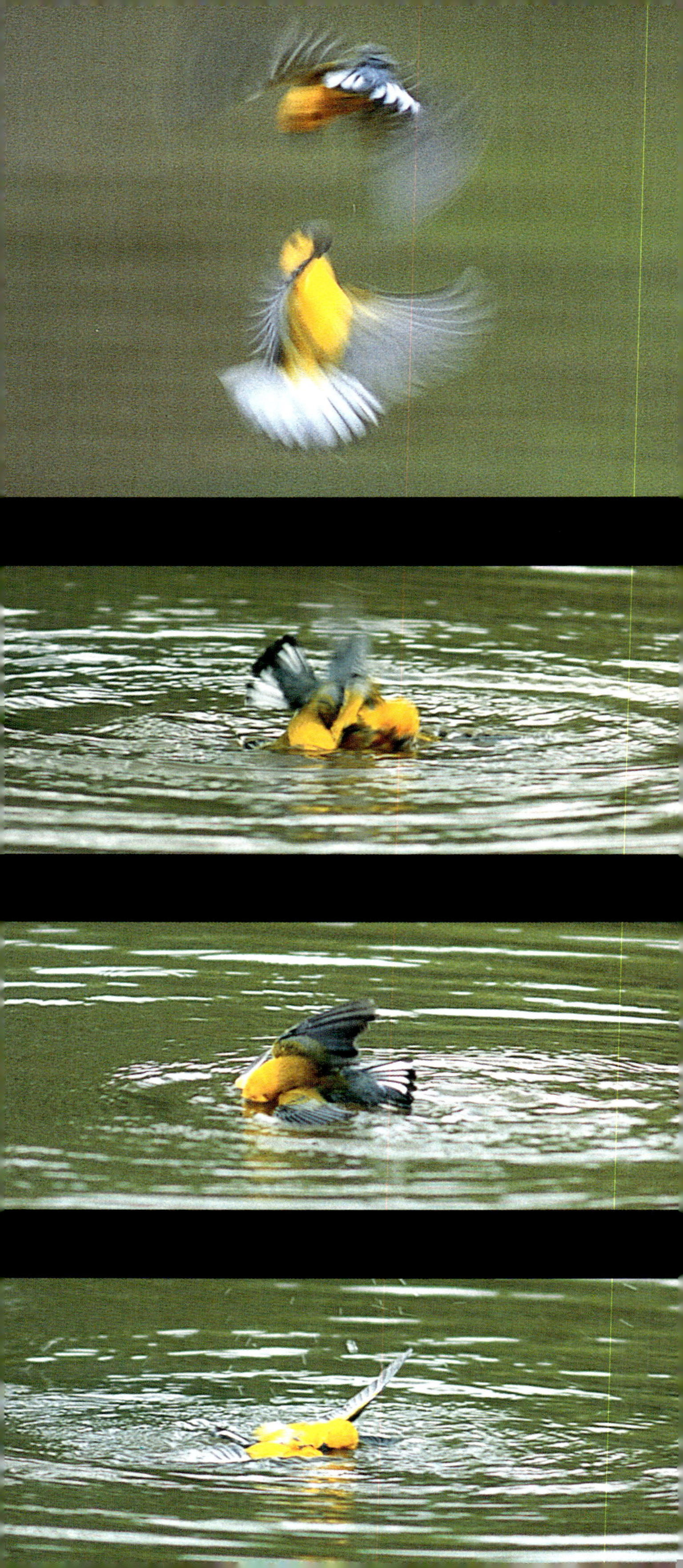

"What we want and what we need are not always the same. I'm glad my life has had all these struggles – they've made me a better person. The bad times have been bad and may have been handed to me without my wanting them, but they've seasoned me, and prepared me for what lies ahead. Moving on is foremost in my mind."

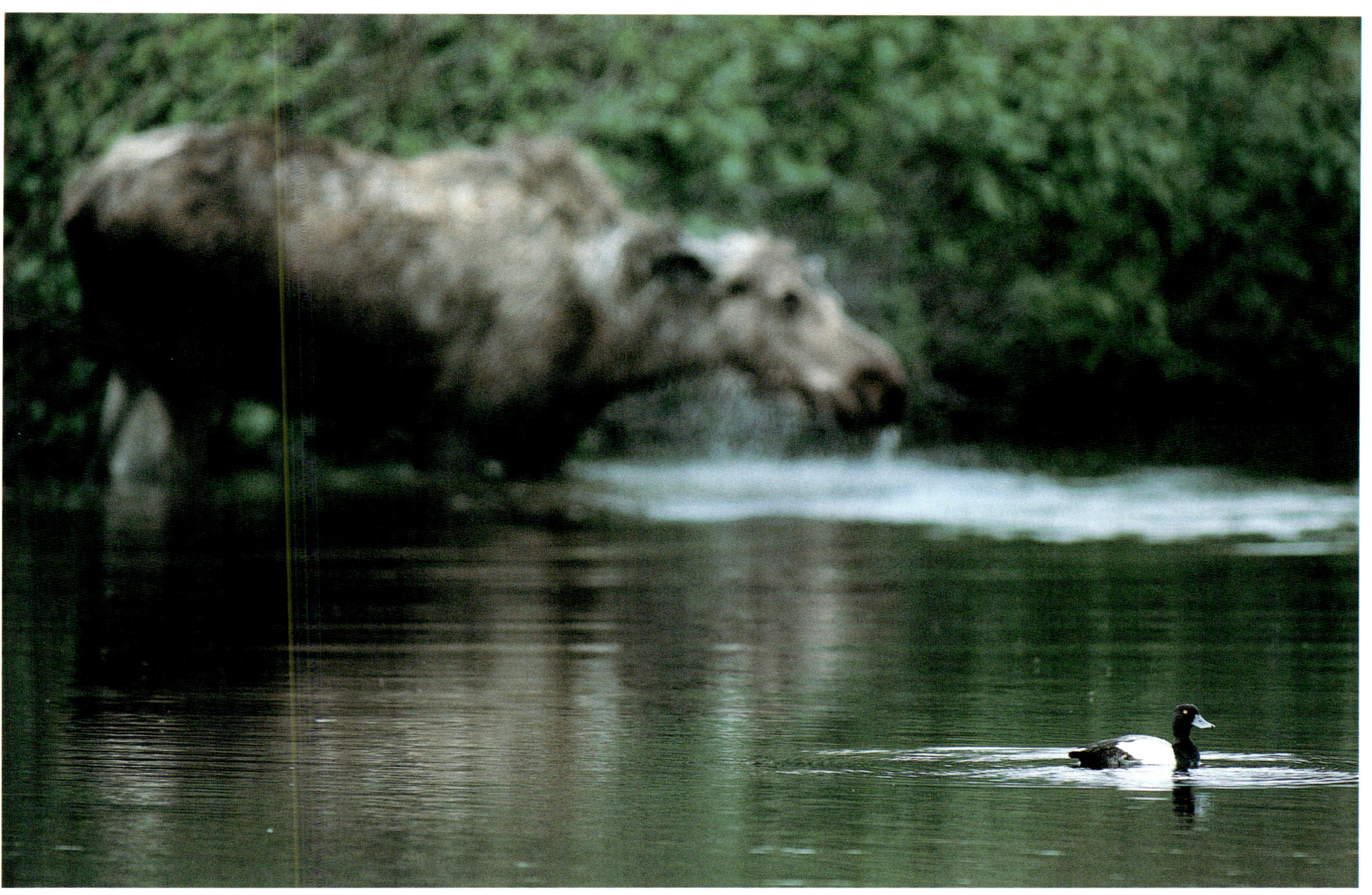

SCAUP AND MOOSE, ALASKA, JUNE 1992

MALE PROTHONOTARY WARBLERS IN TERRITORIAL CONFLICT, MISSISSIPPI, APRIL 1992

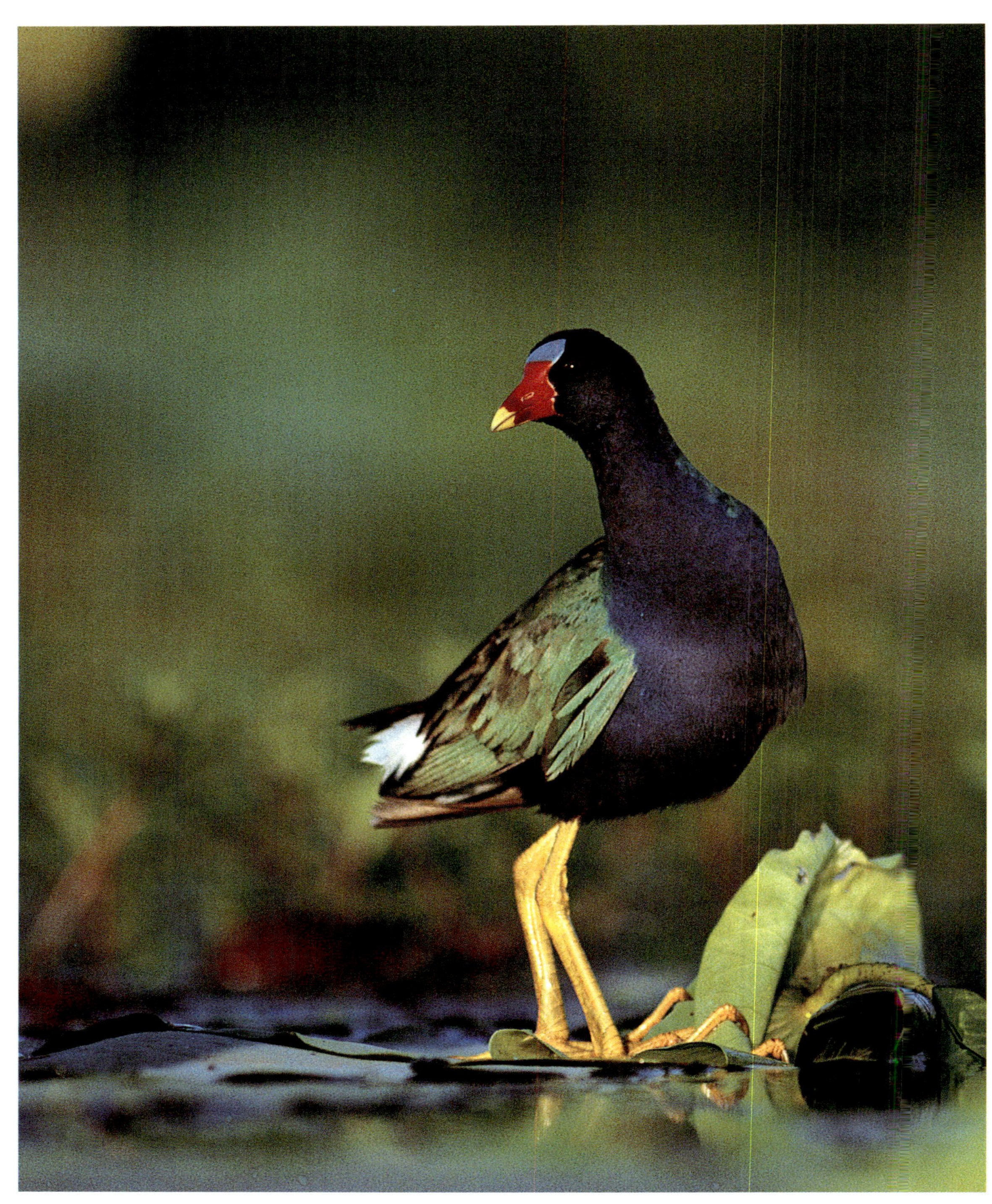

PURPLE GALLINULE, MISSISSIPPI, JULY 1987

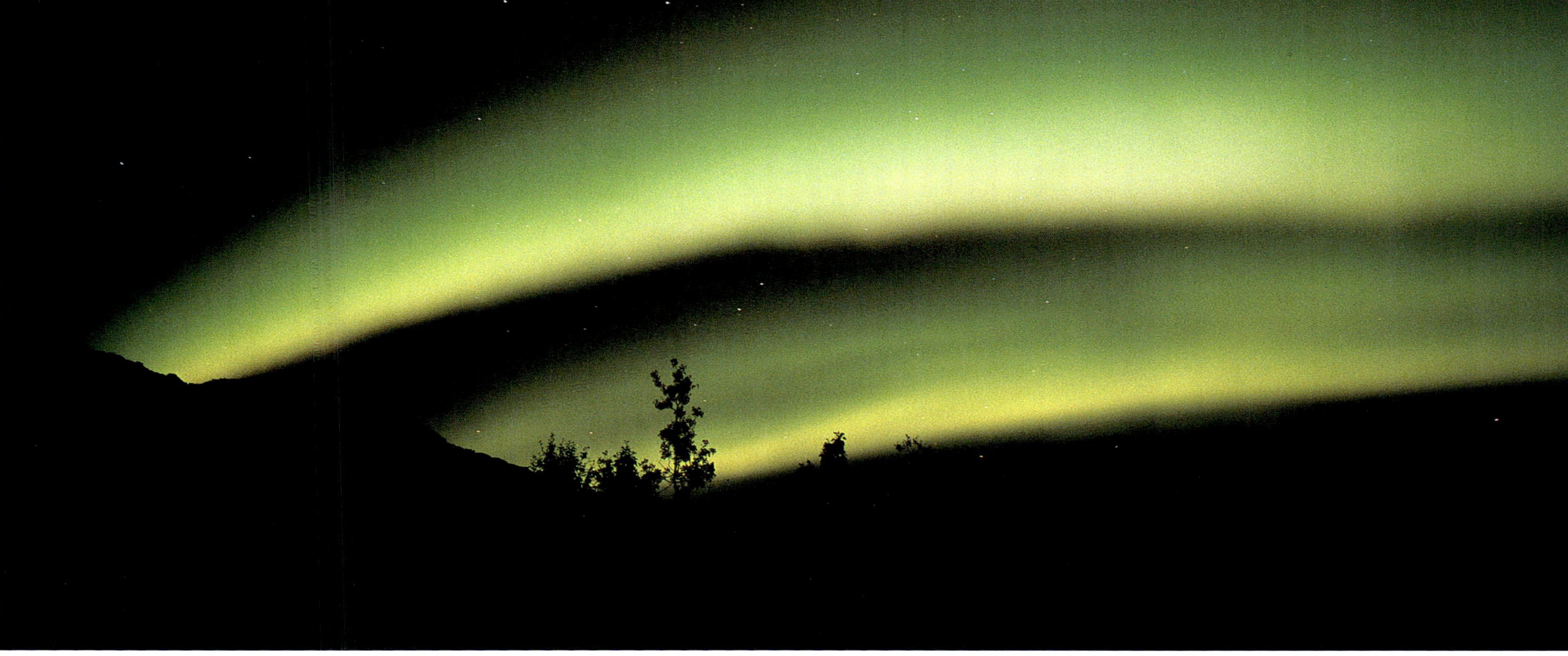

AURORA BOREALIS AND BIG DIPPER, ALASKA, SEPTEMBER 1996

"A recent trip to Alaska was wonderfully refreshing. Every shot, from the moose in Wonder Lake to the aurora borealis performing dancing ribbons, was choreographed by the Creator. God provided it all, and made sure I was always in the right place at the right time."

"Even in our darkest hour, there shines a light leading us home."

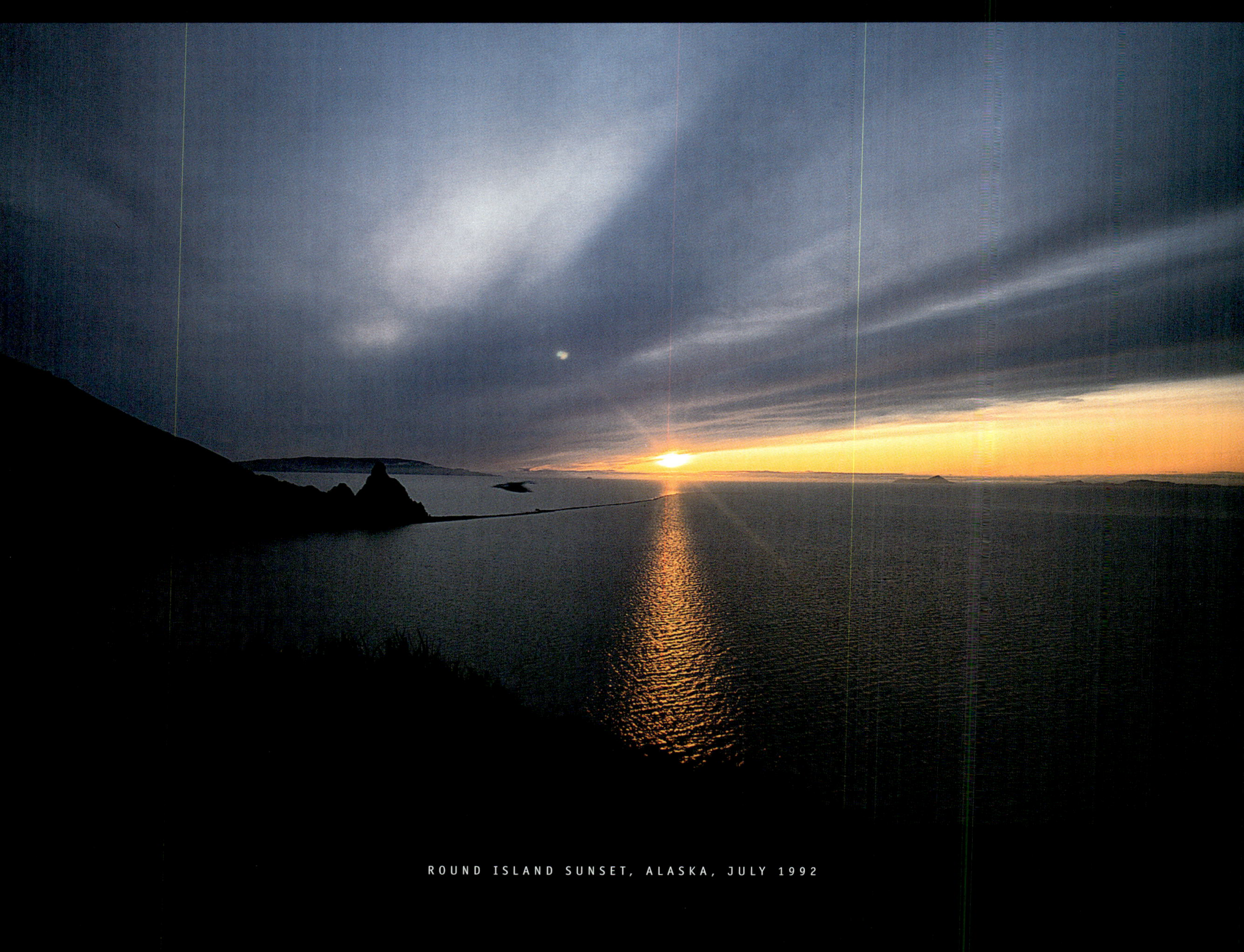

ROUND ISLAND SUNSET, ALASKA, JULY 1992

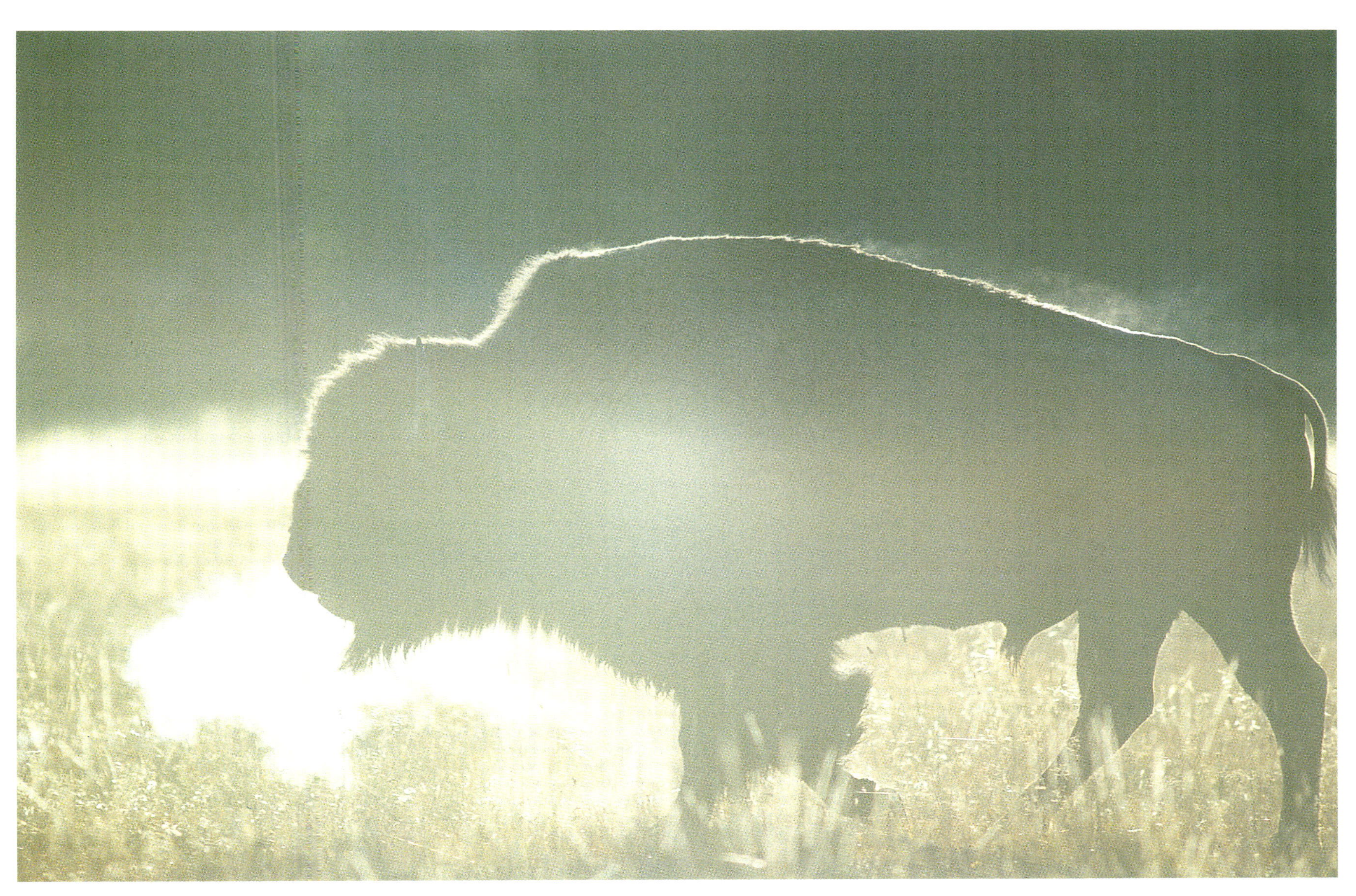

BISON AT DAWN, WYOMING, SEPTEMBER 1990

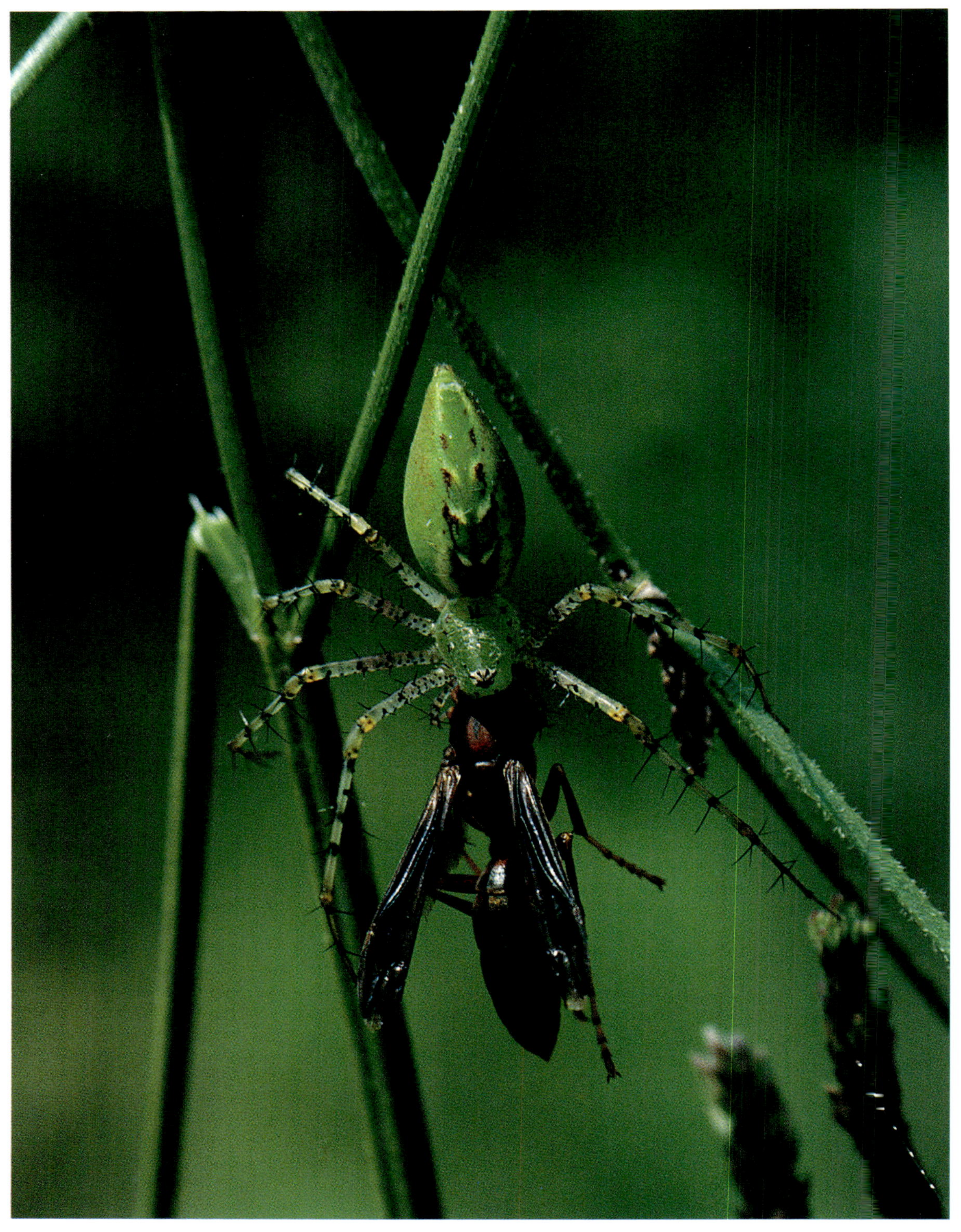

GREEN LYNX SPIDER WITH WASP, MISSISSIPPI, SEPTEMBER 1984

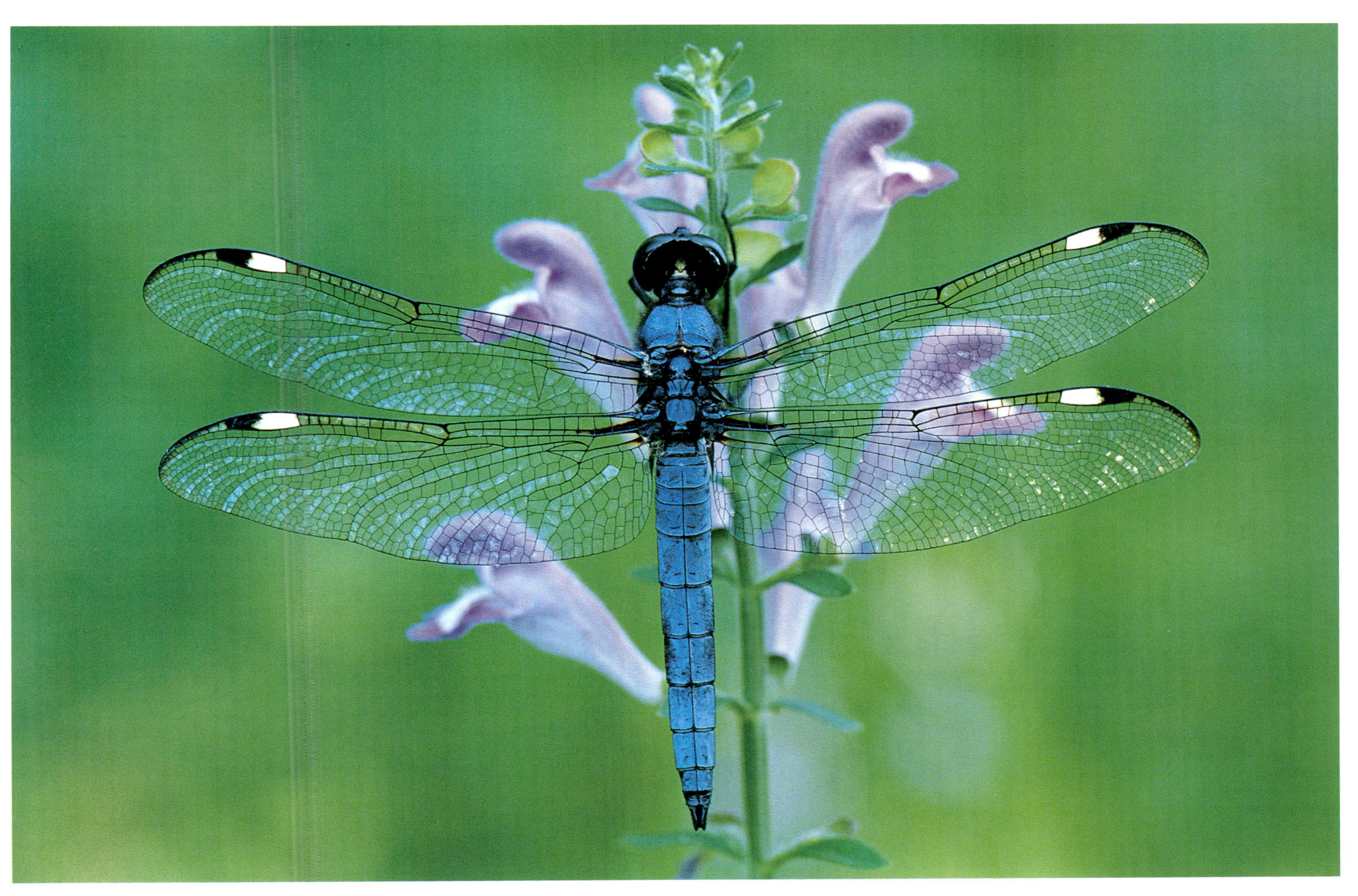

BLACK-FACED SKIMMER ON SKULLCAP, MISSISSIPPI, MAY 1994

FALL 1996

journal entry

"I've decided to use this journal as the basis for a new book. The decision to do this was a difficult one. The book will be very intimate, very personal, and very exposing. *It will also be my most heartfelt work."*

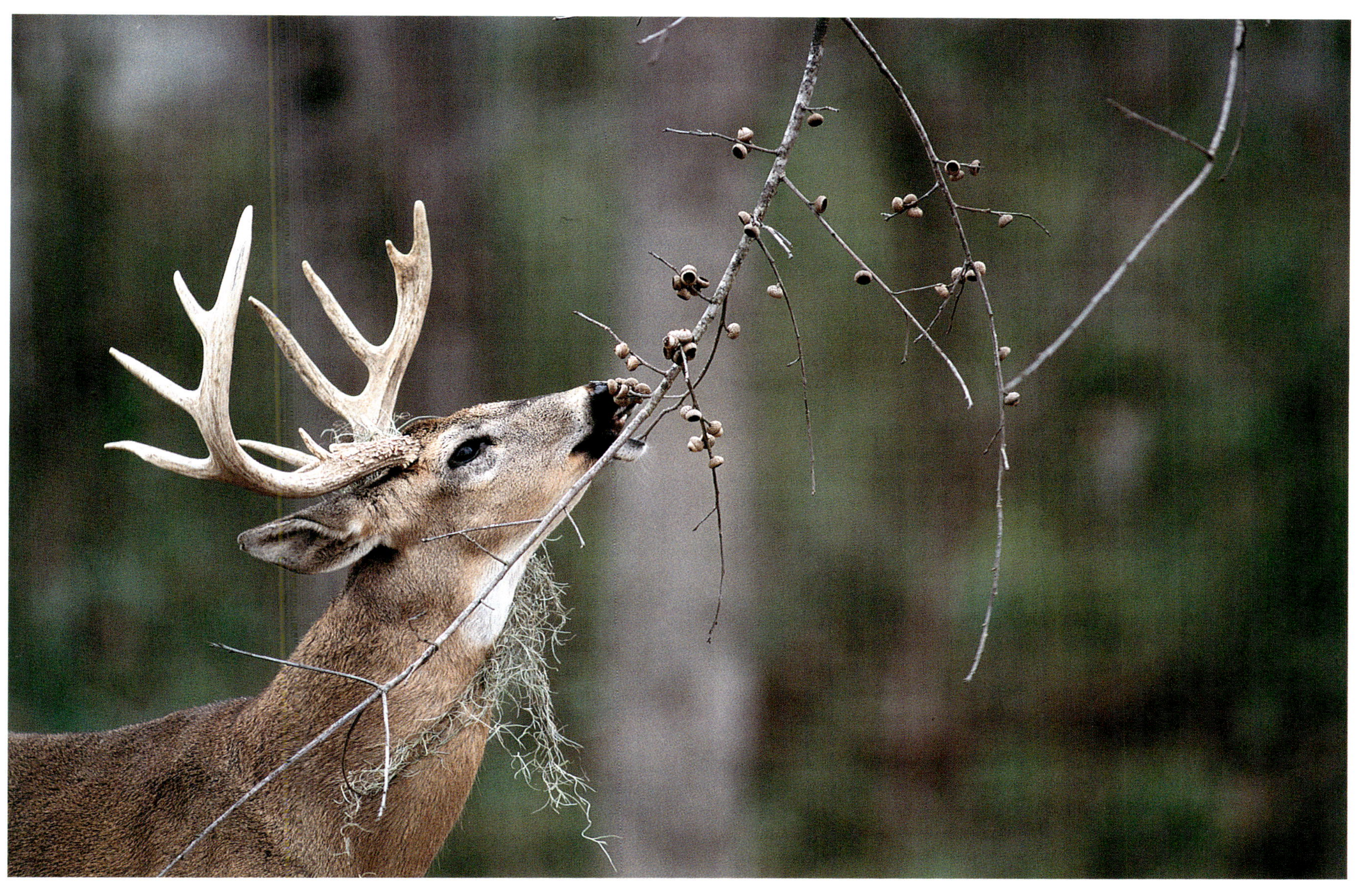

WHITE-TAILED DEER EATING ACORNS, MISSISSIPPI, JANUARY 1991

"I'm looking out over the lake behind the house where God has put me to calm my life. The Spanish moss is blowing in a light southern breeze, and there's a touch of cool in the air.

"Adagio for Strings *drifts across the deck, an appropriate accompaniment to the mood of the day. I've often thought it's the internal stirrings this passionate piece of music inspires that make me enjoy it so. This seems particularly true today."*

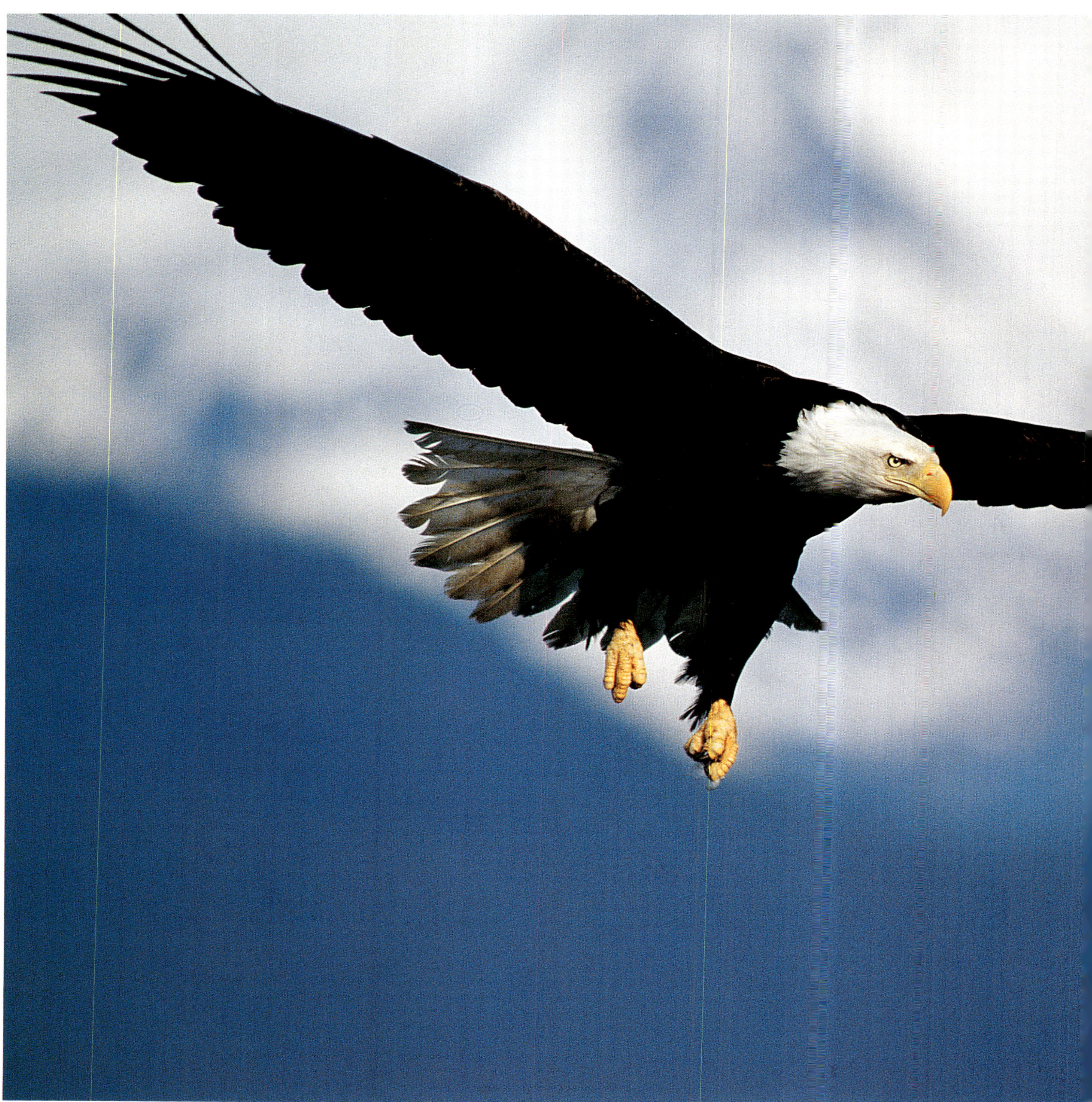

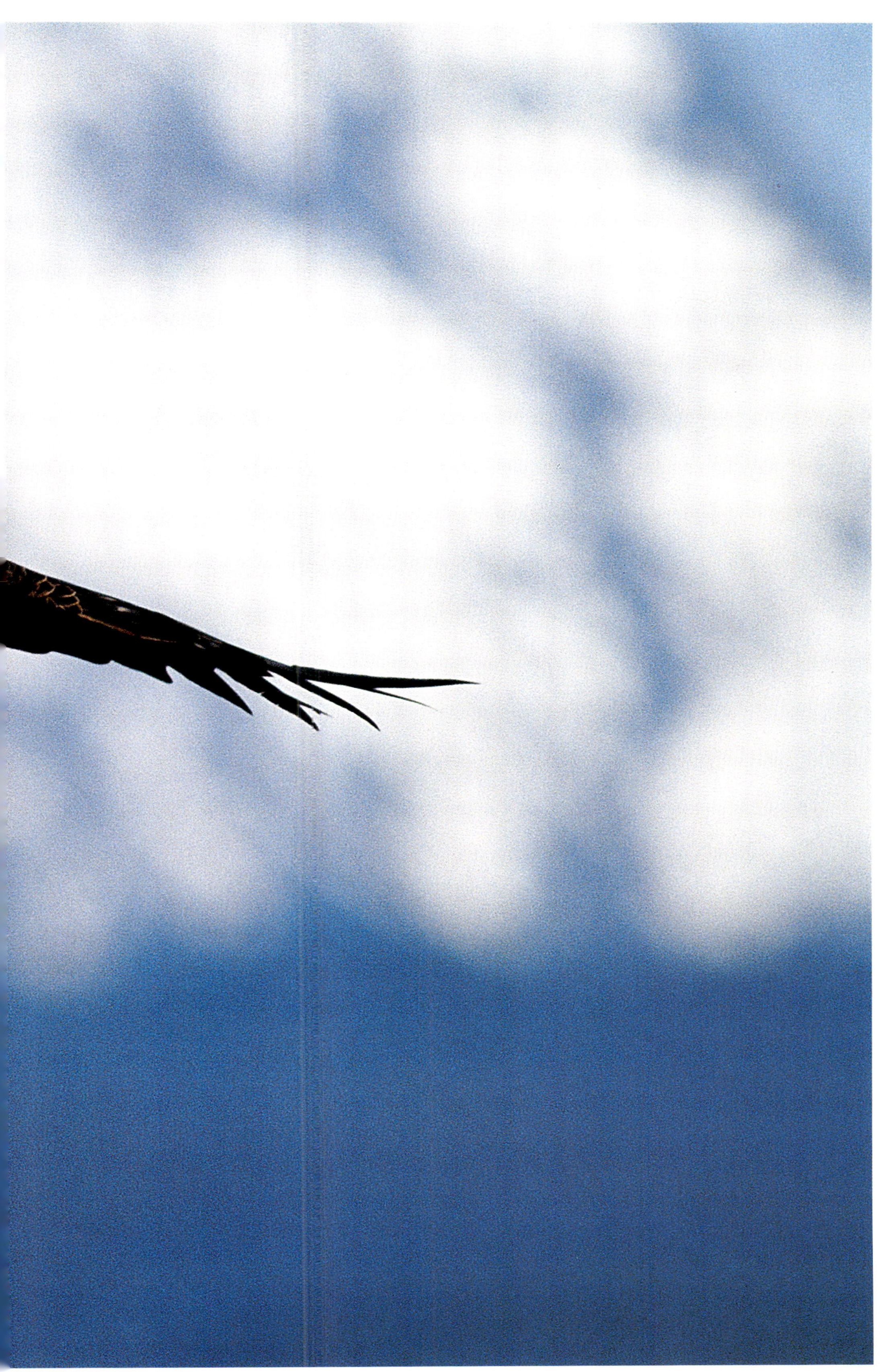

BALD EAGLE IN FLIGHT, ALASKA, MAY 1997

The journal that became *To Catch the Wind* describes an amazing time in my life. The Lord has always led me, but never so clearly as during the most difficult days of those three years. I know I'll continue to be amazed, standing outside myself as I watch God work *on* me as well as *through* me.

The parallels between my life's work and my emotions are revealing and wonderful to watch. The ultimate shot will arrive when it's time – not too soon and not too late.

In the meantime, there's more work to be done. More new territory to explore, more wildlife to photograph, and yes, more questions to be answered. This job can be tough, but my Boss has assured me He'll take care of me. My only assignment is to do what I'm told and hold on tight. The adventure is just beginning.

It's been said that a man can never possess what he's unwilling to pursue. I think that applies to the search for answers and a sense of self as well as more tangible goals.

For now, I'll draw my motivation from the simple fact that I have yet to capture that ultimate shot.

But that's okay. After all, the *real* adventure is not in the image itself, but in its pursuit. The photograph of a lifetime takes a lifetime of photographs.

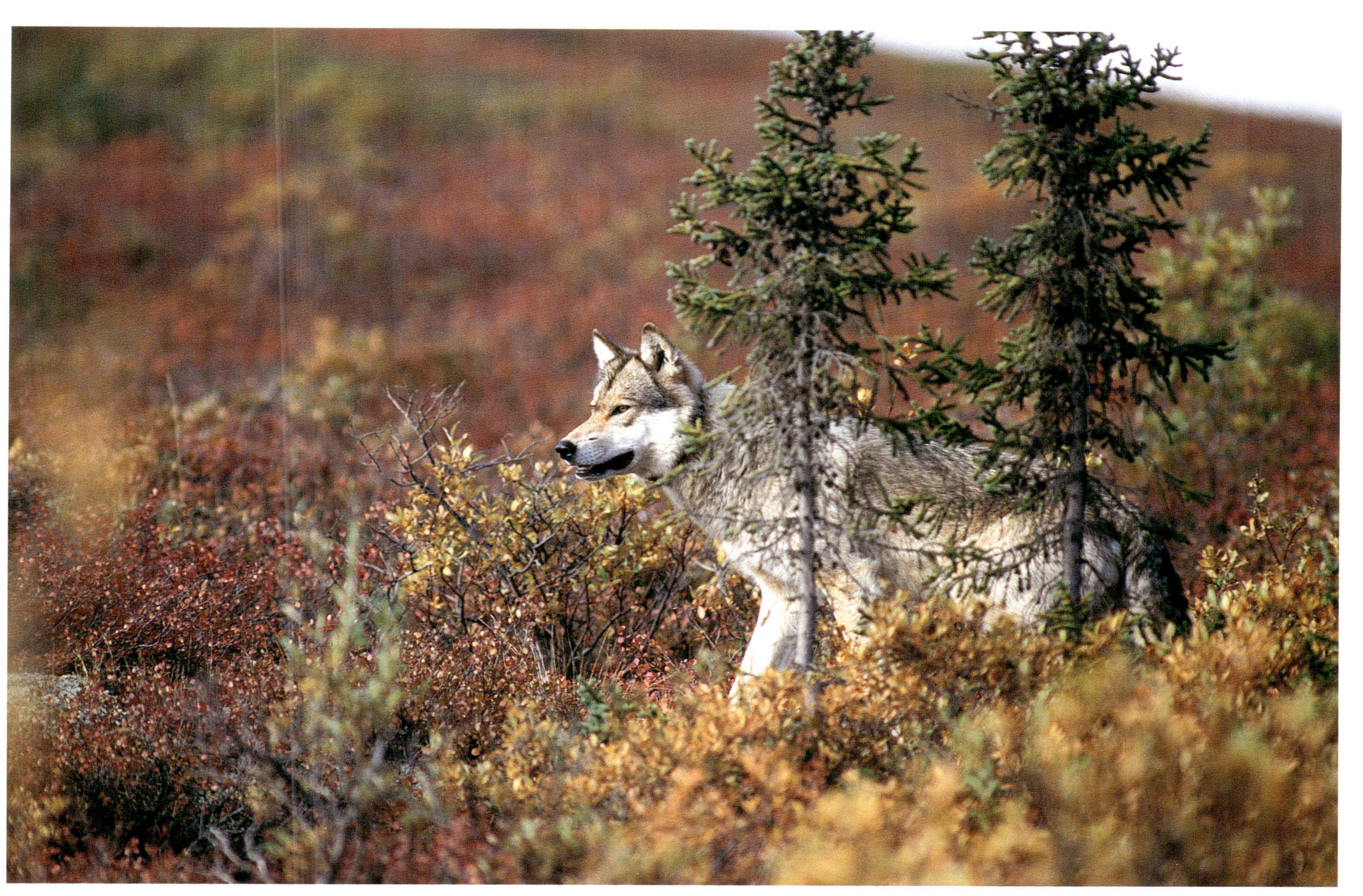

GRAY WOLF, ALASKA, SEPTEMBER 1996

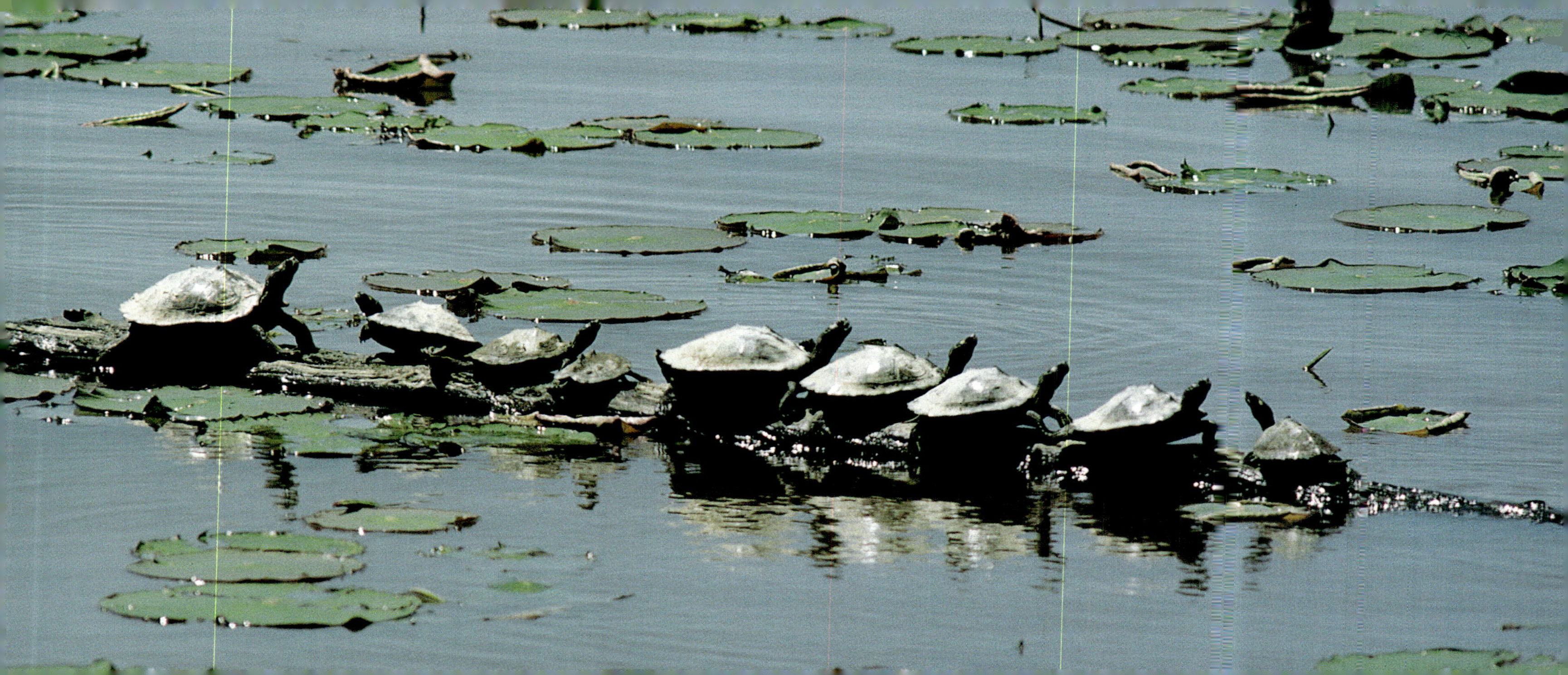

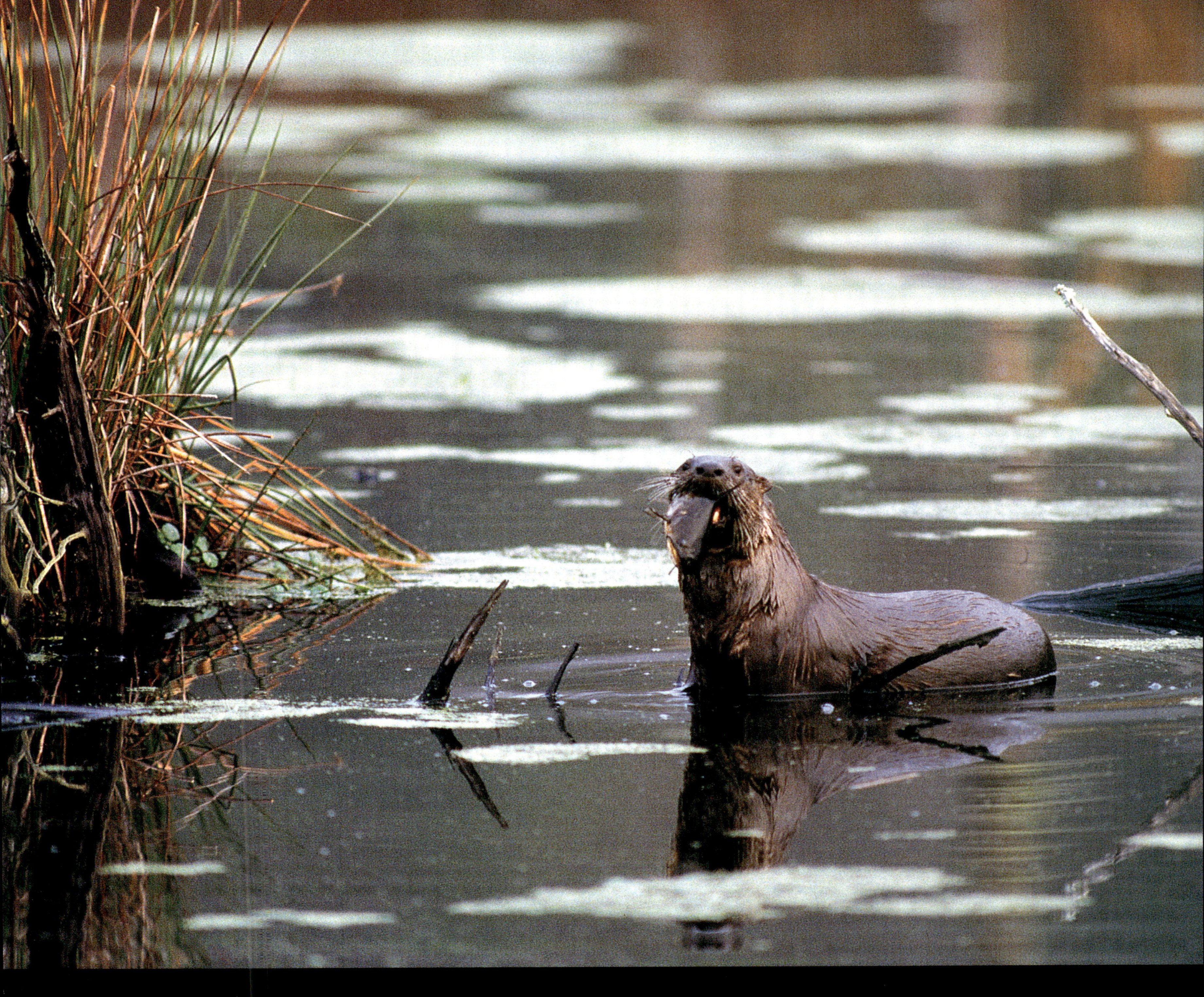

RIVER OTTER WITH CATFISH, SOUTH CAROLINA, FEBRUARY 1997

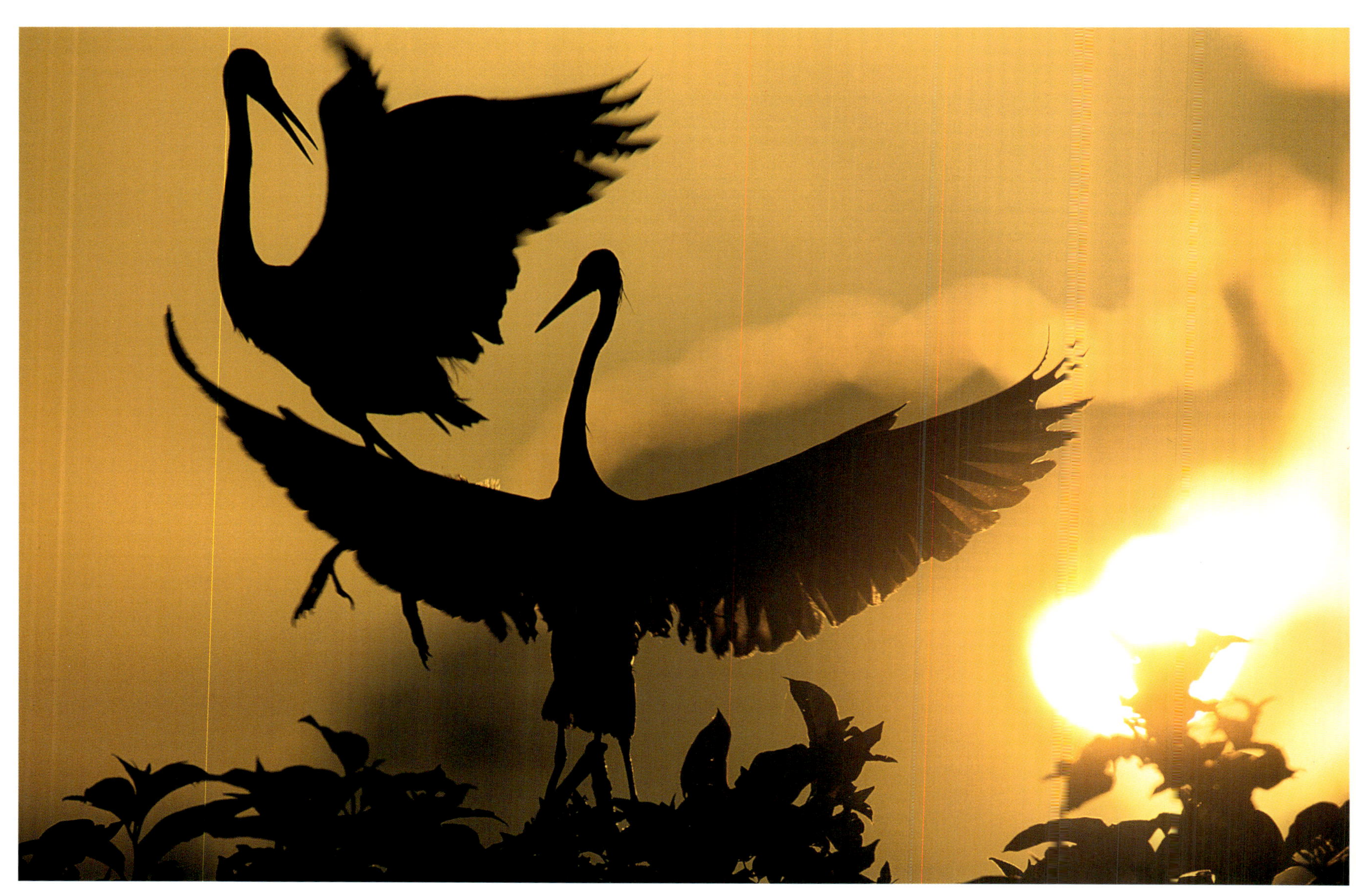

TRICOLORED HERONS AT SUNRISE, LOUISIANA, APRIL 1991

"Somewhere deep inside, I think I really like trying to catch the wind. In my innermost being I know I'll feel it from time to time and see its effects often, but I'll catch it only when I get 'home.' And then, I'll not only grasp it, I'll ride upon it."

STEPHEN KIRKPATRICK, 1997

TWO MOONS ARISING

At times I've reasoned much beyond measure,
Such agonizing, prolonged, selfish death;
And instead of stopping to smell the roses,
I was stopping only to catch my breath.

Then I noticed two moons arising,
The clearer message was in the wind;
This time there is no great inquisition,
Simply, things do come to an end!

STEPHEN KIRKPATRICK, 1997

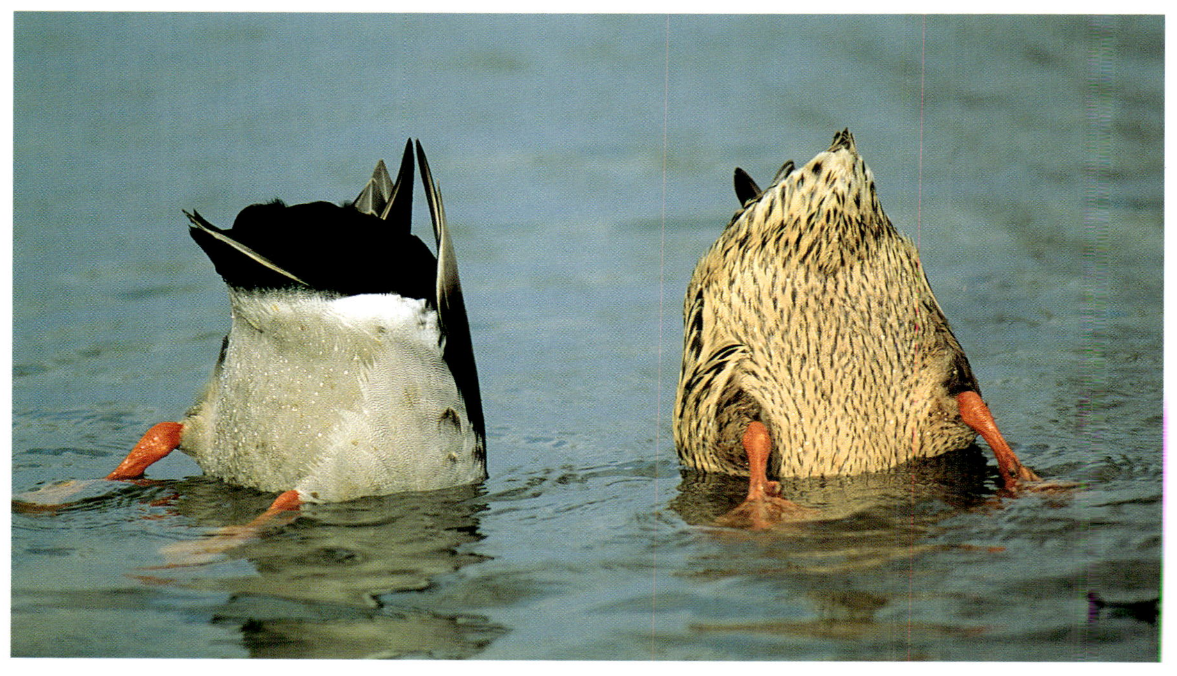

MALLARDS FEEDING, TENNESSEE, JANUARY 1992